ESSEX COUNTY, VIRGINIA

DEED AND WILL BOOK
1692-1693

Ruth and Sam Sparacio

The Antient Press Collection
from

Colonial Roots
Millsboro, Delaware
2016

Colonial
Roots

Helping You Grow Your Family Tree

ISBN 978-1-68034-075-4

Printed February 2016

CONTENTS

[this page intentionally blank]

ESSEX COUNTY, VIRGINIA
ORDERS
1692 - 1693

p.
1

- At a Court held for Essex County May ( ) Ano Dom: 1692

Present Mr. HENRY AWBREY   Capt. EDWARD THOMAS
        Mr. HENRY WILLIAMSON   Mr. BERNARD GAINES
        Capt. JOHN CATLETT   Capt. JOHN BATTAILE
        Capt. WM: MOSELEY   Mr. ROBT. BROOKS
        Mr. THO: EDMONDSON   Capt. ANTHONY SMITH

- A Comision of the Peace for Essex County from the Honble. FRANCIS NICHOL-
SON Esqr: their Majties. Lt. Governr: dated the 30th day of April 1692, was published and
comitted to Record

- A Dedimus from the Rt: Honble: FRANCIS NICHOLSON Esqr. their Maties. Lt.
Governor of Virginia for swaring the Justices of Essex County was published and
comitted to Record

- Capt. EDWARD THOMAS, Mr. BERNARD GAINES, Mr. ROBERT BROOKS, Capt. JOHN
BATTAILE, Capt. ANTHONY SMITH by vertue of a Power from the Rt: Honble. FRANCIS
NICHOLSON Esqr., their Maties Lt. Governor of Virginia took the Oaths enjoyn'd by Act of
Parliamt: instead of the Oaths of Allegiance and Supremacy and the Oath of Justice of
the Peace of Essex County

- Mr. HENRY AWBREY, Mr. HENRY WILLIAMSON, Capt. JOHN CATLETT, Capt.
WILLIAM MOSELEY, Mr. THOMAS EDMONDSON by vertue of a Power from the Rt. Honble.
FRANCIS NICHOLSON Esqr. their Maties. Lt. Governor of Virginia, took Oaths enjoyn'd by
Act of Parliamt. instead of Oaths of Allegiance and Supremacy and the Oath of Justice of
the Peace for Essex County

- According to a Commission from the Rt: Honble. FRANCIS NICHOLSON Esqr.
their Maties. Lt: Governor of Virginia, Mr. HENRY AWBREY was sworn SHERIFF of Essex
County

- Capt. WILLIAM MOSELEY, Capt. EDWARD THOMAS and Capt. JNO. BATTAILE enter
themselves security joyntly and severally with Mr. HENRY AWBREY in the penalty of
One hundred thousand pounds of tobo: & cask to our Sovereign Lord and Lady, the King
and Queen, their heires and Successors, for the said AWBREYs lawfully discharging the
SHERIFFs place. its therefore ordered they give bond accordingly

p.
2

Essex County Court May ( ) 1692

- At the request of Mr. HENRY AWBREY, Sheriff of this County, Mr. GEORGE
PARKE was sworne his SUB SHERIFF for this ensuing year, haveing first taken
the Oaths enjoyn'd by Act of Parliamt: instead of the Oaths of Allegiance and Supremacy

- Capt. EDWARD THOMAS and Capt. ANTHONY SMITH enter themselves security
joyntly and severally with Mr. GEORGE PARKE in the penalty of one hundred thousand
pounds of tobo: to Mr. HENRY AWBREY, Sheriff, for the said PARKEs due performance of
the Office of SUB SHERIFF of the sd County, its therefore ordered they give bond

- FRANCIS MERIWETHER by vertue of a Comision from the Honble: WILLIAM
COLE, Esqr., Secretary of Virginia, was sworn CLERKE of Essex County, haveing first
taken the Oaths enjoyn'd by Act of Parliament instead of the Oaths of Allegiance & Supremacy and his comission comitted to Record

- The Acts of Assembly made at JAMES CITTY the last Session of Assembly, April
Ano: Dom: 1692, were this day published

- Two Orders of Councill dated at JAMES CITTY Aprill ye 2d 1692 and one dated the 12th: were published and comitted to Record
- At the request of Mr. HENRY AWBREY, his Commission to be SHERIFF of this County is admitted to Record
- The two Orders of RAPPA: COURT dated Aprill ye 6th, Ano: 1692 summoning a Grand Jury and several persons &c. are put in force, and ordered that the persons exprest in the sd Orders be summoned to the next Court to be held for this County
- THOMAS TAYLOR, Servant to THOMAS SAINT JOHN, is adjudged Eleven years of age, It is therefore ordered that he serve according to Law
- MOSES ARMITAGE is appointed CONSTABLE in the Upper Precincts of this County

p.   Essex County Court ( ) of May 1692
3   - JOHN PITTS is appointed CONSTABLE in the roome of HUGH CRABB
        - WM: HARPER is appointed CONSTABLE in the roome of LODDIWICK ROWSEY
        - HENRY PICKETT is appointed CONSTABLE in the roome of WM: CHUBBS
        - JNO: WOOD is appointed CONSTABLE in ye roome of DANL: BROWNE
        - THO: PAINE is appointed CONSTABLE in the roome of JNO. BILLINGTON
        - Capt. WILLIAM MOSELEY is requested to take the List of Tithables in the precincts Mr. HENRY AWBREY tooke them the last year: And return the same to the Clerke of this County Courts Office according to Law
        -The other Gentlemen who tooke the Lists of Tithables the last yar requested to take the same this year in their severall precincts, and return severall lists to the Clerke of this County Courts Office according to Law
        - Mr. SAMLL. SALLIE is appointed Survayr: of the Highwaies in the Upper Precincts of St. Marys Parish
        - JNO. GOSS is appointed Survayr: of the Highwaies in the Lower Precincts of St. Marys Parish
        - NICHOLAS COPELAND is appointed Survayr: of the Highwaies in the Upper Precincts of Sittingburne Parish
        - RICHARD STOAKES is appointed Survayr: of the Highwaies in the Lower Precincts of Sittingburne Parish
        - THO: MEADOR is appointed Survayr: of the Highwaies in the Upper Precints of South Parnham Parish
        - RICHD. TAYLOR is appointed Survayr: of the Roads from the head of PISCATAWAY CREEK to KING & QEEEN County
        - Mr. DANL: DOBBINS is continued Survayr: of the Highwaies in the Lower Precincts he formerly was Survayr: off
        - SAMLL. GREEN is appointed Survayr: of the Highwaies in the Lower Precincts of South Farnham Parish
        - Mr. JNO. DANGERFEILD is continued Survayr: of the Highwaies in the Precincts he formerly was Survayr: off

p.   - At a Court held for Essex County June the 10th 1692
4.   Present   Mr. HENRY WILLIAMSON   Capt. EDWARD THOMAS
                     MR. THO: EDMONDSON   Capt. ANTHO: SMITH

        - JNO: WEBSTER appeared in Court and acknowledged a Deed of Sale of a parcell of land to JNO: SAVAGE, to be his real act and deed, the same is admitted to record
        - It is ordered that RICHARD COVINGTON be Survayr: of the Highwaies from

RICHARD TAYLORs Swamp to KING & QUEEN County and from THOMAS DAYEs to the
MAINE ROAD to THO: CROWs.

- THO: COOPER appeared in Court and acknowledged a Deed of Sale of a parcell of
Land to RICHARD BRISINDON, to be his real act and deed, the same is admitted to record

- Mr. JNO. ALMOND and Mr. THOMAS HUCKLESCOTT are nominated and ordered to
examine, state and settle ELIZABETH LINSEY's Account of her Husbands Estate, and make
report thereof to this Court

- WM: BEEZLEY being return'd non est Inventus at the Suit of FARRATT EVERS,
was call'd to come forth & answer the same, but made no appearance; An Attachmt: is
granted the said FARRETT EVERS against the Estate of ye sd WM. BEESLEY for Five hundred and fifty pounds of sweet sented toba: & cask and costs, returnable to the next Court
for Judgmt.

- The difference depending between Mr. LEONARD HILL, Admr: of BENJA: SHEF-
FEILD, Plt. and ANDREW DUDDING Deft., is dismist, the Defendt. declareing upon Oath
that he had no Estate in his hands relateing to the said SHEFFEILDs Estate

p.   Essex County Court 10th of June 1692
5   - (On Margin) Ex: July 19th 1692: May ye 29th: 1693 Then delivered ye within
       Precept & levied upon wthin: Exo: on three Cows & Steer Earling, p GEO PARKE
S.S.E.C. May ye 29th: 1693. Ye Subscribers being summoned as Appraissors on ye Estate
of RICHD: FRYER do appraise ye above sd 3 cows & steer yearling at Fourteen hundred
pounds of Tobo: Witness our hands THOMAS GREEN, WM: HARDING, John marke
MORGAN. May ye 29th 1693. Sworne before me ANTHO: SMITH Vere Recordatr. Test
FRAN: MERIWETHER Cl Cur

- WILLIAM JOHNSON brought an Informacon to this Court against RICHARD
FRYER and therein set forth that the said FRYAR did on the 29th: day of May last steal a
Hog that did belong to a Seaman of Capt. JOHN PURVIS's Ship, which Hog JONATHAN
DRILL did sell to the abovesaid Seaman which is of the said DRILLs proper marke, contrary to the 125th Act of Assembly, for which your Informer humbly prayes order
against RICHARD FRYAR for One thousand pounds of tobo: & cask according to the above
said Act with all cost

To which the Defendant appeared & pleaded not guilty and a Jury being impannelled
and sworn to try the truth of the premisses who (Vizt) Mr. RICHARD COVINGTON, Mr.
ANDREW HARRISON, Mr. THO: GREEN, Mr. WM: LEAKE, Mr. RALPH WHITTON, Mr.
RICHARD BUSH, Mr. WM. ACRES, Mr. JNO: MOSS, Mr. THO: HINDS, Mr. RICHARD HOLT;
Mr. THOMAS WATKINS, Mr. JNO. WEBSTER return their verdict in these words: The Jury
doth find the Defendant Guilty of Hogstealing to the Plaintiff p. me RICHARD COVING-
TON, which verdict this Court doth confirm and order that the said RICHARD FRYER pay
damage according to Law, with cost

- The Difference depending between JAMES ORCHARD Plantiff & THOMAS TOM-
LIN Defendt., is dismist, neither appearing

- The difference between ROBERT LUMKIN Plt. and THO: COOPER Defendt. is
dismist neither appearing

- Judgment is granted RICHARD BROOKS against Mr. LEONARD HILL, Admr. of the
Estate of BENJA: SHEFFEILD, for Eight hundred and five pounds of tobo:, he haveing
made Oath that the same is justly due; It is therefore ordered that the said BROOKS be
paid the sd sum out of the said SHEFFEILDs Estate (provided there be estate sufficient in
the said HILLs Custody, his own debt being first paid) with costs

- The difference between Mr. GEO: HASLEWOOD Plt. and RALPH WHITTON Deft. is
dismist, the Plt. not appearing to prosecute

- The difference between Mr. GEO: HASLEWOOD and REES EVANS Deft. is dismist, neither appearing

p.   Essex County Court 10th of June 1692
6   - The difference between WALTER PAVY Plt. and ROBT: HALSY Defendt., is dismist, neither appearing
       - Judgment is granted WILLIAM BROWNE against JAMES GREDIT for Two hundred pounds of Tobo: and caske, due by Bill under hand and seal dated the 7th: day of Janry: 1690, And ordered that he pay the same with costs
       - Whereas RICHARD MATHEWS was by the Sheriff return'd arrested at the suite of WILLIAM BROWNE, Assignee of RICHD. FEAGLE, which said MATHEWS was called to come forth and answer the same, but made no appearance and no security being return'd, Judgment is therefore granted to said WILLIAM BROWNE, assignee as aforesd: against the Sheriff for three hundred and sixty pounds of Tobo: & costs, provided the said MATHEWS do not appear at the next Court and answer the same
       - Judgment haveing this day past against the Sheriff for the sum of Three hundred and sixty pounds of Tobo: and cost for the non appearance of RICHARD MATHEWS at the suit of WILLIAM BROWNE, assignee of RICHARD FEAGLE, the said Sheriff moved that an attachment against the Estate of the said MATHEWS for the sd sum & costs which is granted him returnable to the next Court
       - Capt. JOHN BATTAILE added
       - Whereas SAMUELL GRIFFEN was by the Sheriff return'd arrested at the suit of THOMAS GRIFFEN, which said SAMLL. GRIFFEN was call'd to come forth and answer the same but made noe appearance and no security being return'd, Judgment is therefore granted to the said THOMAS GRIFFEN against the Sheriff for Two thousand pounds of tobo: and caske & costs, provided the said SAMLL. GRIFFEN do not appear at the next Court and answer the same

p.   Essex County Court 10th of June 1692
7   - Judgment haveing this day past against the Sherriff for the sum of Two thousand pounds of tobo: and caske and costs; for the non appearance of SAMLL. GRIFFEN, at the suit of THOMAS GRIFFEN, & said Sherriff moved for an attachmt., against the Estate of the said SAMLL. GRIFFEN for the same sum and costs, which is granted him returnable to the next Court
       - WILLIAM CREEMER confest Judgment to Capt; EDWARD THOMAS for Two hundred sixty and nine pounds of Tobo:, It is therefore ordered that the said Capt. THOMAS be paid the same by the said CREEMER with costs
       - Mr. FRA: TALIAFERRO and Mr. JNO. TALIAFERRO by vertue of a Commission from the Rt. Honble: FRANCIS NICHOLSON Esqr., their Maties Lt: Governr: of Virginia, took the Oaths enjoyn'd by Act of Parliamt: instead of the Oaths of Allegiance and Supremacy and also the Oath of Justice of the Peace for this County
       - Mr. ROBERT COLEMAN enters Mr. ABRA: BROADLEY his Attorney in the difference inter him and Mr: JOS: GOODRICH
              - Mr. THOMAS EDMONDSON, absent
       - A Warrant of Attorney from Mr. EDWARD CHILTON to Mr. HENRY WILLIAMSON, was produced in Court and admitted to Record
              - Capt. WILLIAM MOSELEY added
       - Judgment is granted Mr. EDWARD CHILTON (for the use of JAMES BOWLER) against RICHARD TALBOT for Five hundred pounds of sweet sented Tobo: and caske, it being due for rent of ye said BOWLER's Plantation; It is therefore ordered that the said TALBOT pay the same with costs

- Capt: ANTHONY SMITH, absent
- (On margin): Exe. July 17: 1692. Executed Febry. 8th 1693/4. Executed ye within Precept on a Sorrell Gelding markt wth: On ye near Buttock. GEO: PARKE Sub Sherriff.)
- Whereas WM. BROTHERS was by the Sherriff return'd & summoned a Grand Jury man to be sworne this Court & not appearing, is fin'd according to Law and ordered that he pay the same with costs

p.   **Essex County Court 10th of June 1692**
8
- Whereas JOHN WILLIAMS was by the Sherriff return'd summoned a Grand Jury man to be sworne this Court and not appearing is fin'd according to Law and ordered that he pay the same with costs
- Whereas JOHN SMITH SENR. was by the Sherriff return'd summoned a Grand Jury man to be sworne this Court, and not appearing, is fin'd according to Law, and ordered that he pay the same with costs
- Whereas ROBT. MOSS was by the Sherriff returned summoned a Grand Jury man to be sworne this Court, and not appearing, is fin'd according to Law, and ordered that he pay the same with costs
- Whereas NICHO: COPELAND was by the Sherriff returned summoned a Grand Jury man to be sworne this Court, and no appearing, is fin'd according to Law, and ordered that he pay the same with cost
- Mr. DANL. DOBBINS, Mr. THOMAS WEBB, Mr. JOHN SOUTHERNE, Mr. JOHN MITCHELL, Mr. JOHN SAVAGE, Mr. JOHN WEBSTER, Mr. DANLL. BROWNE, Mr. THOMAS THORPE, Mr. THOMAS WHEELER, Mr. JOHN PICKETT, Mr. THOMAS HINDS, Mr. JOHN MOSS were this day sworn a Grand Jury for the body of this County
- ROBERT CADE confest Judgment to MARY HODGIS for Five hundred and fifty pounds of sweet sented Tobo: & cask due by Bill, It is therefore ordered that ye said HODGIS be paid the same by the said CADE with costs
- The difference between WM: COVINGTON SENR. Plt. & RICHARD KING and MARY his Wife, Defts., is dismist, the Plantiff not appearing to prosecute
- The difference between RICHARD COVINGTON Plt. and THOMAS WATKINS Defendt., is refer'd till next Court

p.   **Essex County Court 10th of June 1692**
9
- Mr. ROBERT COLEMAN peticoned to this Court for a Lycense to keep and ORDINARY in this County, wlhich is granted him for this ensuing year, and ordered that he give bond with security at the next Court for the lawfull performance thereof
- Capt. EDWARD THOMAS brought his accon to this Court against RICHARD TALBOT. And by his Complaint sett forth that the said TALBOT being in your Complainants Debt did order a hogshead of Tobo: of the Plantacon of Mr. JAMES BOWLER, where sd TALBOT made his crop last year, your Complainant expecting some fraud in the case sett down on said Hogshead only weighed, And caused it to be rowled to another House on the same Plantacon, where your Complainant resolved to cause all the Tobo: to be taken out of the said hhd., so to tare the Caske, which accordingly was done where yor: Complainant found that the said RICHARD TALBOT did sett down and counterfeit the Coopers Marke false tare and false pack, the sd hhd: Tobo: haveing put in between every two layrs. of Tobo: ground leaves, stalks, stones and the sweeping of the Tobo: House, which the Complainant is ready to prove; Therefore humbly prayes order that the said RICHARD TALBOT may receive such punishment as the Law in such cases provides
To which the Defendt. appeared and pleaded not guilty, And a Jury being impannelled

and sworn to try the truth of the premisses, who (Vizt) Mr. RICHARD COVINGTON, Mr. ANDREW HARRISON, Mr. THOMAS GREENE, Mr. WM. LEAKE, Mr. RALPH WHITTON, Mr. RICHARD BUSH, Mr. WILLIAM ACRESS, Mr. JOHN MOSS, Mr. THOMAS HINDS, Mr. RICHARD HOLT, Mr. PHILL: PARR, Mr. JNO. WEBSTER, returned their verdict in these words: This Jury doth find that the Hogshead of Tobo: when it was opened by the Evidences to be false packed, p me RICHD. COVINGTON, which verdict this Court have confirmed, And order'd that the said TALBOT loose the said Hogshead of tobo: and stand fastened to the WHIPPING POST ye space of halfe an hour, and pay all costs

- The difference between THOMAS MARMADUKE Plt. and EDWARD JEFFREYS Defendt. is dismist, neither appearing

p.   Essex County Court 10th of June 1692
10   - The difference inter Mr. JOSEPH GOODRICH Plantiff and Mr. ROBERT COLEMAN
        Defendt., is dismist, the Plantiffs Attorney not haveing sufficient power to
prosecute
        - The difference between Mr. ROBERT COLEMAN Plt. and Mr. JOS: GOODRICH Deft. is dismist, the Plantiff not appearing to prosecute
        - The difference between Mr. BENJA: GOODRICH Plantiff and ROBT. KING Defendt. is refered till the next Court at the Defts. request
        - Judgment is granted HENRY LONG against MARY WARD, Admx. of the Estate of SAMLL. WARD, for One thousand pounds of Tobo: and cask due by Bill, And ordered that he be paid the same out of the said WARDs Estate with costs
        - The difference inter Mr. WM. SHERWOOD Plantiff and THOMAS WOOD Defendt., is dismist, the said SHEWOODs Attorney not having sufficient power to prosecute
        - Nonsuit is granted Capt. PHILL: HARWOOD Defendt. against Mr. WM. STROTHER, Plantiff, he the said STROTHERS not appearing to prosecute his accon; he is therefore ordered to pay damage according to Law
        = Whereas THOMAS WOOD was by the Sherriff returned arrested at the suit of LUCY BURNETT, which said THOMAS WOOD was call'd to come forth and answer the same, but made no appearance and noe security being return'd, Judgmt: is therefore granted to the said LUCY BURNETT against the Sherriff for Ten thousand pounds of tobo: and caske and costs, provided the sd THO: WOOD do not appear at the next Court and answer the same
        - Judgment this day past against the Sherriff for the sum of Ten thousand pounds of tobo: and cask and costs for the non appearance of THOMAS WOOD at the suit of LUCY BURNETT, ye said Sherriff moved for an attachmt., agt: ye Estate of the sd WOOD for the said sum and costs which is granted him returnable to the next Court

p.   Essex County Court 10th of June 1692
11   - In the difference depending between EDWARD JEFFREYS Plantiff and JOHN
        JONES Defendt., its ordered that the Sherriff cause the said JONES to make his
personall appearance at the next Court to be held for this County to answer the said JEFFREYS Complaint
        - In the difference depending between EDWARD JEFFREYS Plantiff and RICHARD JONES Defendt., its ordered that the Sherriff cause the said JONES to make his personall appearance at the next Court to be held for his County to answer the sd JEFFREYS Complaint
        - Whereas JNO: PRICE was by the Sherriff return'd arrested at ye suit of JAMES FULLINGTON, which said JOHN PRICE was call'd to come forth and answer the same, but made no appearance and no security being return'd, Judgmt: is therefore granted the

said JAMES FULLINGTON against the Sherriff for Thirty pounds Sterl.,and costs provided ye said JOHN PRICE do not appear at the next Court and answer the same

- Judgment haveing this day past against the Sherriff for the sum of Thirty pounds Sterl. and costs for the non appearance of JOHN PRICE at the suit of JAMES FULLINGTON, ye said Sherriff moved for an attachment against the Estate of the said JNO: PRICE which is granted him with costs returnable to the next Court

- WM: ACRES confest Judgmt: to SIMON COPNALL for Two hundred and sixty pounds of sweet sented tobo: and cask due by Bill; Its therefore ordered that he be paid the same by ye said ACRES with cost als Exo.

- Nonsuit is granted ` :. ALICE FORBES Defendt. against JOHN CAMMILL, Plantiff, he the said CAMMILL not appearing to prosecute his Accot:, he is therefore ordered to pay damage according to Law with costs

- Ordered that RICHARD HUTCHINS who was summoned an Evidence on behalfe of Capt. EDWARD THOMAS against RICHD. TALBOT, be paid by the said Capt. THOMAS for one dayes attendance according to Law with costs

- Ordered that EDW: DRACUS who was summoned an evidence on behalfe of Capt. EDWARD THOMAS agt: RICHARD TALBOT be paid by the said Capt. EDWARD THOMAS for one dayes attendance according to Law with costs

p.   Essex County Court 10th of June 1692
12   - Ordered that ROBT: WEBB who was summoned an evidence on behalfe of Capt.
        EDW. THOMAS against RICHD. TALBOT be paid by the said Capt. EDWARD THOMAS for one dayes attendance according to Law with costs

- The difference depending between RICHARD HUTCHINS Plt. and Mr: LEO: HILL, Admr. of BENJA: SHEFFEILD, Defendt., is refer'd till next Court by consent of both parties

- Nonsuit is granted ANDREW HARRISON Deft., against Mr. HUGH FRENCH, Plantiff, the Plantiff not entering his Declaracon according to Law, he is therefore ordered to pay damage according to Law with costs

- RACHELL HOLDING, Servant to ELIZA: BROWNE, being summoned to this Court for haveing a bastard Child, and the said BROWNE praying the Benefit of the Law as in such cases, its therefore ordered that the said HOLDING serve the said BROWNE according to Law after her time by Indenture is expired, or by Law shee ought to serve, as also halfe a year for satisfaccon of her fine paid by the said BROWNE

- ELIZA: BROWNE in Court assumes to pay RACHELL HOLDINGs fine for haveing a bastard Child, its therefore ordered that shee pay the same according to Law with costs

- Its ordered that GEORGE PARKE, Sub Sherriff, do bring LORANA TAYLOR to the next Court to be held for this County

- ELIZA: MEADS being summon'd to this Court for having a bastard Child by THOMAS SMITH, It is ordered that the Sher: bring the sd MEADS and SMITH to the next Court to be held for this County

- WM: LEAKE did assume in Court to pay ELIZA: MEADS fine for haveing a bastard Child, It is therefore ordered that he pay ye same according to Law with costs

- The difference inter WM. LEAKE, assee: of PHILL: PENDLETON, Plt., and RICHD. FRYAR, Defendt., is refer'd to next Court

- WM. LEAKE enters JAMES BAUGHAN his Attor: in ye difference inter him & RICHD. FRYAR

- The difference inter Mr. WM. COLSTON Plt. and RICHD. FRYAR deft. is refer'd till next Court

- The difference inter WM: LEAKE Plt. and RICHD. FRYAR Deft. is refer'd till next Court

p.   — At a Court held for Essex County July the 11th ano 1692
13   Present   Capt. JOHN CATLETT   Mr. BERNARD GAINES
                     Capt. WM: MOSELEY   Mr. ROBT: BROOK
                     Capt. EDW: THOMAS   Capt. JOHN BATTAILE

- MARY COGWELL, minor, came into Court and freely and voluntarily made choice of Capt. JOHN BATTAILE to be her Guardian, her Mother being present and consenting thereto, the same is allowed off by this Court

- A Deed of Sale of a parcell of land from THOMAS HILLIARD to WILLIAM SMITH acknowledged before Capt. JOHN CATLETT and Mr: FRA: TALIAFERRO was produced in Court And at the said SMITHs request admitted to record

- An Attachment is granted to THOMAS GRIFFEN for his Freedom Cloathes and costs against the Estate of JOHN SEARLE (who hath absented himselfe out of this County) returnable to the next Court for Judgment

        - Mr. EDMONDSON added

- Whereas at the last Court WM. BROTHERS was fin'd for not appearing to be sworne a Grand Jury man but now appearing and upon Oath declared that he was sick and not able to come, he is therefore excused from the said fine

- An Order of Councill dated at JAMES CITTY Aprill 27th: 1692, and another dated Aprill ye 2d: 1692, were this day published in Court and comitted to Record

- Judgment is granted WM. LEAKE, assignee of PHILL. PENDLETON, against RICHARD FRYAR for Five hundred pounds of sweet sented tobo: and caske, and ordered that he be paid the same by the said FRYAR with costs

- Judgment is granted to Mr. BENJA: GOODRICH, assignee of THOMAS SHEPHARD, Assignee of JOHN SOPER, against ROBERT KING for five hundred pounds of sweet sented tobo: and caske, and ordered that he be paid the same by the said KING with costs

p.   Essex County Court 11th of July 1692
14   - The difference depending between RICHARD HUTCHINS Plantiff and Mr.
        LEONARD HILL, Admr. of BENJA: SHEFFEILD Defendt., is refer'd till next Court
- Nonsuit is granted to HENRY WODNOT Defendt., against RALPH WHITTON Plantiff, he the said WHITTON not entering his peticon according to Law, he is therefore ordered to pay damage according to Law with costs

        - Mr. BER: GAINES, absent

- JAMES FULLERTON brought his accon of Trespass to this Court against JOHN PRICE, And in his peticon sett forth; Whereas your Peticonr: has Right to a certaine tract of land in fee lying in RAPPA: COUNTY and on the South side of Rappa: River upon the Maine Swampe of PISCATAWAY CREEKE, containing Seven hundred acres as may appear by a Patent granted to your Peticonrs: Father, JAMES FULLERTON deced, bearing date the 29th: day of September 1667 up and above ye Land of WM. AKUS, upon the Maine Pocoson of PISCATAWAY CREEKE bounding as followeth, Beginning at WM: AKUS his upper Corner tree & running by his line North by East One hundred and sixty pole, West North West four hundred & eighty pole over certaine branches of the Pocoson, thence North One hundred and one pole, thence West South West sixty six pole, thence parrallell with the first line three hundred and twenty pole to the pocoson & downe the pocoson where it first begin bounding upon the Maine Run, and JOHN PRICE contrary to Law or Right is seated within yor: Peticonrs: land and doth dayly trespass altho: he has been lawfully for:warned to your peticonrs: greate damage of Thirty pounds Sterl: Therefore your peticonr: has brought his accon against JOHN PRICE and humbly prayes that their Majts: Writt of habere facias may issue out of this Court to the Sheriff of the

County to put yor: peticonr: in peaceable possession of his lands with all costs &
damages; On consideracon hereof, this Court doth order the Sherriff of this County do
impannell an able Jury who being sworne before some Justice of this County are, in the
Company of Capt. EDWIN THACKER, Surveyr: of the Lower part of this County, on the
first Tuesday in August next, if fair, if not the next fair day, to lay out the lands in difference according to the antient reputed bounds

p.   Essex County Court 11th of July 1692
15   of the same, haveing regard to all evidences that shall be produced by either
        Plantiff or Defendt., of which a report is to be return'd to the next Court
                        - Capt. BATTAILE, absent
        - JOHN MILLS acknowledged JAMES BAUGHAN to be his Attorney in the Dif-
ference inter him and ELIZA: LINCH
        - The difference between LUCY BURNETT Plt. and THOMAS WOOD Deft., is dismist,
the Plantiff not laying her Declaracon right
        - Whereas JOHN WILLIAMS was at the last Court fin'd for not appearing as a
Grand Jury man to be sworne, but now appearing and alleadging that he was not summoned by the Sherriff he is therefore excused from the said fine
                        - Capt. BATTAILE, present
        - Judgment is granted THOMAS GRIFFEN against SAMLL. GRIFFEN for Thirteen
hundred eighty six pounds of tobo: and cask being due on ballance of a Bill for 60
thousand pounds of tobo: & cask and ordered that the he be paid the same by the said
SAMLL. GRIFFEN with costs.
                        - Mr. GAINES, present
        - ROBERT RICHARDSON confest Judgment to Mr. ROBT: PLEY for three pounds
fifteen shilllings due by Bill, And ordered that ye said PLEY be paid the same by the said
RICHARDSON with cost
        - EDWARD JEFFREYS acknowledged Mr. JNO: TAVERNER his Attorney in the dif-
ference between him and RICHD. JONES & JOHN JONES
        - The difference depending between EDW: JEFFREYS Plt. and RICHARD JONES &
JOHN JONES Defendts., is referr'd till next Court
                        - Mr. GAINES, absent
        - ELIZA: MEADS being summoned to this Court to declare who is the Father of her
bastard Child, and in Court declareing upon Oath that THOMAS SMITH is the Father of
the said Child; It is therefore ordered that the said SMITH give security to keep the sd
Child and save South Farnham Parish harmless from the same
        - JAMES BAUGHAN and RICHARD COVINGTON acknowledged themselves security
joyntly & severally with THO: SMITH that the said SMITH should keep & maintaine ye
bastard Child laid to him by ELIZA: MEADS and also save Southfarnham Parish harmless
from ye same

p.   Essex County Court 11th of July 1692
16   - Judgment upon attachment is granted EVAN JONES against ye Estate of JOHN
        SORRILL for Eleven hundred twenty four pounds of tobo: in the hands of RO:
BROOKE, he haveing made Oath that ye same is justly due and ordered that he be paid the
same
        - RICHARD KING confest Judgment to THOMAS PHELPS for Foure hundred ninety
and six pounds of sweet sented Tobo: & cask due on Ball. of a Bill, and ordered that the
said PHELPS be paid the same by the said KING with costs
        - The difference between RALPH WHITTON Plt. & JOSUA NASON Defendt., is dis-
mist, the Plt. not entering his peticon according to Law

- At the request of JNO. BURNETT, a Deed of Sale of a parcell of land from THOMAS GAINES to JOHN BURNETT ye abovesd. JNO: BURNETT's Father, is admitted to Record, as also a Survey of the said Land

- RICHARD HOLT JUNR. by a peticon set forth to this Court, that he is very much afflicted with Lameness insomuch that he is incapable of working, And therefore humbly pray'd to be levy free, On consideracon whereof, this Court doth Exempt sd HOLT from paying Levey this year

- The difference between MATHEW NELSON and JOHN BAUGHAN is dismist

- The difference depending between WM. CATLETT Plantiff and Mrs: ELIZA: BLUMFEILD, Admx. of Capt: SAMLL. BLUMFEILD deced, Deft., is refer'd till next Court

- ELIZA: BROWNE peticoning to this Court that RACHELL HOLDING, her Servant, is very sickly and incapable of working, & humbly pray'd that she might be levy free, On consideracon whereof this Court doth exempt the said ELIZA: BROWNE from paying Levy for the said HOLDING

- The difference between JOHN NELLSON Plantiff and FRA: DYES Deft. is refer'd till next Court

p. 17 **Essex County Court 11th of July 1692**

- Ordered that JOHN RICHARDS who was summoned an Evidence on behalfe of WILLIAM COVINGTON against RICHARD KING and MARY his Wife be paid by ye said COVINGTON for one dayes attendance according to Law with costs

- The difference between WILLIAM COVINGTON Plt. and JOHN KING and MARY his Wife, Defendts., is dismist

- The difference between JOHN KING and MARY his Wife, Plantiffs, and WILLIAM COVINGTON, Defendt. is dismist

- Judgment is granted JAME BAUGHAN against RICHARD HOLT for five hundred pounds of sweet sented tobo: and cask due by Bill, And ordered that he be pay'd ye same by ye said HOLT with costs

- Judgment (nisi causa) is granted to JOHN MILLS against ELIZA: LINCH, Admx. of WM. LINCH deced, for five hundred pounds of tobacco and Cask due by Bill to be paid with cost of suit

- The difference depending between Capt. SAMLL. TRAVERS Plt. and Capt. EDW: THOMAS and Capt: JOHN BATTAILE, Securities of REES EVANS, Defendts., is referr'd till next Court at ye Defendts. request

- Mr. JOHN WATERS acknowledged Mr. JAMES BAUGHAN his Attorney in ye difference between him and HENRY PICKETT

- Judgment is granted RICHARD GREENSTED against JOHN SOUTHERNE for Twenty shillings by account, And ordered that he be paid ye same by ye said SOUTHERNE with costs

- Nonsuit is granted JOHN SOUTHERNE Defendt., against RICHD: GREENSTED Plantiff, he ye said GREENSTEAD not bringing his Accon right, He is therefore ordered to pay damage according to Law with costs

- Whereas JOHN STIMSON was by ye Sherriff return'd arrested at suit of Capt. JNO: BATTAILE which said JOHN STIMSON was call'd to come forth and answer ye same, but made noe appearance and noe security being return'd, Judgment is therefore granted ye said Capt. JNO. BATTAILE againt ye Sherriff for One pound thirteen Shill;, & sixty pounds of tobo: & cask provided ye said STIMSON do not appear ye next Court & answer ye same

p.   <u>Essex County Court 11th of July 1692</u>
18   - Judgment haveing this day past against ye Sherriff for One pound thirteen
       shillings and sixty pounds of tobo: for the non appearance of JOHN STIMSON at
ye suit of Capt. JOHN BATTAILE, ye said Sherriff therefore moved for an attachment
against ye said STIMSONs Estate fore ye said sum and costs, which is granted him returnable to ye next Court
       - Mr. JOSEPH GOODRICH being returned non est inventus at ye suit of Mr. ROBERT
COLEMAN, was call'd to come forth and answer ye same but made noe appearance; an
attachment is granted ye said Mr. ROBERT COLEMAN against Estate of the said GOODRICH
according to Declaracon wth costs returnable to ye next Court for Judgment
       - Whereas RICHARD GREENSTED was by ye Sherriff returned arrested at ye suit
of JNO: SOUTHERNE, which said RICHARD GREENSTED was call'd to come forth and answer
the same, but made noe appearance & noe security being return'd, Judgment is therefore granted ye said JNO. SOUTHERNE against ye Sherriff for Two thousand pounds of
tobo: and cask and costs provided ye said RICHARD GREENSTED do not appear at ye next
Court and answer ye same
       - Judgmt. haveing this day past against ye Sherriff for two thousand pounds of
tobo: and cask & costs; for ye non appearance of RICHARD GREENSTED at ye suit of JOHN
SOUTHERNE, ye said Sherriff therefore moved for an attachment against ye said GREEN-
STEDs Estate for ye sd sum and costs which is granted him returnable to ye next Court
       - The difference between Mr. ROBERT PLEY & JOHN WILLIAMSON is dismist

p.   <u>Essex County Court 11th of July 1692</u>
19   - It is ordered that ye Sherriff summons Mr. JOHN TALIAFERRO to appear at ye
       next Court to be held for this County to answer an Informacon brought against
him by HENRY CURRY, for planting Tobacco contrary to Law
       - It is ordered that ye Sherriff summons Mr. ROBT: TEAY & ROBERT THOMAS to
testifie their knowledge next Cort: concerning ye informacon brought against Mr.
JOHN TALIAFERRO by HEN: CURRY for planting tobo: contrary to Law
       - DAVID LOYD being returned non est inventus at ye suit of HENRY PICKETT was
call'd to come forth and answer ye same but made noe appearance, an attachment is
granted ye said PICKETT against ye said LOYDs Estate for three hundred forty pounds of
tobo: and costs returnable to ye next Court for Judgment
       - The difference depending between ROBERT HALSY Plt. and THOMAS HUCKLE-
SCOTT Defendt., is refer'd till next Court
       - The difference depending between HEN: PICKETT Plantiff and Mr. JOHN
WATERS Defendt., is refer'd till next Court at the Defendts. request

       - At a Court held for Essex County August ye 10th Ano: 1692
       Present   Capt. WM: MOSELEY   Mr. ROBT. BROOKE
                    Mr. THO: EDMONDSON   Capt. BATTAILE   Justices
                    Mr. JOHN TALIAFERRO

       - Mr. JOHN SMITH appeared in Court and acknowledged a Deed of Sale of a par-
cell of land to Mr. JOHN TALIAFERRO to be his real act and deed, ye same was admitted to
Record
       - Capt. JOHN BATTAILE by vertue of a power from Mrs. ELIZA: SMITH, Wife to ye
above named Mr. JNO: SMITH, relinquished her ye said ELIZABETHs right of dower of in
& to a pcell of land sold by her Husband, Mr. JNO. SMITH, to Mr. JNO. TALIAFERRO, ye
same is admitted to Record

p.   <u>Essex County Court 10th of August 1692</u>
20   - FRANCIS MERIWETHER by vertue of a power from HUGH OWEN acknowledged a
      Deed of Sale of a parcell of land made by the said OWEN to ROBERT BEVERLEY and
it was admitted to Record

      - ROBERT CADE appeared in Court and acknowledged a Deed of Sale of a parcell of
land to RICHARD STEPHENS of MIDDLESEX County to be his real act & deed, ye same was
admitted to record

      - LETTIS CADE, Wife to ye above named ROBERT CADE, appeared & did freely and
voluntarily relinquish her right of Dower of in & to a parcell of land sold by ye said
ROBERT CADE to RICHARD STEPHENS of MIDDX. County ye same was admitted to Record

      - JNO: HARPER appeared in Court and acknowledged a Deed of Sale of a parcell of
Land to ALEXANDER DENAIN to be his real act and deed ye same was admitted to Record

      - LYDIA HARPER, Wife to ye above named JOHN HARPER, appeared in Court and
did freely & voluntarily relinquish her right of dower of in & to a parcell of land sold
by the said JOHN HARPER to ALEXR: DENAIN, ye same was admitted to Record

      - Attachment is granted to Mr. JNO. TAVERNER against ye Estate of JOHN SORRELL
for five hundred pounds of tobo: and caske and costs returnable to ye next Court for
Judgment

      - The difference between Mr. WM: CATLETT and Mrs. ELIZA: BLUMFEILD &c., is
refer'd till next Court

      - Whereas JOHN DOORS is by the Sherriff return'd security for the appearance
of FRANCIS DYES at the suit of JOHN NELSON, which said FRANCIS DYES, was call'd to
come forth and answer to the same but makeing noe appearance, Judgment is granted
to ye sd JNO: NELSON agt: ye said JOHN DOORS for One thousand and sixty five pounds of
Tobo: and cask & costs provided ye said DYES do not appear at ye next Court and answer
thereto

p.   <u>Essex County Court 10th of August 1692</u>
21   - Judgment is granted Capt. SAMUEL TRAVERS against Capt. EDWARD THOMAS and
      Capt. JOHN BATTAILE, securities of REES EVANS, for Seven thousand three hun-
dred eighty and seven pounds of tobo: & caske being in full satisfacon of a Bond under
their hands and seales dated November ye 27: 1690, And ordered that ye said Capt.
SAMLL. TRAVERS be paid ye sume by ye said Capt. EDWARD THOMAS and Capt. JOHN
BATTAILE with cost of suit

      - REES EVANS confest Judgment to Capt. EDWARD THOMAS and Capt. JOHN BAT-
TALIE for Seven thousand three hundred eighty seven pounds of tobacco and cask, (it
being for a Judgment past against them, ye said THOMAS and BATTAILE as securities of
ye sd EVANS for ye sd sum) to be paid with cost of suit

      - Judgment is granted Capt. JOHN BATTAILE against JOHN STIMSON for thirty five
shillings, it being for a case of Pistolls and Houlsters received of EDWARD CRESFEILE on
ye account of Mr. RICHD. TALIAFERRO and by the said STIMSON assumed to be paid to ye
said Capt. JNO. BATTAILE; Its therefore ordered that he pay ye same with costs
                            - Capt. EDWARD THOMAS added

      - JOHN WATERS JUNR. appeared and acknowledged a Deed of Sale of a parcell of
land to PHILL PARR to be his real act & deed, ye same was admitted to Record

      - Whereas at ye last Court it was ordered in ye difference between JAMES FUL-
LERTON and JNO: PRICE that ye Sherriff should impannell an able Jury who being
sworne before a Justice were in ye company of Mr. EDWIN THACKER, Survayor: to lay
out ye land in difference according to ye ancient reputed bounds thereof, & to have regard to all evidences that should be produced by either Plt. or Defendt., of which a report was to be returned to this Court; And ye Jury and Survayr: now returning their

Report to this Court & ye Court on pusall thereof finding   Juaryes report not to be positive whereby to ground any Judgment thereon, do therefore order that ye Sherriff summons ye sd Jury (ye Plt. and Defts. haveing timely notice) to appear at ye next Court & there to give in a positive report concerning ye same under their hands & seales in writeing, haveing regard to all evidences that shall be produced by either Plt. or Defendt.,. Capt. SPICER & JAMES BAUGHAN appear'd Attor: for ye Plt., Mr. JA: TAYLER & Mr. JNO: TAVERNER appeared Attor: for ye Defendt.

p.   Essex County Court 10th of August 1692
22   - Mr. WM. CLAIBORNE of KING and QUEEN County appeared in Court and acknow-
      ledged a Deed of Sale of a parcell of land to RICHARD COVINGTON to be his real act
and deed, ye same was admitted to Record
      - Mr: LEONARD HILL summoning WM: YOUNG in Chancery to give (on his Cor-
porall Oath) of a Booke, writings and papers belonging to ye Estate of BENJA: SHEF-
FEILD deced, & also to deliver what of them were in his possession to ye said HILL as he
was Admr. of ye sd SHEFFEILD; The Court therefore ordered that ye said YOUNG should
draw up his answer to ye same and give it into ye Court upon Oath, which is as followeth: In Answer ye Deft: knowes nothing of the bookes, writeing or papers
belonging to ye Estate of BENJA: SHEFFEILD.   WM. YOUNG
      - Mr. JNO. TAVERNER appeared Attor: for ye Plt.
      - Ordered that the Sherriff summons Mr. PHILL PARR and RICHARD CARTER to
appear at ye next Court to answer a Bill in Chancery exhibited against them by Mr.
LEONARD HILL, Admr. of BENJA: SHEFFEILD
      - WM. LEAKE brought his accon to this Court against RICHARD GREGORY and de-
clares that he did in Febry: last receive a hhd: of tobo: of JNO. KING at ye Defts. Plantacon in this County conteyning Five hundred neat and did sett his proper marke upon
it and went with a man to Rowl it away, and ye Deft. contrary to Law or right did by
force of armes take ye said hhd: of tobo: from the Plt: and rowled it into his House and
locked his door and have since sold it to ye Plts. damage One thousand pounds of tobo:
and cask: wherefore ye Plt. has brought his accon against ye Deft., and prayes order
against him for Five hundred pounds of tobo: and cask with all costs and damages; to
which the Deft. appeared and pleaded no guilty, And a Jury being Impannelled and
sworn to try the truth of ye premisses who Vizt. THOMAS GAINES, HENRY MOSS, JNO.
LANDRUM, HENRY PIGGET, RICHARD CARTER, HENRY BOOTH, DAVID WILSON, WM.
JOHNSON, JNO: SOUTHERN, ANDREW HARRISON,

p.   Essex County Court 10th of August 1692
23   RICHARD GRINSTED, DAVID JENKINS, return their verdict in these words: Wee
      of the Jury do find for ye Plt. Five hundred pounds of tobo: and cask and damage
fifty pounds of tobo:; THOMAS GAINES; Which verdict this Court doth confirm and order
that ye Deft. pay ye same to ye Plt. with cost of suit
      - Mr. JAMES BAUGHAN appeared Attor: for ye Plt., and Mr. JAMES TAYLOR ap-
peared Attorney for ye Deft
                  - Capt. BATTAILE present
      - WM. CRYMES complaineth to this Court against JOHN SCOTT of this County in a
plea of Debt and declareth that he render unto him ye sum of Eleven hundred & two
pounds of tobo: and cask, Five barrells and two bushells of Indian Corne with fifty three
pounds of tobo: Cost upon a Judgment for ye same; And ye sum of three pounds ten shillings Sterl. money of England all & every which said sums of Tobo: Corne and money he
ye said SCOTT to ye Plt. oweth and unjustly detayneth for that that is to say he ye said
JOHN SCOTT did by two severall Obligacons signed by ye said JOHN bearing date ye 17th

day of June in ye year of our Lord 1691 as also by a Judgment of the Worpll. Court of
GLOSTER by the Plt. obteyned ye 16th day of June in ye year 1691 aforesaid, for ye said
five barrells and two bushells of Indian Corne as by the said writeings or obligacons
here in Court and ye said Judgment bearing date as aforesaid ready to be produced doth
& may more at large appear, notwithstanding ye said JOHN SCOTT, ye Deft., ye aforesaid
severall sums of Tobo: and money as also the said Indian Corne or any part or parcell
thereof to ye said Plt. heretofore; tho: by him often thereunto required, hath not contented or paid but ye same he doe hitherto hath altogether refused and still doth refuse
to ye Plts. damage One thousand pounds of Tobo: Whereupon he hath brought his accon
& prayes Judgment with costs and damages in his part so unjustly susteyned &c., And it
appearing to this Court that ye said SCOTT hath satisfied and paid ye above recited Judgment of GLOCESTER Court for Five barrells and two bushells of Indian Corne & fifty
three pounds of tobo: & costs of ye sd Judgmt., but ye above said Tobo: and money still
unpaid, Judgmt. is therefore granted ye said CRYMES against ye sd SCOTT for Eleven
hundred & two pounds of sweet sented tobo: & cask to conteyne ye same due by Bill dated
June 17th: 1691; and three pounds ten Shillings Sterl., due by Bill dated 17th June 1691
with cost of suit. Capt. SPICER appeared Attorney for ye Plt.

p.   Essex County Court 10th of August 1692
24   - DAVID JENKINS peticon into this Court that he hath kept an Orphan boy name
        JAMES CORKER that was formerly bound to DARCUS INGRAM, and prayed that ye
said boy might be bound to him; In consideracon whereof this Court do order that the
said boy remain bound as formerly
        - An Imparlance is granted to JOHN SCOTT at ye suit of WM: CRYMES till next
Court
        - The difference between Capt. BATTAILE &c. Plt. and THOMAS CLOWSON Deft. is
refer'd till next Court
        - Capt. ARTHUR SPICER apopeared Attorney for the Deft.
        - Whereas at ye last Court JOHN SOUTHERNE obteyned an order against ye Sher-
riff for Two thousand pounds of tobo: and cask and costs for ye non appearance of
RICHARD GREENSTEAD at his suit and ye said GREENSTEAD now appearing and alleadging that he was not lawfully arrested and makeing ye same appeare, ye said suit is dismist   Mr. JNO: TAVERNER appeared Attor: for ye Plt. and Capt. ARTHUR SPICER appeared
Attor: for ye Deft.
        - Mr. ROBERT CADE in Court acknowledged Mr. JAMES BAUGHAN his Attorney
        - Non suit is granted Mr. THOMAS HUCKLESCOTT Deft., against Mr. ROBERT HAL-
SEY Plt., he ye said HALSEY not appearing to prosecute his accon; he is therefore ordered to pay damages according to Law with costs
        - HUGH FRENCH & MARGARET his Wife complaine against ANDREW HARRISON of
this County in a Plea on ye Case for that, that is to say, she ye said MARGARET did in ye
time of her widdowhood & on ye 30th day of November in ye year 1683, sett & to farme
lett unto ye aforesaid ANDREW his heires &c. ye use of Four hundred acres of land next
and adjoyning to the lands of ROBT: PAINE for & dureing ye terme

p.   Essex County Court 10th of August 1692
25   or time of Eight years then next following & to come, In consideracon of all
        which he ye said ANDREW was obliged to make ye same a Plantacon & build
houses thereon, & ye same so built to leave tenantable and Plant on one hundred apple
trees and ye same to dress & manure according to ye Judgmt. of the Neighbors, as by ye
Law Instrumt: of Lease (here in Court ready to be produced) doth and may fully appear;
Now yor: Complts. in fact say that ye said ANDREW HARRISON his severall covenants &

agreemts. as aforesaid on his pt. hath nowaies pformed, but altogether on ye contrary neglected and hath done & comitted & suffered to be done and comitted much waste & spoile thereon destroying all or ye most part of ye fencing & apple trees layed open & destroyed by Cattle or otherwise as also by pulling the very nailes out of ye housing that were built & other damages & enormities to ye Plts. have done to ye value of Five thousand pounds of tob: & therefore have brought this suit &c. & pray Judgmt. with costs &c., To which ye Deft. by Mr. JNO: TAVERNER, his Attorney, appeared & pleaded that whereas ye Deft. obteyned a non suit in June Court last agt: ye Plts. at this suit, would not answer thereto now unless that ye Plts. would imediately at ye bar pay downe ye sd nonsuit; and insisted whereon, for that, it has been practiced in RAPPA. Court, & ye Plts. by Capt. ARTHUR SPICER, their Attorney, said that ye Plts. are and alwaies were ready to pay ye Deft. ye said nonsuit but that ye Deft. never demanded it, And as to the paying ye same now downe at ye Barr they could by no possibility it being Fifty pounds of tobo: besides costs neither was it ever so intended by the Law that gives it to the Deft. And that if it were other wise so to be done it would have been by Rule of Court it being a meer matter of Practice and all Rules of Court, Sett & ordered were to be observed by every one practiceing in such Court, and demanded that ye Deft. should show such Rule of ye sd Court otherwise the Plts. ought not to be barred of their accon but ought to proceed, On due consideracons whereof & ye pleas offered on both sides, it is ye Judgmt. of this Court & accordingly ordered that ye Plts. pay ye Deft. ye sd nonsuit before their accon be admitted to Tryall, from which Judgmt., ye Plts. appeale to ye 6th: day of ye next Genll. Court to have a rehearing of ye matter before ye Rt. Honble. ye Lt. Governor & Councill. Mr. REES EVANS enters himself security in an assumsit of Five thousand pounds of tobo: & cask for ye appeallants due prosecution of ye sd appeale. And Mr. JNO. TALIAFERRO enters himself security in an assumsit of Five thousand pounds of tobo: & cask for the appellee duly answering sd appeale

p.   Essex County Court 10th of August 1692
26   - Judgment is granted HENRY PICKETT against DAVID LOYD for Three hundred
      and forty pounds of tobo: due by Account sworn to in Court, and ordered that ye
said LOYD pay ye same to ye sd PICKETT with cost of suit
      - A nonsuit is granted JNO. WATERS Deft., against HENRY PICKETT Plt., noe cause
of accon appearing, ye said PICKETT is therefore ordered to pay damage according to
Law with costs
      - A nonsuit is granted Mr. JNO. TALIAFERRO Deft. against HENRY CURRY Plt., he
ye said CURRY not appearing to prosecute his accon; he is therefore ordered to pay
damage according to Law with costs
      - Capt. ARTHUR SPICER appeared Attorney for Mr. TALIAFERRO at ye suit of
HENRY CURRY
                  - Capt. WM. MOSELEY, absent
      - The difference between JNO: MILLS and ELIZA: LINCH is refer'd till next Court
      - The difference between Capt. ARTHUR SPICER Plt. & JOHN ELLITT Deft. is refer'd
till next Court
      - The difference between Capt. ARTHUR SPICER Plt. & WM. YOUNG Deft. is refer'd
till next Court
      - The difference between Capt. ARTHUR SPICER Plt. & RICHARD FRYAR Deft. is
refer'd till next Court

p.   Essex County Court 10th of August 1692
27   - On ye peticon of Mr. HENRY AWBREY, he is exempted from paying of Levy for
      his Negro, Juno, this year

- On ye mocon of Mr. HENRY WILLIAMSON, he is exempted from paying ye Levy for his Negro woman named Frank this year
- The difference between RICHARD GREENSTED and JOHN SOUTHERNE is refer'd till next Court
- The difference between THO: WOOD Plt. and JOHN POWELL &c. Defts., concerning Hogstealing is dismist, ye Plt. not reciteing any Law in Declaracon
- Mr. JNO: TAVERNER appeared Attorney for ye Plt.
- JAMES BAUGHAN & JAMES TAYLOR appeared Attor: for ye Defts.
- The difference between SAMLL. GREEN & JNO. BRAISSER is dismist, they neither appearing
- Whereas JOSHUA NASON was by the Sherriff return'd arrested at ye suit of RALPH WHITTON which said JOSHUA NASON was called to come forth and answer ye same but made noe appearance and noe security being return'd, Judgment is therefore granted ye said RALPH WHITTON against ye Sherriff for two thousand pounds of tobo: and cask & costs provided ye said NASON do not appear at ye next Court and answer ye same
- Judgment haveing this day past against ye Sherriff for Two thousand pounds of tobo: & Cask & costs for ye non appearance of JOSHUA NASON at ye suit of RALPH WHITTON, ye sd Sherriff therefore moved for an attachment agt: ye said NASONs Estate for ye said sum & costs, which is granted him returnable to next Court
- The difference between PATRICK JACKSON & WM: COPELAND is dismist, no cause of accon appearing to ye Court

p. 28   Essex County Court 10th of August 1692
- The difference inter JNO. CAMMILL Plt. & MRS. ALICE FORBES &c. Deft. is at ye request of ye Defts. refer'd till next Court
- The difference between RALPH WHITTON & JNO. KING is dismist
- Mr. JAMES BAUGHAN appeared Attor: for ye Plt., & Mr. JNO. TAVERNER appeared Attorney for ye Deft.
- A nonsuit is granted HENRY WOODNUTT Deft. against RALPH WHITTON Plt., no cause of accon appearing, he is therefore ordered to pay damage according to Law with costs
- Capt. SPICER & Mr. TAVERNER appeared Attorneys for HENRY WOODNUTT vs. Whitton. JAMES BAUGHAN appeard Attorney for RALPH WHITTON
- RACHEL POTTER complaines to this Court against JNO. SEYMOUR in a plea on ye case that he ye said JOHN SEYMOUR render and restore unto her the Plt. seven head of Cattle Vizt. cowes, calves & one steer, to ye value of Three thousand pounds of tobo:, which he unjustly detyenes &c. and whereof he is and hath been possessed and saith that ABEDNINLECK POTTER, ye Plts. Father, did about nine years last past make over unto JOHN BATES of RAPPA. County deced in put and only under Colour to preserve them for ye said ABEDNINLECK agt: Doctr: ROBERT SYNOCK who daily threatened to take them from him, one Cow & Calfe, ye Cow ye sd POTTER had againe but ye said Calfe remained running at ye said JOHN BATES's Plantacon & so hath continued to do ever since, wth: her encrease to ye number aforesd., And for that he ye said JOHN SEYMOUR, ye Deft. as Marrying with ye Widow & Relict of ye sd JOHN BATES (long since deced) became possessed or at leastwise

p. 29   Essex County Court 10th of August 1692
made himselfe so, of ye said or some of sd Cattle as were then at ye time of his Marriage upon ye sd Plantacon together with what encrease they have come to since amounting to seven head as aforesaid notwithstanding; ye Plt. in fact saith that

he ye Defts: ye said seven head of Cattle as aforesaid, tho often demanded and required doth still keep and deteyene as aforesaid to ye Plts. damage one thousand pounds of tobo: and therefore hath brought her suit & prayes Judgmt. &c., And it appearing by sufficient evidence that he Plt. hath a good right to ye above sd Cattle, It is therefore ye Judgmt. of this Court and accordingly ordered that ye Deft. deliver up ye said seven head of Cattle to ye Plt. and pay all cost of suit als Exo.

        - Ordered that ROBERT RUDDERFORD who was summoned an evidence on ye behalfe of RACHELL POTTER agt: JOHN SEYMOUR be paid by ye said POTTER for two dayes attendance according to Law with costs (On margin: This Exo. inter RACHEL POTTER & JNO: SEYMOUR is agreed on Septr: 20th 1692/3; GEO: PARKE, Sub Sher:)

                                Vere Recordatr FRANCIS MERIWETHER Cl Cur

        - A nonsuit is granted JOHN BLAISE Deft.: against Capt. EDWARD THOMAS Plt. he ye Plt. not proveing his Declaracon, he is therefore ordered to pay damage according to Law with costs

        - Ordered that this Court be ajourned till ye 10th: day of September next

p.   - At a Court held for Essex County ye 10th: Ano 1692
30   Present   Capt. JOHN CATLETT   Mr. BERNARD GAINES
                       Mr. THO: EDMONDSON   Capt. JNO. BATTAILE

        - A Proclamacon concerning Seamen &c. dated ye 18th: of August 1692 was this day published in Court & comitted to Record

        - THOMAS PARKER SENR. appeared in Court and acknowledged a Deed of Gift of a parcell of Land to his Son, JEREMIAH PARKER, to be his real act & deed, ye same is admitted to Record

        - An Order of Councill dated at JAMES CITTY July 5th 1692 was this day published in Court and comitted to Record

        - Whereas WM: TOMLIN was by ye Sherriff return'd arrested at ye suit of DAVID WILSON which said WM. TOMLIN was call'd to come forth and answer ye same but made no appearance & no security being return'd, Judgmt. is therefore granted ye said DAVID WILSON against the Sherriff for Four hundred and thirty pounds of tobo: & cask & costs provided the said TOMLIN do not appear at ye next Court and answer ye same

        - Judgment haveing this day past against ye Sherriff for Four hundred and thirty pounds of Tobo: and cask and costs for ye non appearance of WM. TOMLIN at ye suit of DAVID WILSON, the Sherriff therefore moved for an attachment agt: ye said TOMLINs Estate for ye sd sum & costs which is granted him returnable to ye next Court

        - The difference inter WILLIAM MERRITT & JOHN MAGUFFEE is dismist

        - Mr. JAMES BAUGHAN appeared Attorney for Mr. JOS: GOODRICH at ye suit of Mr. ROBT. COLEMAN

p.   Essex County Court 10th of September 1692
31   - Capt. ARTHUR SPICER appeared Attorney for Mr. ROBERT COLEMAN agt: Mr. JOS: GOODRICH

        - Mr. ROBERT COLEMAN bringing his accon to this Court as Admr. of THOMAS EVANS deced agt: Mr. JOS: GOODRICH and ye sd COLEMAN not being quallified as aforesd. nonuit is therefore granted ye sd GOODRICH agt: ye sd COLEMAN with costs

        - Judgment upon attachment is granted to Mr. JNO. TAVERNER agt: ye Estate of JOHN SORRELL in ye hands of Mr. ROBERT BROOKE for five hundred pounds of tobo: and caske due by Bill sworn to; to be paid with costs

        - Judgment is granted Mr. WM. CATLETT against Mrs. ELIZA: BLUMFEILD, Relict and Admx. of Capt. SAMLL. BLUMFEILD deced, for Fifty five pounds eight Shillings to be paid with cost of suit

- Capt. ARTHUR SPICER appeared Attor: for Mrs. ELIZA: BLUMFEILD at ye suit of mr. WM. CATLETT

- FRANCIS DYES confest Judgmt. to JNO. NELSON for One thousand sixty five pounds of tobo: and cask due by Bill under hand and seale dated Augt: ye 25th 1691: Therefore ordered that he pay ye same with costs of suit

- Capt. SPICER appeared Attor: for JNO. NELSON vs DYES

- The difference inter Mr. LEONARD HILL, Admr. of BENJA: SHEFFEILD deced, Plt. & Mr. PHILL: PARR and RICHARD CARTER Defendts, is dismist, ye Plt. not appearing to prosecute

- WILLIAM CRYMES complaineth against JOHN SCOTT of this County in a plea on ye Case for that Whereas he ye said JNO. SCOTT did by his certaine Deed of Conveyance or Instrument in Writeing bearing date ye eleventh day of Febry: in ye year 1688/9, bargain and sell unto ye Plantiff his heirs and assignes for ever all and singular tha Tract or divident of land situate lying and being in ye County aforesaid; then called County of RAPPAH:, and by the said Deft.

p.   Essex County Court 10th of September 1692
32   bought and purchased of ye Plt., as also four English Servants by name JOHN
      BELL, THOMAS GRAVES, THOMAS COUCH and ELIZABETH ELLSER, also twelve head of Cattle that is to say nine Cowes and three two yeare old a peice and three horses named or known by ye names of Tom, Jack branded wth the Letter I S on ye neer buttoak as by ye said Deed or Instrument in writeing relacon being thereunto had doth and may more fully and at large appear, Nothwithstanding which ye Plantiff in fact saith that ye Deft. ye aforesaid Tract or Dividend of land so as aforesaid to him granted bargained and sold doth by force & armes keep and withold the possession of the same from ye Plt. as also ye said Servants, stock of cattle & horses doth by like force keep & detaine Wherefore he hath brought his accon and prayes Judgmt. for ye said Land and that their Maties Writt of habere facias seisinam may be directed to ye Sherriff of ye said County to put him in peaceable and quiett possesion of ye said Land, And the Plt. in fact farther saith that he is damnified and damage hath susteyned to ye value of Ten thousand pounds of tobo: by reason of the Defts. deteyning of ye aforesaid Servtts., Cattle and horses for all which he prayes Judgment together with his damages and costs to him to be adjudged &c., And Whereas ye Defendt. had an Imparlance granted him in this suit from ye last Court to this and not appearing, Now Judgment on nil dicit is therefore granted to ye Plt. against ye deft. for ye above said Land, Servant, Cattle & horses with costs of suit als Exo:. Mr. EDMONDSON dissented from ye Courts Judgment

- The Judgment (nisi causa) granted ye last Court to JNO: MILLS against ELIZABETH LINCH, Admx. of WM. LINCH deced, for five hundred pounds of Tobo: and cask due by Bill is made void, ye Deft. appearing now and pleading that ye Bill was out of date and it appearing so, ye Court have therefore dismist ye suit

- Nonsuit is granted to Mrs. ALICE FORBES Deft. agt: JNO: CAMMILL Plt., he ye Plt. not makeing anything appear, Its therefore ordered that he pay ye same with costs

- Capt. ARTHUR SPICER appeared Attorney for Mrs. FORBES

p.   Essex County Court 10th of September 1692
33   - The difference inter Capt. ARTHUR SPICER Plt: and WILLIAM BALL Defendt., is
      refer'd till next Court

- The difference inter Capt. ARTHUR SPICER Plt. & JNO: ELLITT is refer'd till next Court

- The difference inter Capt. ARTHUR SPICER Plt. & WM.. YOUNG Deft., is refer'd till next Court
- The difference inter Capt. ARTHUR SPICER Plt. & RICHARD FRYAR is refer'd till next Court
- The difference inter Capt. JNO BATTAILE Plt. & THOMAS CLOWSON Deft. is continued till next Court
- The difference inter RICHD. GRINSTED & JNO: SOUTHERNE is refer'd till next Court
- JAMES FULLERTON complaineth against JNO. PRICE in a plea of Trespass.

Whereas yor: peticonr: hath right to a certaine tract of land in fee lying in RAPPA. COUNTY & on ye South side of Rappa. River upon ye Maine Swamp of PISCATAWAY CREEKE cont: Seven hundred acres as may appear by a Patent granted to yor: peticonrs: Father, JAMES FULLERTON deced, bearing date ye 29th day of September 1667, up & above ye land of WM. AKUS upon ye Maine Pocoson of PISCATAWAY CREEKE bounding as followeth; beginning at WM: AKUS his uper corner tree & running by his line North by East One hundred and sixty pole, West North West four hundred and eighty pole over certaine branches of ye Pocoson, then North one hundred & one pole, thence West South West sixty six pole, thence parallel with ye first line three hundred and twenty pole to ye Pocoson; and down ye sd Pocoson where it first began, bounding upon ye Maine Runn: And JNO. PRICE contrary to ye Law or right is seated within yor: Peticonrs: land and doth daily trespass, altho he has been Lawfully forewarned, to yor: peticonrs. great damage of thirty pounds Sterl.; Wherefore yor: peticonr: has brought his accon agt: JNO: PRICE and humbly prayes that their Mats: Writt of habere facias may issue of this Court to ye Sheriff of ye County to putt yor: Petrs. into peaceable possession of his land with all costs and damages;

Whereupon this Court by their Order bearing date ye 11th: day of July last did order that the Sheriff of this County should Impannell an able Jury, who being sworne before some Justice of ye sd County were in ye Company of Mr. EDWIN THACKER, Surveyr:, on the first Tuesday in August then next following to lay

p   Essex County Court 10th of September 1692
34   out ye lands in difference according to ye amount reputed bounds thereof
       haveing regard to all evidences that should be produced by either Plantiff or
Defendt., of which a Report was to be return'd to ye next Court; which said Jury together with ye Surveyr: meeting upon ye sd land did survey and lay out ye same according to ye before recited Order and drew up & delivered their verdt: into this Court (In August last, together with the Draught or Platt of ye said land protracted by ye said Surveyr: and ye Court on view thereof finding ye Juries verdt: Imperfect did further order that ye same Jury should be summoned by ye Sheriff (the Plt. & Defendt., haveing notice) to appear at ye next Court and given in a perfect verdt: considering ye same haveing regard to all evidences that should be produced by either Plt. or Deft. And said Jury now appearing by name ROBT. COLEMAN, THOMAS GAINES, JOHN MEADOR, ROBERT MILLS, JNO. FERGESON, WM.: COVENTON, RICHARD HALLE, THOMAS COVINGTON, ROBT: HALSEY, THO: WHEELER, JNO: MOSS: DANIEL BROWNE, give in this following verdict to the Court under their hands & seals (vizt.) In Obedience to an Order of Court to this County dated ye 10th day of August 1692, wee of the Jury have in ye presence of Mr. EDWIN THACKER, laid out ye lands in difference between JAMES FULLERTON Plt. & JNO: PRICE Deft., according to evidence and do find that JNO: PRICE is seated within ye bounds of our Survey; which verdt: this Court have ordered to be confirmed; from which order of ye Court, ye Defendt. appeales to ye 6th day of ye next Genll. Court to have a rehearing of ye matter before ye Rt. Honble. ye Lt: Govr: and Councill;

Mr THO: WOOD SENR. enters himselfe security in ye sum of Five thousand pounds of
Tobo: & cask for the appellants due prosecution lof the sd appeal

JAMES BOUGHAN enters himselfe security in ye sum of Five thousand pounds of tobo: &
cask for the appellees due answering the said appeal

p.   Essex County Court 10th of September 1692
35   - Mr. HENRY AWBREY is by this Court requested to discourse ye Gent. of
          RICHMOND COURT concerning ye laying of ye Levy as also to appoint a time for
ye doing of ye same
          - Ordered that ye Court be adjourn'd till ye 29th: day of this Instant

          - At an Adjourn'd Court held for Essex County 7br: ye 29th 1692
          Present   Mr. THOMAS EDMONDSON   Capt. JOHN BATTAILE
                           Capt. EDWARD THOMAS   Capt. ANTHO: SMITH

          - GEORGE WARD appeared in Court and acknowledged a Deed of Sale of a parcell
of land to JNO: MOODIE to be his real act and deed, ye same is admitted to Record
          - Judgmt. upon attachment is granted THOMAS GRIFFEN against ye Estate of JNO:
SORRELL in ye hands of Mr. ROBERT BROOKE, for Two hundred pounds of tobo: in lieu of
his Freedom Cloaths. he haveing made oath that he hath received no satisfaction for ye
same by ye said SORRELL; to be paid with cost of suit
          - Judgment upon attachmt: is granted to ye Church Wardens of South Farnham
Parish for ye use of ye sd Parish agst: ye Estate of MARY ONGLEY for three barrells of
Indian Corne in ye hands of Capt. EDWARD THOMAS to be paid with cost of suit
          - Nonsuit is granted to SILVESTER TANDY Deft., agt: JNO: WATSON Plt., he ye Plt.
not appearing to prosecute. to be paid with costs
          - Mr. JNO. TAVERNER appeared Attor: for SIL: TANDY vs WATSON
          - Whereas WM. MERRIOTT was by ye Sheriff return'd arrested at ye suit of THO:
HUCKLESCOTT wch: said WM. MERRIOTT was called to come forth & answer ye same, but
made noe appearance & noe security being return'd, Judgmt: is therefore granted to ye
sd THO: HUCKLESCOTT agt: ye Sheriff for Two hundred & fifty pds: of tobo: & caske due by
Bill & costs provided if he WM: MERRIOTT do not appear at ye next Court & answer ye
same

p.   Essex County Court 10th of September 1692
36   - Judgment haveing this day passed agt: ye Sheriff for Two hundred and fifty
          pounds of tobo: and costs for ye non appearance of WM. MERRIOTT at ye suit of
THOMAS HUCKLESCOTT, ye said Sheriff moved an Attachmt: agt: ye said MERRIOTTs Estate
for ye sd sum & costs, which is granted him returnable to ye next Court
          - The difr: intr: MARTIN JOHNSON & Capt. EDW: THOMAS is refer'd till next Court
          - The difference inter JOHN SCOTT and Mr. WM: CRYMES is refer'd till next Court
          - Mr. TAVERNER appear'd Attor: for JNO: SCOTT
          - The difference inter JNO. SOUTHERNE Plt. & RICHD. GRINSTED Deft., is refer'd
till next Court: And that ye Plt. hath Liberty granted him to draw his Declaracon agt: ye
next Court
          - RALPH WHITTON complaineth agt: JNO: KING in a Plea of ye Case. that JOHN
KING did on ye 25th day of xbr: in ye year of our Lord 1688 run away and carried away
with him one Servant woman that did belong to yor: petr: contrary to Law or right to
yor: petrs: damage Ten thousand pounds of sweet sented tobo: and cask, all which your
Petr. is ready to make appear; Wherefore yor: Plt. has brought his accon agt: JNO: KING
and humbly prayes yor: worsps. Order for present paymt: of ye sum above with all costs;

And noe cause of action appearing in ye Defendts. mocon. this Court have granted him a nonsuit agt: ye Plt., with costs. Mr. JAMES BAUGHAN appeared Attorney for ye Plt. Mr. JNO. TAVERNER appeared Attorney for ye Deft.

- The difference inter RALPH WHITTON Plt. & JNO: KING Deft. is dismist ye accon not right brought

- Mr. JAMES BAUGHAN appeared Attorney for ye Plt. and Mr. JNO: TAVERNER appearead Attorney for ye Deft.

- ROBT. JOHNSON being return'd non est inventus at ye suit of ALICE SHIPLEY was call'd to come forth & answer ye same, but made noe appearance, an attachmt. is granted ye sd ALICE SHIPLEY agt: ye sd JOHNSON for Four hundred and fifty pds: of tobo: & cask & costs returnable to ye next Court for Judgmt.

p.   Essex County Court 29th of September 1692
37   - The difference inter CHRISTOPHER ROBINSON Plt. & ROBERT THOMAS Defendt.. is refer'd till next Court

- Capt. SPICER appear'd Attorney CHRS: ROBINSON Esqr.

- GEORGE LAMBETH being call'd to come forth & answer ye suit of FRANCIS MERRIWETHER, assignee of WM. SMITH, & not makeing his appearance, ye Sheriff makeing Oath that he had left a copie of ye Writt according to ye Law, an attachmt. is therefore granted to ye sd FRANCIS MERRIWETHER agt: ye said LAMBETHs Estate for Two pounds three Shills: and two pence Sterl., due by Bill under hand and seale and costs returnable to ye next Court for Judgmt.

- Judgment is granted STEPHEN WELLS against BENJA: MARSH for thirty gallons of Rum according to Specialty to be paid with costs of suit

- Mr. JNO. TAVERNER appeared Attorney for ye Plt.

- Whereas ELIZABETH LINCH was by ye Sheriff return'd arrested at ye suit of RICHARD TAYLOR. which said ELIZA: LINCH was call'd to come forth and answer ye same, but made noe appearance and noe security being return'd, Judgment is therefore granted ye said RICHARD TAYLER agt: ye Sherriff for two thousand pds: of sweet sented tobo: and cask and costs provided ye said LINCH do not appear at ye next Court and answer ye same

- Judgmt. haveing this day past agt: ye Sheriff for two thousand pds: of sweet sented Tobo: and caske & costs, for ye non appearance of ELIZA: LINCH at ye suit of RICHARD TAYLER, ye sd Sher: therefore moved for an attachment agt: ye sd LINCHes Estate for ye sd sum & costs returnable to ye next Court

- The difference intr: THO: WOOD JUNR.. Plt., & JNO: POWELL &c. Defendts. is refer'd till next Court. Mr. JNO: TAVERNER appeared Attorney for ye Plt. Mr. JAMES BAUGHAN appeared Attor: for ye Defendt.

- Whereas at ye last Court, Mr. WM. CRYMES obteyned a Judgmt. on (Nil dicit) agt: JNO: SCOTT for a parcell of land, four English Servants, twelve head of Cattle and three horses, & ye Deft. appearing now on his motion alledging that he hath matter of equity: an Injunction in Chancery granted him till next Court

p.   Essex County Court 29th of September 1692
38   - Mr. JNO. TAVERNER appeared Attorney for JNO: SCOTT at ye suit of Mr. WM. CRYMES

- Ordered that ye Sheriff or his Deputy summons Mr. PHILL: PARR to appear at ye next Court to answer a Bill in Chancery exhibited agt: him by Mr. LEO: HILL. Admr. of BENJA: SHEFFEILD

- Mr. GAINES. present

_The difference intr: Capt. JNO. BATTAILE. &c. & THOMAS CLOWSON is refer'd till next Court

- The diff: inter DENNIS MACARTIE &c. & Mrs. ELIZA: BLOOMFEILD &c. is refer'd till next Court. Mr. JNO: TAVERNER appeared Attor: for Mr. DENNIS MACARTY

- Whereas WM: COVINGTON was by ye Sher: return'd arrested at ye suit of RICHD. KING, which said WM. COVINGTON was call'd to come forth and answer ye same, but made noe appearance & noe security being return'd, Judgmt. is therefore granted ye sd RICHARD KING agt: ye Sher: for Three thousand pounds of sweet sented tobo: & caske & costs provided ye sd WM. COVINGTON do not appear at ye next Court & answer ye same

- Judgmt. haveing this day past agt: ye Sheriff for Three thousand pounds of sweet sented tobo: and caske & costs for the non appearance of WM: COVINGTON at ye suit of RICHD. KING, ye sd Sheriff moved for an attachmt: agt. ye sd COVINGTONs Estate for ye sd sum & costs, which is granted him returnable to ye next Court

- Ordered that ye Court be adjourn'd till the 10th: day of October next

p.   At a Court held for Essex County October ye 10th 1692
39   Present   Capt. WILLIAM MOSELEY   Mr. ROBERT BROOKE
                      Mr. THOMAS EDMONDSON   Capt. JOHN BATTAILE
                      Mr. BERNARD GAINES   Capt. ANTHO: SMITH

- A Proclamacon for a PUBLICK THANKSGIVING was this day published in Court and committed to Record

- Also a Proclamacon for continuing all Officers &c. was this day published in Court and committed to Record

- A Ltre: of Attorney from DAVID COGHILL to Mr. ROBERT MYNES or CHILION WHITE to acknowledge a Deed of Sale of a parcell of land sold by him ye sd COGHILL to Capt. RICHARD BOOKER was proved in Court by the Oaths of WM. LOBB & WM. RYDER & admitted to Record

- ROBERT MYNNE by vertue of a Power from DAVID COGHILL appeared in Court and acknowledged a Deed of Sale of a parcell of land sold by ye sd DAVID COGHILL to Capt. RICHARD BOOKER to be his ye sd COGHILLs real act & deed; ye same is admitted to Record

- Two bonds for performance of Covenants in ye above menconed Deed of Sale are at ye request of ye above said Capt. RICHARD BOOKER admitted to Record

- Capt. JOHN BATTAILE in right of himselfe and as Guardian to MARY COGWELL, a minor, brought his accon of Trespass agt: THOMAS CLOWSON of this County and declares that ye said THOMAS CLOWSON with force and armes and contrary to ye Peace of our Soevereigne Lord and Lady King William & Queen Mary, keeps and deteynes from ye Plantiff quallified as above said, One messuage Tenement and Tract of land conteyning Six hundred acres scituate lying & being in ye Parish of Sittingbourne and in ye aforesaid County & of right belonging & apperteyning to ye Plt. & he said MARY COGWELL, And although ye Plt. quallified as aforesd., hath divers times forewarned ye said CLOWSON from ye same, yet keeps ye possession thereof to ye Plts. damage quallified aforesaid Twenty thousand pounds of Tobo: for which prayes Judgment and that ye Plt. with ye sd MARY

p.   Essex County Court 10th of October 1692
40   COGWELL may have your Worships Writt of habere facias possessionem directed
      to ye Sheriff of this County, And that ye said CLOWSON may pay all cost of suit,
   To which ye Defendt. by Capt. ARTHUR SPICER, his Attorney, appeared and pleaded
Justification and craved reference from ye last Court till this; that he might have his

evidence summoned to proved ye said land lapsed by JAMES COGWELL and ye Defendt. produceing his evidences to this Court & it appearing by ye Deposition of NICHOLAS COPELAND that there was Corne growing on ye said Land above twenty yeares since, And that a man his Wife & family lived on ye said land since that; which were put there by ye said JAMES COGWELL, & that there was fruit trees growing thereon, It is therefore ye Judgment of this Court and accordingly ordered that their Mats: Writt of habere facias pssessionem be directed to ye Sheriff of this County to put ye Plt. (quallified as aforesd.) into peaceable and quiet possession of ye above sd Land and appurtenances & that ye Deft. pay all cost of suit als Exo.

From wch: order ye Deft. appeales to ye Seventh day of ye next Genll. Court to have a rehearing of ye matter before the Honbl: Governr: & Councill

Mr. HENRY AWBREY together with Mr. THOMAS EDMONDSON enter themselves security in an assumpsit of Five thousand pounds of tobo: & cask for ye appeallant due prosecution of ye sd. appeale

Capt. WM. MOSELEY together with Mr. BER: GAINES enter themselves security in an assumpsit of Five thousand pounds of tobo: and cask for ye appellee due answering of ye sd appeale

   - JOHN SCOTT confest Judgmt. to Mr. WM. CRYMES for Nine thosuand pounds of sweet sented tobo: & caske; Its therefore ordered that he pay ye same to ye sd CRYMES with cost of suit

   - Its ordered that NICHOLAS COPELAND, who was summoned by Mr. THOMAS VICARIS, as an evidence in ye suit depending between Capt. JOHN BATTAILE Plt. & THOMAS CLOWSON Deft. be paid by ye sd Mr. THO: VICARIS for four dayes attendance according to Law with costs

p. 41   **Essex County Court 10th of October 1692**

   - Its ordered that JAMES BOWLER, who was summoned by Mr. THO: VICARIS as an evidence in ye suit depending between Capt. JOHN BATTAILE Plt. and THOMAS CLOWSON Deft., be paid by said Mr. THO: VICARIS for two dayes attendance according to Law with costs

   - Mr. THO: HUCKLESCOTT enters JAMES BAUGHAN his Attorney
   - The Court adjourn'd till tomorrow morning Eight a Clock

   - At a Court held for Essex County October ye 11th 1692

Prsent   Capt. WM. MOSELEY   Mr. ROBERT BROOKE
            Mr. BERNARD GAINES   Capt. JOHN BATTAILE   Justices

   - Whereas WM. BALL being by ye Sheriff return'd arrested at ye suit of Capt. ARTHUR SPICER was call'd to come forth and answer ye same, but made noe appearance & noe security being return'd, Judgmt. is therefore granted sd Capt. ARTHUR SPICER agt: ye Sheriff for One thousand pds. of sweet sented tobo: and cask with costs, provided ye sd BALL do not appeare at ye next Court and answer ye same

   - Judgment haveing this day past against ye Sheriff for One thousand pounds of sweet sented tobo: and caske with costs for ye non appearance of WM. BALL at ye suit of Capt. ARTHUR SPICER, ye sd Sheriff therefore moved for an attachmt: agt: ye said WM. BALLs Estate, which is granted him for ye sd sum returnable to ye next Court

   - Whereas JOHN ELLIT being by ye Sheriff return'd arrested at ye suit of Capt. ARTHUR SPICER was call'd to come forth & answer ye same, but made noe appearance & noe security being return'd, Judgment is therefore granted ye sd Capt. ARTHUR SPICER agt: ye Sheriff for Fifteen hundred pounds of sweet sented tobo: & caske wth: costs provided sd ELLIT do not appeare at ye next Court & answer ye same

p   Essex County Court 11th of October 1692
42   - Judgment haveing this day past against ye Sheriff for Fifteen hundred pounds
         of sweet sented tobo: & caske with costs for ye non appearance of JOHN ELLITT at
ye suit of Capt. ARTHUR SPICER, ye sd Sheriff moved for an attachment against ye sd
ELLITT's Estate for ye sd sum and cask with costs, which is granted him returnable to ye
next Court
         - Whereas WM. YOUNG being by the Sheriff return'd arrested at ye suit of Capt.
ARTHUR SPICER was call'd to come forth & answer ye same, but made noe appearance &
noe security being return'd, Judgment is therefore granted to ye sd Capt. ARTHUR
SPICER agt: ye Sheriff for Five hundred pounds of sweet sented tobo: & cask with costs
provided ye said YOUNG do not appear at ye next Court and answer ye same
         - Judgmt. haveing this day past against ye Sheriff for Five hundred pounds of
sweet sented tobo: & cask with costs for ye non appearance of WM. YOUNG at ye suit of
Capt. ARTHUR SPICER, ye sd Sheriff therefore moved for an attachment agt: ye sd
YOUNGs Estate for ye sd sum & cask with costs, which is granted him returnable to ye
next Court
         - Whereas RICHARD FRYER being by ye Sheriff return'd arrested at ye suit of
Capt. ARTHUR SPICER was call'd to come forth & answer ye same but made noe appearance and noe security being return'd, Judgmt. is therefore granted ye said Capt. ARTH:
SPICER agt: ye Sheriff for One thousand & ten pounds of sweet sented tobo: and cask
wth: costs, provided ye sd FRYER do not appear at ye next Court & answer ye same
         - Judgmt. haveing this day past agt: ye Sheriff for One thousand & ten pounds of
sweet sented tobo: and cask wth: costs for ye non appearance of RICHARD FRYER at ye
suit of Capt. ARTHUR SPICER, ye sd Sheriff therefore moved for an attachmt: agt: ye sd
FRYERs Estate for ye sd sum & cask with cost, which is granted him returnable to ye
next Court

p.   Essex County Court 11th of October 1692
43   - The difference intr: RICHARD GREENSTED & JOHN SOUTHERNE is refer'd till next
         Court
         - Capt., ARTHUR SPICER appeared Attorney for RICHD. GREENSTED vs. JOHN
SOUTHERNE
         - Judgmt. on (Nil Dicit) is granted to Mr. THOMAS HUCKLESCOTT against WM.
MERRIOTT for Two hundred & fifty pds. of tobo: & cask due by Bill. with cost of suit
         - The difference intr: CHRISTOPHER ROBINSON Esqr. Plt. & ROBERT THOMAS Deft.,
is continued till next Court
         - The difference intr: Mr. LEO: HILL, Admr. of BENJA: SHEFFEILD deced, and
PHILL PARR is dismist for want of prosecution
         - Nonsuit is granted to Mrs. ELIZA: BLOMBEILD, Administrx. of Capt. SAML. BLOM-
FEILD deced, Deft. agt: Mr. DENNIS MACARTY, Assignee of Capt. GEO: COOPER Plt., he ye
Plt. not appearing to prosecute to be paid with costs
         - Capt. ARTHUR SPICER appear'd Attorney for Mrs. BLUMFEILD
         - The difference inter RICHARD KING Plt. & WM. COVINGTON Deft. is dismist, for
want of prosecution
         - The difference inter MARTIN JOHNSON Plt. & Capt. EDWARD THOMAS Defendt., is
refer'd till next Court
         - Capt. ARTHUR SPICER appeared Attorney for ye Defendt.
         - The difference inter Mr. BENJA: CLEMENTS Plt. & JOHN SCOTT, Defendt., is
dismist for want of prosecution

p   Essex County Court 11th of October 1692
44   - Whereas EDWARD BRACEY being by ye Sheriff return'd arrested at ye suit of
       WM. LEAKE was called to come forth & answer ye same but made noe appearance
& noe security being returned, Judgmt. is therefore granted ye sd WM. LEAKE agt: ye
Sheriff for six hundred pounds of sweet sented tobo: & caske wth: costs, provided ye sd
BRACEY do not appear at ye next Court & answer ye same
       - Judgmt. haveing this day past agt: ye Sheriff for Six hundred pounds of sweet
sented tobo: & cask wth: costs for ye non appearance of EDWARD BRACEY at ye suit of
WM. LEAKE, ye sd Sheriff therefore moved for an attachmt. agt: ye Estate of ye sd ED-
WARD BRACEY for ye sd sum & cask wth: costs, wch: is granted him returnable to ye
next Court
       - The difference inter RICHD. RHODES Plt. & WM. VEALE Defendt., is dismist for
want of prosecution
       - A Letter of Attorney from Mr. JOHN WATERS to Mr. JAMES BAUGHAN was
proved in Court by ye Oath of Mr. ROBT. COLEMAN and admitted to Record
       - The difference inter Capt. ARTHUR SPICER Plt. & JOHN WATERS Defendt., is
refer'd till next Court
       - RALPH WHITTON & ELIZA: his Wife bringing their accon to this Court agt: JOHN
KING sheweth that ye sd KING stands indebted to them in ye sum of One thousand
pounds of sweet sented tobo: & caske payable upon their Plantacon where they now
live, all which they are ready to make appear & prayes order for present paymt: of ye
same with costs of suit; And ye Defendt. appearing & haveing Nine hundred & thirty six
pounds of tobo: in discount of ye sd Debt sworn to in Court, Its therefore ordered that ye
Defendt. pay ye Plts. Sixty four pounds of sweet sented tobo: and cask, it being ye ballance of ye sd Debt with cost of suit.
       - JAMES BAUGHAN appeared Attorney for ye Plts.
       - Capt. ARTHUR SPICER appared Attorney for ye Defts.

p.   Essex County Court 11th of October 1692
45   - JOHN CAMMILL brought his accon to this Court against Mr. ALICE FORBES &
       declares that ye said Mrs. ALICE FORBES stands indebted to him a Cow and a year-
ling that belonged to MARY KILLMAN. Daughter of JOHN KILLMAN, late of ye County of
RAPPA: deced, as also Nine hundred and seventy five pounds of tobo: & cask; now ye said
MARY KILLMAN being deced ye right descends upon him as marrying SARAH, younger
Sister to ye said MARY, who hath often demanded ye said Cattle & tobo: of ye said Mrs.
ALICE FORBES, Admx. and Relict of Mr. THOMAS GOULDMAN, late of RAPPA: deced, who
came possessed of the Estate of ye said JOHN KILLMAN in behalfe of ye Orphans, he
therefore prayes Judgmt. for his aid Cattle wth: their encrease since they have been
demanded & for his tobo: wth: cost of suit,
   To which ye Defendt. by her Attorney appeared & demanded that ye Plt. should make
ye Laws same appear; Whereupon ye Plt. produced an order of RAPPA. Court wherein
ye sd KILLMAN's Estate was to be sold at an Out Cry and that ye said Mr. THOMAS GOULD-
MAN was appointed to take ye Judgmts. & give an account of ye same as also an account
of ye sd Estate sould by ye sd GOULDMAN according to ye before recited order whereon it
appears that ye said tobo: is due to ye Plt. but not makeing it appear to ye Court that ye
sd Mr. THOMAS GOULDMAN was possest with ye above Cattle, Judgmt. is granted to ye sd
JOHN CAMMILL agt: ye sd Mrs. ALICE FORBES, Admx. & Relict of Mr. THOMAS GOULDMAN
deced. for Nine hundred & seventy five pounds of tobo: to be paid with cost of suit
       - Capt. ARTHUR SPICER appear'd Attor: for Mrs. ALICE FORBES at ye suit of JNO:
CAMMILL   JAMES BAUGHAN appeared Attor: for JOHN CAMMILL vs FORBES

- Nonsuit is granted SILVESTER TANDY Defendt.. against JNO WATSON Plt.. he ye Plt. not appearing to prosecute. to be paid with costs
    - JAMES BAUGHAN appear'd Attorney for SIL· TANDY vs WATSON

p   **Essex County Court 11th of October 1692**
46   - A nonsuit is granted to Mrs. ALICE FORBES Defendt.. agt: DAVID WILSON Plt..
he ye Plt. not appearing to prosecute, to be paid with costs
    - Capt. ARTHUR SPICER appeared Attorney for Mrs. FORBES vs D. WILSON
    - The difference intr: RICHARD TAYLER Plt. & ELIZA: LINCH is continued till next Court
    - Judgmt. on attachmt. is granted to Capt. EDWARD THOMAS against ye Estate of JOSEPH KEMBALL for a Sow & three piggs with costs als Exo.. and ordered that ye Sheriff summons JOHN JONES and RICHARD GREENSTED to appraise ye said Sow and Piggs & return an account thereof to the next Court
    - JAMES BAUGHAN appear'd Attorney for RICHARD TAYLER vs. ELIZA. LINCH
    - Capt. ARTHUR SPICER appear'd Attorney for ELIZA: LINCH at ye suit of RICHD. TAYLER
    - Mr. MARTIN JOHNSON acknowledged Mr. JAMES BAUGHAN to be his attorney agt: Capt. EDWARD THOMAS

p.   **Essex County Court 10th of November 1692**
47   - At a meeting of their Maties Justices for Essex and RICHMOND Counties (for-
    merly RAPPA.) at the Court House of the said County of Essex this 10th day of
November Ano Dom 1692 for receiving County Claimes. in order to ye Laying of a Levy
for both the said Counties

Mr. HEN· WILLIAMSON		
Capt. JNO. CATLETT		
Capt. WM: MOSELEY	Capt. GEO: TAYLER	Justices
Mr. THO. EDMONDSON	Capt. WM. BARBER	
Mr. BER· GAINES	Capt. ALEX· SWAN	
Mr. ROBT BROOKE		
Capt. JNO BATTAILE		
Capt. ANTHO. SMITH		

Essex County Dr. 1692

To Capt. WM. MOSELEY for one wolfe killed by Gun	0200
To THOMAS MUNDAY for four wolves kill'd by Pitt	1200
To EDMOND PAGETT for one wolfe kill'd by Pitt	0300
To JNO: SOLMON for one wolfe kill'd by Pitt	0300
To Mrs. REBECCA TOMLIN for one wolfe kill'd by gun	0200
To THOMAS HOWARTON for one wolfe kill'd by gun	0200
To Capt. JNO. CATLETT for six wolves kill'd by gun	1200
To Idm one wolfe kill'd by Pitt	0300
To BRYAN WARD for one wolfe kill'd	0200
To Mr: HEN: AWBREY for two wolves kill'd by Gun	0400
To Mr. BER. GAINES, Assee. of GEO: WILSON for one wolfe kill'd by Pitt	0300
To Mr. CHARLES TALIAFERRO for one wolfes head	0200
To Mr. DANLL: DOBYNS for his Charge about the Prisonr: JNO. DEVALL	0500
To Capt JNO. BATTAILE for one tithable over charged to DAVID WILSON	0098
To Idm one Tith JOS. HENLY dead	0200
To JNO. MEADOR for one wolfe head kill'd by Gun	0200
To Mr. ROBT COLEMAN one omitted last yeare	2000

To Mr GEO: PARKS for trouble in conveying Esqr. WOMELEYs Negro over the River	0200
To Mr. ROBT: COLEMAN for accomodateing the Court	0666`
To EDWARD NEWTON for accomodateing the Court on the North side	0450
To Mr GEO: PARKE. Sub Sheriff. for Extraordinary services	1000
To Mr. EDW. JONES. for Extraordinary services	1000
To Mr. HEN: AWBREY for Burgesses Charges	8000
To FRA: MERIWETHER, Clk., for halfe a yeare extraordinary services	0750
(Does not add up)	19963

p.   Essex County Court 10th of November 1692
48   Richmond County Dr.

To Mr. MAX: ROBINSON for keeping SOUTHINS FERRY	3500
To THO: LEWIS for keeping TOTASKEY FERRY	3500
To Idem for reparing the Marsh to the said FERRY	0500
To THO: GLASCOCK JUNR. for one wolfes head by Pitt	0300
To JACOB DELA BELLO for keeping PISCATAWAY FERRY	2500
To WALTER FRANCIS for one wolfes head	0200
To Mr. JNO. DEANE for one wolfes head	0200
To Capt WM. BARBER three wolfes heads	0600
To Mr. ALEXR DONIPHAN one wolfes head	0200
To RICHARD GREENE one wolfes head	0200
To WM. SMITH JUNR. two wolfes heads by Pitt	0600
To JNO BOWLES one wolfes head	0200
To ELIAS WILSON one wolfes head by Pitt	0300
To Idm. one wolfes head by Pitt	0300
To JNO. PATRIDGE one wolfes head	0200
To three wolfes to Mr. THO: LOYD. he returning his Certificate into the Office	0600
To WM. SMITH one wolfes head by Pitt	0300
To JA: ORCHARD one wolfes head	0200
To JNO. ALLAWAY one wolfes head by Pitt	0300
To THO: HARRIS one wolfes head by Pitt	0300
To THO. WALKER one wolfes head	0200
To FRAN: JAMES one wolfes head	0200
To Mr. WM. BROKEN BURROW for his attenance upon a Venire at JAMES CITTY	0500
To 18 Tithables overcharged to Coll. LOYDs List of Tithables last year to Coll. STONE	1314
To Col. JNO: STONE credit to the County last year	0111
To Idm. pd: Secretaries fees for two Condishions of ye Peace for Rappa County Ano 1691	0320
To EDW NEWTON for menteyning a Criminall Negro in Prison two months 18 dayes	1000
To FRA. SUTTLE for mending the Prison	0100
To EDW JONES. Sub Sheriff for secureing ANN CAMBELL by Warrant from two of the Councill	0500
To Mr: DENNIS MA:CARTY for prosecuteing Prsentmts: and fornicators &c. in RAPPA. County	1800
To WM: COLSTON Clk. of RAPPA. County for Extraordinary business	1500
To Mr. ARTHUR SPICER for his appearance as Attorney for the sd County	0800
To WM. COLSTON Burgesses Charges	8000

To WM. COLSTON Clk. for a Deputy to officiate dureing his attendance as
      Burgess at JAMES CITTY   1000
To SHADRICK WILLIAMS, one wolfes head   0200
                                    (Does not add up)   33745

p.   Essex County Court 10th of November 1692
49   Essex and RICHMOND Counties Dr. November Ano: 1692   Tobo.
          To Creditt delivered into Essex County amounting to   19963
To Creditt delivered into RICHMOND County   33745
To Ball. of the whole sum of 53708   05370
To Cask for ditto sum   04296
To the Levy from the Assembly   32174
To the Clerke of the Assembly by Acct.   00350
                                                         95898

Out of the Fractions EDW· THOMAS for Wolfes head 200
To 739 lbs. of Tobo. being the fraction given by the Respective County
      Courts to their severall Clerkes   00739
                                                         96637

                      p Contra: Cr:
By Creditt to the Counties from the Assembly   00400
By 1887 tithables at 50 p poll is   96237
                                                         96637

      - At a Court held for Essex County November 10th: Ano. 1692
      Present Capt. JNO: CATLETT   Mr. ROBT: BROOKE
              Capt. WM: MOSELEY   Capt. ANTHO: SMITH

      - JNO: BAKER apper'd and acknowledged a Deed of Sale of a parcell of land to
ROBT. FOSTER to be his real act & deed & the same is admitted to Record
      - Also the above named Mr. JNO: BAKER appear'd and acknowledged a Bond for
performance of Covenants in the abovesaid Deed to ye sd ROBT: FOSTER to be his act &
deed, ye same is admitted to Record
      - Mr. JNO: BAKER appear'd and acknowledged a Deed of Sale of a parcell of land to
JNO. GARNETT to be his real act & deed & ye same is admitted to Record
      - Also the said Mr. JNO: BAKER appear'd & acknowledged a Bond for performance
of Covenants in the abovesd Deed to the sd JNO: GARNETT to be his act & deed, ye same is
admitted to Record

p.   Essex County Couirt 10th of November 1692
50   - Mr JNO. BAKER appear'd and acknowledged a Deed of Sale of a parcell of Land
       to WM: HOWLETT to be his reall act & deed, ye same is admitted to Record
      - Also a Bond for performance of Covenants in the abovesd Deed to ye sd HOW-
LETT to be his reall act & deed, ye same is admitted to Record
      - Mr. JNO. BAKER appear'd & acknowledged a Deed of Sale of a parcell of Land to
JNO: FOSTER to be his real act & deed, ye same is admitted to Record
      - Also ye abovesd. Mr. JNO: BAKER appear'd and acknowledged a Bond for per-
formance of Covenants in the abovesaid Deed to JNO: FOSTER to be his act and deed, ye
same is admitted to Record
      - Mr JNO. BAKER appear'd & acknowledged a Deed of Sale of a parcell of Land to
WM. SMITHER to be his real act & deed ye same is admitted to Record

- Also th said Mr. JNO: BAKER appear'd & acknowledged a Bond for performance of Covenants in the above menconed Deed to ye sd WM: SMYTHER to be his act & deed, ye same is admitted to Record

- Mr. JNO: BAKER appear'd & acknowledged a Deed of Sale of a parcell of land to Capt. WM. MOSELEY to be his real act & deed, ye same is admitted to record

- BRYAN WARD appear'd and acknowledged a Deed of Sale of a parcell of Land to JNO: ALMOND to be his real act & deed, ye same is admitted to Record

- WM. FREEMAN appear'd and acknowledged a Deed of sale of a parcell of land to FRANCIS BROWNE to be his real act & deed, ye same is admitted to Record

- The Court is adjourned till tomorrow morning 8 a Clock

p.   - At a Court held for Essex County Febry: ye 10th 1692
51   Present Capt. JNO: CATLETT   Mr. FRA: TALIAFERRO
                  Mr. THO: EDMONDSON   Mr. ROBT: BROOKE
                  Capt. EDW: THOMAS   Capt. JNO: BATTAILE

- Mr. HENRY WILLIAMSON & Capt. JNO: CATLETT are appointed Feoffees in Trust for the TOWN LAND in this County (On the margin: Mr. HENRY WILLIAMSON & Capt. JNO. CATLETT are appointed Feoffees in Trust with Mr. HEN: AWBREY in ye stead of Colnll. WM. LOYD & Mr. THOS: GOULDMAN for Conveying ye TOWN LANDs of this County)

- RICHARD FREEMAN appear'd and acknowledged a Deed of Sale of a parcell of Land to WM: FREEMAN to be his real act & deed. the same is ordered to be recorded

- VINCENT VAUSE appear'd and acknowledged a Deed of Sale of a parcell of Land to Capt. EDWARD THOMAS to be his real act and deed. the same is ordered to be recorded

- ANN VAUSE, Wife to the above named VINCENT VAUSE, appear'd and acknowledged a Deed of Sale of a parcell of land sold by her Husband, VINCENT VAUSE, and she the sd ANN VAUSE to Capt. EDWARD THOMAS, ye same is ordered to be recorded

- The private Examination of ANN VAUSE concerning the abovesd. land is at the request of Capt. EDWARD THOMAS ordered to be recorded

- CORNELIUS NOELL appear'd and acknowledged a Deed of Sale of a parcell of land to THOMAS CLOUTSOME to be his real act and deed, ye same is ordered to be recorded

- CORNELIUS NOELL appear'd and acknowledged a Deed of Sale of a parcell of land to EDMOND CONELE to be his real act and deed, ye same is ordered to be recorded

- THOMAS CLOUTSOME appear'd and acknowledged a Deed of Sale of a parcell of land to CORNELIUS NOELL to be his real act & deed, ye same is ordered to be recorded

- EDMOND CONELE by Vertue of a Power from MARY CLOUTSOME appear'd and acknowledged all the sd MARYs right title interest and claime to a parcell of land sold by her Husband, THO: CLOUTSOME & her selfe to CORNELIUS NOELL, ye same is ordered to be recorded

p.   Essex County Court 10th of February 1692/3
52   - Certificate according to Act of Assembly is granted to CORNELIUS NOELL for
          Two hundred and fifty acres of land, due for the Importacon into this Colony of DAVID TEMERTON. THOMAS CLARKE, ELIZA: WATERMAN, HENRY PYELL, MARY PUE

- RICHARD WILSON appear'd and acknowledged a Deed of Sale of a parcell of land for Eighty nine yeares to WM. COMPTON to be his real act & deed, ye same is ordered to be recorded; Also MARY WILTON, Wife to the above named RICHD. WILTON, appear'd and acknowledged the above mencon'd land to WM: COMPTON to be her real act and deed. the same is ordered to be recorded

(On margin: Certificate according to Act of Assembly is granted to WM: CLAP-HAM for Nineteen hundred acres of land due for ye Importacon of Thirty eight persons into this Colony whose names are VALLINTINE MAYO; ABGALL BASETT, THO: KING, RICHD. GOLDON, SUSANA GOBETT; MARGARET GRIFFES; DAVID PURVIS, RICHD. MON JOY FRANCES GEORGE, HENRY LASH, JOS: STRANGE, KATHERINE YEATES, PETTER DALLE, ANN CRUMSURE, JNO. SPENGE, JOHN COLLERRELL, RICHD: NORTH; JNO: BRYAND, JNO. HASELL, JNO: PERSEFULL, ANN GWINES, HEN: WILLIAMS, EDMOND WHEDEN; FRA: JENNINGS; JONATHAN BATHOW, ELIZA: CHAMBERS, MARY PUTLEY, ANN FACK; JNO: THOMAS, ANN FOY, DAVID ROME, JNO. SPIERS, JNO. WILLKISSON, JNO: WILLCOK, JNO: CROOKE, EDMUND COLLENERY, HEN: DYER, JAMES DANIELL, Cert: issue out)

- URSULA CLARKE being by her Master, Mr. JNO: JONES, brought to this Court for haveing a bastard Child in the time of her service, And the said JONES praying the benefit of the Law as in such cases; This Court have therefore ordered that the said CLARKE serve ye sd JONES or his assignes Two yeares after her time by Indenture or Custome is expired, it being for the loss & trouble her sd Master sustains by her haveing the sd bastard
- Capt. EDWARD THOMAS as Security for THO: STOESLEY confest Judgment to the Parish of South Farnham for Two hundred pounds of tobo: it being for URSULA CLARKEs fine for the sin of fornication, and ordered that the same be paid with costs als Exo.
- Ordered that URSULA CLARKE serve THO: STOESLEY halfe a year after her time by Indenture or Custome is expired, it being in consideracon of her fine paid by the sd STOESLEY for her comitting the sin of fornication
- JNO. HUTSON appear'd and acknowledged a Deed of Sale of a parcell of Land to BARTHOLOMEW VAWTER to be his real act & deed, ye same is ordered to be recorded
- Order of Administration is granted to Mrs. ANN HASLEWOOD on the Estate of her deced Husband, Mr. GEO: HASLEWOOD, in this County, giveing bond according to Law (ELIZA: HAZLEWOOD marked out)
- Ordered that Capt. JNO. CATLETT, Mr. FRA: TALIAFERRO, Mr. JNO. TALIAFERRO & Mr. SAMLL. SALLIS or any three of them doe on the fifth day of May next meet at the Plantacon of Mr. GEO: HASLEWOOD deced in this County, and being first sworne, appraise what Estate of the said deceds Estate as shall be presented to them by Mrs. (ELIZA. marked out) HASLEWOOD. Admx. of the sd deced, and Capt: JNO. BATTAILE be there to swear ye appraisers

p.   Essex County Court 10th of February 1692./3
53   - The last Will and Testament of JNO: EVANS deced was this day proved by the
        Oaths of the witnesses, and a Probate thereof granted to SUSANNA EVANS, Execu-trix therein named
- Ordered that JNO: BRYAN serve Capt. EDWARD THOMAS fifteen dayes after his time by Indenture or Custome be expired, it being for his service spent in seeking his Freedom
- RICHARD CAUTHORNE by his peticon made choice of Mr. JOHN GRIFFIN to be his Guardian, the same is allowed of by this Court
- Judgment on attachment is granted to RALPH WHITTON against JOSHUA NASON for three hundred and fifty pounds of tobo: and ordered that the same be paid with cost
- Mr. JNO: EVERIT appear'd Attorney for JOSHUA NASON and JAMES BOUGHAN appear'd Attor: for RA: WHITTON
- Ordered that a Court of Claims be held at the Court House of this County on the

25th day of this Inst. Febry: for all persons to give in their claimes and Agrieveances
- Capt. JNO. BATTAILE, absent
- Judgmt. on attachment is granted to Capt. EDW: THOMAS, assignee of Capt.
ARTHUR SPICER, against the Estate of ELIZA: PIGG as Exx. in her own wrong of JNO. PIGG
deced, for foure hundred and fifty pounds of sweet tobo: and caske in the hands of WM.
MARSH, to be paid with cost
- Capt. EDW: THOMAS, Absent; Capt: ANTHO: SMITH, present
- Mr. JNO. ALMOND appear'd Attor: for JACOB DOBOLLOW vs ANN COOPER, and Mr.
JA: BOUGHAN appear'd Attorney for ANN COOPER
- The Court is adjourn'd till tomorrow morning 8 a Clock

- At a Court held for Essex County Febry: ye 11th: ano 1692
Present Capt. WM: MOSELEY   Capt. JNO: BATTAILE
        Mr. FRA: TALIAFERRO   Capt. ANTHO: SMITH

- Certificate according to Act of Assembly is granted to Capt. WM. MOSELEY for
Two hundred and fifty acres of land due for the Impartacon into this Colony of ANN
PANTREP & four Negroes

p.   Essex County Court 11th of February 1692/3
54   - The difference inter CHRISTOPHER ROBINSON Esqr. & ROBT. THOMAS is con-
        tinued till next Court by consent
                Mr. THO: EDMONDSON, Prsent
- The difference inter RICHARD GREENSTED & JNO: SOUTHERNE is dismist for want
of prosecution
- The difference inter JNO: SOUTHERNE and RICHD: GREENSTED is dismist for want
of prosecution
- The Judgmt. on nihil dicit granted last October Court to Mr. THO: HUCKLESCOTT
against WM: MERRIOT for Two hundred and fifty pounds of tobo: & caske due by bill &
costs, is by this Court confirm'd and ordered that ye sd MERRIOT pay the same to the sd
HUCKLESCOTT with cost of suit
- The Judgmt. granted last October Court to WM: LEAKE against the Sheriff for ye
non appearance of EDW: DRAINS at the suit of sd LEAKE for Six hundred pounds of sweet
sented tobo: & caske & costs is by this Court confirm'd and ordered to be paid with costs
- Mr. JAMES BAUGHAN appear'd Attor: for LEAKE
- The difference inter DAVID WILSON Plt. & WM. TOMLIN Defendt., is dismist, the
Plt. not laying his Declaracon right
- An Imparlance is granted to JNO: ALMOND at ye suit of Mr. RICHARD ROBINSON
till next Court
- The difference inter Capt. AR: SPICER and RICHARD MATHEWS is refer'd till
next Court
-Capt. JNO. CATLETT, present; Mr. THO: EDMONDSON, Mr. FRA: TALIAFERRO, absent
- Judgmt. is granted to Capt. ARTHUR SPICER against JNO. WATERS for Six hun-
dred pounds of sweet sented tobacco and cask due by bill: to be paid with cost of suit

p.   Essex County Court 11th of February 1692/3
55   - ELIZABETH WARKEMAN brought her accon against BRYANT TURNER and De-
        clar'd that the sd TURNER did oblige himselfe by Bond to make her Two hundred
pair of mens and womens shoos, but he being required to performe the same, hath and
doth absent himselfe and denyeth the fullfilling ye same, for wch: she hath brought
her accon and prays Judgmt., with cost of suit &c.

- To which the Defendt. by Capt. ARTHUR SPICER, his Attorney, appear'd and pleaded to the insufficiency of the Declaracon and moved for a nonsuit; Whereupon the Court on view of the Declaracon & finding the same insufficient have granted the Defendt. a nonsuit agt: the Plantiff to be paid with costs als Exo.

- Mr. JNO: EVERIT appear'd Attorney for ELIZ: WARKEMAN
- Capt. ARTHUR SPICER appear'd Attorney for BRY: TURNER
- The difference inter Capt. WM: SMITH & JNO: FREEMAN is dismist for want of prosecution
- The difference inter JNO: JONES and JNO.EARINTON is dismist for want of prosecution
- The difference inter JNO: ALMOND & HEN: GORE is dismist for want of prosecution
- The difference between Mrs. ALICE FORBES and SAMLL. HARWAR is dismist for want of prosecution
- The difference between THOMAS PARKE and JNO: DIXSON is dismist for want of prosecution
- The difference between PAUL MICOU and REBECCA TOMLIN is dismist for want of prosecution
- The difference between THO: PHELPS and TOBY LEVERIT is dismist for want of prosecution
- The difference inter ROBT: HALSEY and THO: CRISPE is dismist for want of prosecution
- The difference inter ROBT: HALSEY & JNO: CRASKE &c. is dismist for want of prosecution
- The difference inter SIMON COPNALL and THO: COGGIN is dismist for want of prosecution
- The difference inter JAMES BOUGHAN and RALPH WHITTON is dismist for want of prosecution

p.   Essex County Court 11th of February 1692/3
56   - RALPH WHITTON brought his accon against JNO: DAVIS and declar'd that the said DAVIS is indebted to him Six hundred and ten pounds of tobo: due from the said DAVIS to JAMES NEWBEL & denies paymt., Wherefore he humbly pray'd Judgmt. for the same with costs &c., to which the Defendt., by Capt. ARTHUR SPICER, appear'd and pleaded that the Plt. had noe cause of accon against ye sd Defendt. & therefore humbly pray'd for a nonsuit against ye Plt., Which this Court have granted on & ordered that ye Plt. pay the sume to the Deft. with costs

- Capt. ARTHUR SPICER appear'd Attorney for JNO: DAVIS vs. WHITTON
- The difference inter Mr. WM: CRYMES & JNO. SCOTT is dismist for want of prosecution
- THOMAS COOPER SENR. brought his accon against ARTHUR HODGES and declared that the said HODGES did on the 11th: day of July last assume for to pay to him Three hundred pounds of Swt: tobo: & cask for the use of RICHARD BRISINDIN, wch: he is ready to prove and refuses paymt: Wherefore he humbly pray'd order for present paymt: with costs &c., and the Plantiff being required to prove the same, could not, Therefore the Court have dismist ye accon

- Mr. JAMES BAUGHAN appear'd Attorney for THO: COOPER vs ARTHUR HODGES
- The difference between ROGER LOVELESS and THO: COGGIN is dismist for want of prosecution
- The difference inter THO: COOPER JUNR. and WM. MORRIS is dismist for want of prosecution

- The difference inter JONAS SMITH and WM: JEFFERIES is dismist for want of prosecution
- The difference inter JONAS SMITH and WM: JEFFERIES is dismist for want of prosecution
- The difference inter JONAS SMITH & ROBT. DEPUTY is dismist for want of prosecution
- Mr. JNO. EVERIT appear'd Attorney for JONAS SMITH (marked out) DAVID MERRIDAY vs JONAS SMITH
  - Mr. THO: EDMONDSON, Mr. FRA: TALIAFERRO, Capt. ANTHO: SMITH Present
    Capt. WM. MOSELEY, Capt. JNO. BATTAILE, Absent

p.   Essex County Court 11th of February 1692/3
57   - JNO. WATERS brought his accon against WM. JOHNSON & declared that the said
      JOHNSON stood indebted to him in the sume of Foure hundred sixty foure pounds
of sweet sented tobo: and cask due upon the ballance of a Bill of Nine hundred pounds of
tobo: and caske & refused paymt: he therefore humbly prayes order for paymt. with
cost of suit &c., but no cause of accon appearing to this Court, upon the Defendants
mocon, a nonsuit is granted him against the Plt. and ordered that the same be paid with
costs
      - Mr. JAMES BAUGHAN appear'd Attorney for JNO. WATERS
      - The difference inter THO: THORPE and THO: SHORT is dismist for want of prosecution
      - The difference inter JAMES BOUGHAN and HENRY LONG is dismist for want of prosecution
      - The difference inter RICHD. WILTON and ABNER GRAY is dismist for want of prosecution
      - The difference inter REBECCA ROBINS and RICHARD & JUDITH LOITON is dismist for want of prosecution
      - The difference inter THO: WILLIAMS and THO: PAINE is dismist for want of prosecution
      - The difference inter JNO: WATSON and DANNLL. PEIRSIL is dismist for want of prosecution
      - The difference inter ROBT: DEPUTY and FRN: LACY is dismit for want of prosecution
      - The difference inter BENJA: MATHEWS & THO: SMITH is dismist for want of prosecution
      - The difference inter HENRY PICKETT &c. & THOMAS GAINES &c. is dismist for want of prosecution
      - RICHARD TAYLOR as being Guardian to ELIZABETH BROWNE by his peticon sett
forth that ELIZA: LINCH of this County did on the first day of July last or thereabout take
up one gray mare about two yeares old in HOBSES HOLE Old Fields belonging to yor:
petitionr: and did brand dock & broake ye sd Mare contrary to Law or right, all which
yor: petr: is ready to prove and refuses to deliver your petr: the Mare to his great
damage of Two thousand pounds of sweet sented tobo: and caske, Wherefore your petr.
has brought his accon against ELIZA: LINCH as being quallified as aforesd., and humbly
prayes your worships order for the present delivery of the said Mare with all costs &
damages &c., to which the Defendt. appear'd and pleaded not guilty

p.   Essex County Court 11th of February 1692/3
58   Whereupon the Court have ordered that a Jury be impannelled and sworn to try
      the truth of the premisses who vizt. THOMAS GAINES, foreman, JNO: GATEWOOD,

DAVID WILSON, FRA: GOULDMAN, JOHN BRAISEIR; HENRY PICKETT, WM. SWETMAN, PHILL PARR, WM: PRICE, WM: JEFFERIES, RICHARD COVINGTON, RALPH WHITTON return their verdict in these words: Wee of the Jury do find for the Plt. ye Mare according to evidence with twenty pounds of tobo: damage; THOMAS GAINES; which verdict (upon the Plantiffs mocon) this Court have confirm'd and ordered that the Defendt. deliver the sd Mare to the Plt. or pay the value thereof and also pay the sd Twenty pounds of tobo: damage with cost of suit

- The difference inter SAMLL. COATES and THO: ST. JOHN is dismist for want of prosecution

- Mr. ROBT. COLEMAN appear'd Attorney for ELIZ: SMITH at ye suit of RICHARD TAYLOR &c.

- HENRY LONG brought his accon against WM: COPLAND & declares that the sd COPLAND stands indebted to him by Bill Foure hundred pounds of tobo: and caske & denies paymt., he therefore prayes Judgmt. for the same with costs &c., but the sd COPLAND being by the Sheriff return'd non est inventus was call'd to come forth and answer ye same but not appearing, an attachmt. is granted the said LONG against ye sd COPLANDs Estate the sd Foure hundred pounds of tobo: & caske with costs returnable to the next Court for Judgment.

- HENRY LONG brought his accon against WM: PRICE and declares that the said PRICE stands indebted to him for his accomodacons one yeare Foure hundred & fifty pounds of tobo: and caske & denies payment; he therefore prayes Judgment for the same with costs &c., To which the Defendt. appear'd and pleaded that he had satisfyed the Plt. for the said Debt, Whereupon the Court (on the Defendts. mocon), have refer'd the same till the next Court, for ye Defendt. to make ye same appear

- ROBERT DEPUTY brought his accon against JOSHUA NASON and declares that the sd NASON stands indebted to him Six hundred & twenty pounds of sweet sented tobbo: p account & denies paymt: he therefore prayes Judgmt. for the same with costs &c., but the Plantiff not appearing to prosecute his accon, upon the Defendts. mocon, a nonsuit is granted him against ye Plantiff and ordered that the same be paid with costs

- Mr. JNO: EVERIT appear'd Attor: for JOSHUA NASON vs DEPUTY

p.   Essex County Court 11th of February 1692/3
59   - The difference inter ROBT: DEPUTY & JAMES NEWBEL is dismist for want of prosecution

- Id: DAVID WILSON, assee. of ELIZA: LINCH vs WM: MERRIT

- JONAS SMITH complaineth against DAVID MERRIDAY in an accon of Trespasse for that the Defendts. Wife did unlawfully take up, ride and make use of a Horse belonging to the Plt. which he is ready to make appear, by which unlawfull act as aforesd he is damnified and damage hath to the value of Five hundred pounds of sweet sented tobo: and caske: Wherefore he hath brought his accon and prayes Judgmt. against the Defendt., for the above sd damage with costs &c.

- To which the Defendt. by Mr. JNO: EVERIT, his Attorney, appear'd and pleaded to the insufficiency of the Declaracon and humbly moved for a nonsuit against the Plantiff, which this Court have granted And ordered that the same be paid with costs als Exo.

- ELIZA: MEADS, who was subpena'd by the Sheriff as an evidence for JONAS SMITH in a difference depending between the sd SMITH & DAVID MERRIDAY, and not appearing, is by this Court fin'd according to Law for her default, And ordered that the same be paid by ye sd MEADS with costs

- ROBERT DEPUTY who was subpena'd by the Sheriff as an evidence for JONAS SMITH in a difference depending between the sd SMITH and DAVID MERRIDAY and not appearing is by this Court fined according to Law for his default, And ordered that the same be paid by the said DEPUTY with costs

- Mr. JNO: TAVERNER brought his accon to this Court against JOHN WATERS and declar'd that the said WATERS stands indebted to him Five hundred pounds of sweet sented tobo: and caske by Bill & denies paymt; he therefore prayes Judgmt. for the same with costs &c., but the Plt. not appearing to prosecute his suit (upon mocon of the Defendts. Attorney) a nonsuit is granted him against the Plt., And ordered that the same be paid with costs

- The difference inter PAUL MICOU and Mrs: REBECCA TOMLIN is dismist for want of prosecution

- Do: Mr. RICH: ROBINSON vs RALPH WHITTON

- DAVID MERRIDAY brought his accon to this Court against ROBERT DEPUTY & declres that the said DEPUTY stands indebted to him Three hundred pounds of tobo: by Acct: and denies paymt; He therefore prayes Judgmt. for the same with costs &c., which sd DEPUTY being call'd to come forth and answer the same but makeing no appearance an attachmt. is therefore granted the sd MERRIDAY against the Estate of the sd DEPUTY for Two hundred thirty three pounds of tobo: & costs (due by account sworn to in Court) returnable to the next Court for Judgmt. (On the margin: Attach: iss. Feb 23d 1692/3; March ye 2d 1692/3. There is no Estate of ye within named ROBT. DEPUTY to be found p DAVID MERRIDAY, Witness G: PARKE, Sub Sher: vere Recordatr. FRANCIS MERRI-WETHER Cl. Cur.)

p.   Essex County Court 11th of February 1692/3
60   - The difference inter HUMP: BOOTH and SAMLL. GRIFFIN is dismist for want of
       prosecution
       - The difference inter JAMES FUGEET & Mr. JNO: GRIFFIN is refer'd till next Court
for Mr. JNO: EVERIT to produce his Power from the sd FUGEET
       - The difference inter JAMES FUGEET &c. & THO: GAINES is refer'd till next Court
       - The difference in Chancery intr: JAMES FUGEET & THO: GAINES &c. is refer'd till
next Court
       - Mr. ROBERT YARD brought his accon to this Court against JNO. WATERS and de-clar'd that the said WATERS stood indebted to him Fourteen pounds Sixteen shillings & six pence Sterl. by account sworn to and denyed payment; Wherefore he pray'd Judg-mt. for ye same with costs, And the Defendt. appearing by Mr. JAMES BOUGHAN his Attorney and offering nothing in Barr thereof, this Court have granted Judgmt. to the said YARD against the said WATERS for the above sd sum of Fourteen pounds sixteen shillings & six pence Sterl: with cost of suit

- Mr. ROBERT YARD Plt. brought his accon to this Court against JNO. WATERS Defendt., and declar'd that the Defendt. stood indebted to him by Obligacon Foure Cowes and Calves & denyed paymt., Wherefore he pray'd Judgmt., for them with costs; And the Defendt. appearing by Mr. JAMES BOUGHAN, his Attorney, and offering nothing in Barr, this Court have granted Judgmt. to the Plt. against the Defendt. for the said Foure Cowes & calves with cost of suit. (On the margin: Exo. Feb: 13th 1692/3. Febry: ye 15th 1692/3 Then executed ye within preceipt & levied this Exo. on three Cowes & Calves and one Cow bigg with Calfe p GEO: PARKE Sub Sher:)

- GEORGE DOBBINS brought his accon to this Court against Mr. ROBT: BROOKE and declar'd that the sd Mr. BROOKE stood indebted to him in the sum of Four hundred and ninety pounds of tobo: and one pound nineteen shilllings and four pence for the which he humbly prays order with cost of suit, but the Plt. failing to enter his peticon, the Court have dismist the suit

- The difference intr: Mr. THO: HUCKLESCOTT & SARAH ROWZEE is dismist for want of prosecution

- Mr. THO: HUCKLESCOTT Plt. brought his accon to this Court agt: Mr. ABRA: NORTH Defendt., & declar'd that the Defendt. stood indebted to him as Marying Mrs. SARAH ROWZEE nine hundred and forty pounds of tobo: for Medicine administred and humbly pray'd Judgmt. against the Defendt., for ye same with costs of suit; But the Plt. not makeing his Debt appear, the Court have dismist the suit

p.   Essex County Court 11th of February 1692/3
61   - Ordered that RICHARD JONES, who was subpena'd an evidence in the difference
         between RICHARD TAYLOR Plt. and ELIZA: LINCH, Defendt., be paid by the Plt. for
10 dayes attendance according to Law with costs, the sd JONES haveing made Oath to ye same

- Nonsuit is granted DAVID MERRIDAY Defendt., against THO: PHELPS, Plt., he the Plt. not appearing to prosecute his accon; And ordered that the same be pay'd with costs

- The difference intr: Mr. WM. TODD & ELIZA: his Wife, Admx. of THO: FOSTER, Plts. & JNO. WATERS, Defendt., is refer'd till next Court

- RICHARD FRYAR of this County complaineth against HENRY PICKETT of the said County in a Plea of Trespass for that, that is to say, he the said PICKETT did by force and armes &c., and against the Peace &c., on the (blank) day of Janry: last past upon the lands of the Plantiff, he the said Plt. being then & there in peaceable & quiet possession by force and armes as aforesaid did enter and stopp molest hinder and breake the Chaine of the Survayr: of the County thereunto lawfully called and by the Plt. employed and ordered to lay out the land aforesaid of the Plt. as aforesaid; And the Plt. in fact saith that by reason of such the Defendts. outcry and force &c., as aforesaid & the afore-sd Survayr: was hindred and impeded by the Defendt. aforesaid in the lawfull and just proceeding in his business and other enormities to him hath done to the Plts. damage three thousand pounds of tobo: Wherefore he hath brought his accon and prayes Judgment &c. for his damages so unjustly susteyn'd with cost of suit &c., To which the Defendt. by his Attorney appear'd and pleaded not guilty;

  Whereupon this Court have ordered that the Sheriff of this County or his deputy Impannell an able Jury of the Neighbourhood who are nowise concern'd by affinity or consanguinity or otherwise who being first sworn are in the Company of the Survayr: of that precinct to goe upon the land in difference on the 23d day of this Instant Febry: if fair (if not, the next fair day) and lay out the same according to the Plts. Patent and return an account of their proceedings to the next Court; And it is further ordered that they have regard to all evidences that shall be produced by either Plantiff or Defendant, and Capt. ANTHO: SMITH is hereby requested to swear the said Jury and Evidences

p.   Essex County Court 11th of February 1692/3
62   - The difference inter Mr. MARTIN JOHNSON and Capt. EDWARD THOMAS is
         refer'd by consent till next Court

- The difference intr: PHILL PARR and WM: YOUNG is refer'd till next Court

- WM. JEFFREYES brought his accon to this Court against ROBT. DEPUTY and de-clar'd that the said DEPUTY stood indebted to him Two thousand seven hundred and fifty seven pounds of Tobo: by Accot:, and denyed paymt: he therefore pray'd Judgmt. for the same with cost &c.; wch: sd DEPUTY being call'd to come forth and answer the same, and not appearing, an attachmt. is therefore granted the sd JEFFREYES against the Estate of the sd DEPUTY for the sd 2757 pounds of Tobo: with costs returnable to the next Court for Judgmt.

- ROBT. DEPUTY brought his accon agt. WM: JEFFREYES & declar'd that ye sd JEFFRIES stood indebted to him Five hundred pounds of sweet sented tobo: by Acct: & denies paymt:, he therefore pray'd Judgmt. for ye same with costs &c., but ye sd DEPUTY not appearing to prosecute his action, upon ye Defendts. mocon, a nonsuit is granted him against ye sd DEPUTY & ordered that ye same be paid with costs
- The Court is adjourn'd till ye 10th: of March next

- At a Court held for Essex County March ye: 10th: Ano 1692
Present Capt. JOHN CATLETT   Mr. BERNARD GAINES
       Capt. WM: MOSELEY   Mr. ROBT: BROOKE
              Capt. ANTHO: SMITH

- A Commission of the Peace for this County dated the 14th of Janry: Ano 1692 was published and committed to Record, Also ye dedimus for swearing the Commissioners
- Capt. JNO. CATLETT, Capt. WM. MOSELEY, Mr. BERNARD GAINES, Mr. ROBERT BROOKE and Capt. ANTHONY SMITH by vertue of a Power from Sr. EDMOND ANDROS Knt. their Maties Lt. & Govr. Gen: of Virga: dated the 14th of Janry: ano 1692; took ye oaths appointed by Act of Parliament to be taken instead of the Oaths of Allegiance and Supremacy & the Test together with ye Oath of Justice of ye Peace
- The Court adjourn'd till tomorrow morning eight a Clock

p.   - At a Court held for Essex County Aprill ye 10th Ano. 1693
63   Present Mr. HENRY WILLIAMSON   Mr. FRA: TALIAFERRO
               Mr./Capt. JOHN CATLETT   Mr. BERNARD GAINES
               Capt. WM. MOSELEY   Mr. ROBERT BROOKE
               Mr. THO: EDMONDSON   Capt. JOHN BATTAILE
               Capt. EDWARD THOMAS   Mr. JOHN TALIAFERRO

- Mr. HENRY WILLIAMSON, Mr. THOMAS EDMONDSON, Capt. EDWARD THOMAS, Mr. FRANCIS TALIAFERRO, Capt. JOHN BATTAILE & Mr. JOHN TALIAFERRO by vertue of a Power from Sr. EDMOND ANDROS Knt., their Maties. Lieut: and Governr: Genll. of Virginia tooke the oaths appointed to be taken by Act of Parliamt: instead of the Oaths of Allegiance and Supremacy & ye Test, together with the Oath of Justices of the Peace
- The last Will and Testament of Mr. JOHN JONES was proved by the Oaths of the witnesses and a probate thereof granted to MILLICENT JONES, Executrix therein named.
- CHRISTOPHER PELL, Servant to Mr. JOHN DANGERFIELD, who came into this Country in ye Shipp, *RESOLUTION,* Mr. RICHD. KELSICK Comdr:, being by the said DANGERFIELD presented to this Court to have inspection into his age, is adjudged thirteene yeares of age and ordered that he serve him ye said DANGERFIELD or his assignes according to Act
- RICHARD HARVEY and MARY his Wife appeared & acknowledged a Deed of Sale of a parcell of land to ABRAHAM STEPP to be their real act & deed, ye same is ordered to be recorded
- JOHN MORGAN confest Judgmt. to Capt. EDWARD THOMAS for Four hundred and fifty pounds of sweet sented tobo: & caske due by Bill, wch: this Court have ordered to be paid with costs als Exo.
                    Mr. BERNARD GAINES, absent

p.   **Essex County Court 10th of March 1692/3**
64   - Judgmt. on attachment is granted to Mr. HENRY AWBREY against the Estate of
WILLIAM THOROGOOD for one black gelding branded on ye neare buttock with
C T with a starr on his forehead and a white snipp on his nose; with costs als Exo. and
ordered that Mr. WM. BENDERY & WM: JONES value ye said Horse and return an account
of the same to ye next Court
        - JOHN DAY in Court made choise of JOHN BILLINGTON to be his Guardian, this
Court have therefore ordered that the said BILLINGTON be possest with ye said DAYes
Estate giveing bond for ye same with good security at ye next Court to be held for this
County
        - Ordered that RICHARD TAYLER by Surveyr: of the High Wayes in the precincts
FRANCIS BROWNE was formerly surveyr: of, And that he cleer all ye Roads which ye
said BROWNE use to cleare
        JOHN MERTEER confest Judgmt. to JOHN SCOTT for One thousand and sixty pounds
of sweet sented tobo: & caske due by Bill which this Court have ordered to be paid with
cost of suit
        - The whole body of the Acts of Assembly made at an Assembly begun at JAMES
CITTY ye second day of March 1692/3 were this day published in Court
        - JAMES SCOTT appeared and acknowledged a Deed of Sale of a parcell of Land to
GEORGE PROCTOR to be his reall act and deed, ye same is ordered to be recorded
        - Mr. BERNARD GAINES by vertue of a power from MARY SCOTT, Wife to ye above
named JAMES SCOTT, appear'd and acknowledged all her, ye sd MARYs, right title & interest to ye above sd land, to ye above sd GEORGE PROCTER, ye same is ordered to be
recorded

p.   **Essex County Court 10th of March 1692/3**
65   - MICHAEL DICKSON, Servant to Mr. HENRY AWBREY, who came into this Country
in ye Ship, *RESOLUCON,* Mr. RICHD: KELSICK Commandr:, being by his Master ye
sd Mr. AWBREY, presented to this Court to have inspection into his age is adjudged Sixteen yeares of age and ordered to serve his sd Master or his assignes according to Act
        - Capt. EDWARD THOMAS in open Court acknowledged Mr. JOHN EVERETT to be his
Attorney
        - Capt. EDWARD THOMAS, Mr. BERNARD GAINES, Mr: FRA: TALIAFERRO Absent
        - ROBERT DEPUTY being by the Grand Jury presented for playing Cards on a Sab-
bath Day, and ye said DEPUTY appearing and confessing ye same is by this Court fin'd of
according to ye 11th: Act of Assembly made at JAMES CITTY Ano 1691 entituled An Act
for ye more effectual Suppressing ye Severall Sins & Offences of Swearing, Carding,
Prophaning Gods holy name, Sabbath abateing, Drunkeness, fornication & adultery,
and ordered to pay ye same with costs als Exo.
        - Ordered that the Grand Jury for this County draw up and deliver their pre-
sentmts. to ye next Court to be held for this County
                                - Mr. RO: BROOKE absent
        - Mr. RICHARD ROBINSON brought his accon against JOHN ALMOND and declar'd
that ye said ALMOND stands obliged to be accomptable to him for Fifty six pounds, Six
Shill: and five pence Sterl: & Ten thousand three hundred eighty nine pounds of tobb:,
as by a writeing under ye sd ALMONDs hand dated ye 2d of Janry: 1690 appears, and
pray'd Judgmt. for ye same with costs &c., To which the Defendt. appear'd at the last &
craved an Imparlance till this Court which was granted him, being call'd to answer ye
same this Court appear'd and pleaded nihil debet. This Court have therefore thought fitt
and accordingly ordered that Mr. DANL. DOBYNS, Mr. EDWARD ADCOCK & Mr. RICHD:
LACKLAND do on ye 9th day of May next meet at ye House of Capt. ANTHONY SMITH &

there audit & examine state & settle all ye accts. in difference between ye Plt. & Defendt. & return an account of their proceedings to ye next Court under their hands

p.   Essex County Court 10th of April 1693
66   - Mr. RICHARD ROBINSON in Court acknowledged Mr. JOHN EVERETT to be his Attorney wch: is at his request ordered to be recorded

- Ordered that the Inhabitants of Sittingbourne Parish do repair to their Pish Church on ye first day of May next and then & there elect & make choice of a VESTRY for ye said Parish, and Capt. WM. MOSELEY, Mr. BER: GAINES and Mr. ROBT. BROOKE or any two of them are by this Court requested to administer ye oaths unto ye sd VESTRY

- The difference inter HENRY LONG Plt. and WM. COPELAND Deft. is dismist

- The difference inter HENRY LONG Plt. & WM. PRICE is dismist, Declaracon and Acct. not agreeing

- Judgmt. is granted to DAVID MERRIDAY against ROBERT DEPUTY for Two hundred thirty and three pounds of tobo: to be paid with cost of suit; (On the margin: Augt: ye 23th 1693. Executed ye wthin preceipt & ordered ye within Exo: on ye body of ye wthin named ROBT. DEPUTY & ye debt wth costs suit satisfyed. GEO: PARKE Sub Sher.)

- A letter of Attorney from JAMES FUGEET to Mr. JNO. EVERETT was at ye sd EVERETTs request admitted to record

- The Court adjourn'd till tomorrow morning eight a Clock

- At a Court held for Essex County Aprill ye 11th Ano 1693
Present Mr. HENRY WILLIAMSON   Mr. FRA: TALIAFERRO
        Capt. JOHN CATLETT   Mr. BER: GAINES
        Capt. WM. MOSELEY   Capt. JOHN BATTAILE

p.   Essex County Court 11th of April 1693
67   - JAMES FUGEET and DOROTHY his Wife, Daughter & Devisee of THOMAS PETTITT, late of ye County of RAPPA: deced, in all humility complains that her deced Father, THOMAS PETTITT, in and by his last Will in Writeting bearing date September ye 13th 1663 did give & devise unto her, ye Complainant, and to her heires forever, all his land then lying and being in ye County of RAPPA: now this County, being perticularly One hundred acres of land taken up & patented by the said THOMAS PETTITT and Two hundred & eighty acres adjoyning thereto by him purchased & by Conveyance assured to him as by ye said Will more at large doth & may appeare

Now so it is, may it please yor: Worps: that ye Complts. have great cause to suspect that the said Patent Deed Writeing conveyance & Charter did all of them come into ye hand and Custody of THOMAS GAINES & KATHERINE his Wife, late ye Wido: of ye said deced PETTITT,, or into ye hands of one of them, and may still in possibility be in their or one of their Custody keeping and possession; And ye sd Complts. humbly conceive that ye said Patent, deed, writeing, conveyance or Charters justly belong to them and they, ye Complts., being utterly remediless at ye Comon Law to recover ye same, humbly pray that by the Decree of this Court ye Respondts., THOMAS GAINES & KATHERINE his Wife may be compelled upon their Corporall Oaths to lett forth and declare what Patents deeds, writeing, conveyances, charters or other evidences they or either of them at any time before or since ye death of ye abovesd PETTITT have had in their hands, custody and possession, & what and how many of them and that yor: Worps: will please to decree that they, the said THOMAS GAINES & KATHERINE his Eife, do forthwith surrendr: & deliver up to these Complts., all ye said writeings, papers and evidences relateing to ye said lands as shall seem most agreeable to Equity in such cases & that they pay costs pleaded, To which ye said THOMAS GAINES appeared and alledged that the summons did

not agree with ye Docqts: & therefore pray'd that ye suit might be dismist, Wherefore
the Court have dismist ye same.

p.   Essex County Court 11th of April 1693
68   - JAMES FUGEET and DOROTHY his Wife, Daughter & Devisee of THOMAS PETTITT
        late of RAPPA. County deced, complaines against THOMAS GAINES in a Plea of
Trespasse, for that, that is to say, the Complt. DOROTHY hath good right title & interest
by the Guift of & devise of her deced Father, THOMAS PETTITT, in his last Will in
writeing menconed & exprest, of in and to Three hundred & Eighty acres of land more
or less situate lying and being in this County, and was the proper Estate and freehold of
him ye sd deced PETTITT, & of which he dyed seised, into which the said THOMAS GAINES
with force and armes &c. on or about ye Month of December now last past did then
enter & the Timber and Trees thereon growing did cutt fall maul and destroy, and did &
many other Injuries & Trespasses before and since dayly hath and doth comitt, And ye
possession thereof from ye Complts. do wrongfully keep & withold, all wch: is contrary
to ye Lawes & to ye Complts. damage One hundred pounds Sterl:, for which they bring
their suit and pray Judgmt. with costs and that the Sheriff be commanded by Writt of
habere facias seisinam to eject the said GAINES and to put the Complts. into quiet and
peaceable possession of the premisses
        To which ye Deft. appear'd and pleaded that ye Writt did not agree with the Doc-
quet & therefore pray'd that the suit might be dismist, Wherefore this Court have
dismist ye same
        (the following crossed out: JAMES FUGEET & DOROTHY as Marrying DOROTHY PETTIS &
Legatee to THO: PETTIS deceast brought their accon of Trespass to this Court agt. THO-
MAS GAINES to wch: ye Deft. appear'd & pleaded that ye Writt by wch: he was arrested
did not agree with ye Docqt: & therefore pray'd that ye suit might be dismist, Wherefore
this Court have dismist)

p.   Essex County Court 11th of April 1693
69   - WM. TODD and ELIZABETH his Wife, Administratrix of THOMAS FOSTER, humbly
        shew to this Court that JOHN WATERS is indebted to them in the said quality
thirty pounds Sterl: money being due by three Bills, vizt. one Bill payable to ye said
THOMAS FOSTER ye 10th: of Octobr: 1690; one other Bill payable to ye said FOSTER ye 10th:
of 8br: 1691; and a third Bill payable to ye said FOSTER ye 10th of 8br: 1692, all which
said Bills bear date the Eight day of July 1689 as by the said Bills here ready to be produced in Court may fully appear, And the said JOHN WATERS omitteth and refuseth to
pay the said money but the same from ye Plts. he thereunto hath unjustly detained and
as ye doth deteyne, And hereupon they bring suit and pray Judgmt. for the said sum of
thirty pounds Sterl. with costs &c. To wch: the Defendt. by Mr. JAMES BOUGHAN, his
Attorney, appear'd at the last Court and moved that ye same might be refer'd, which
according was, and now appearing but offering nothing in barr thereof, this Court
have granted Judgmt. to ye Plantiffs quallified as aforesaid against the Deft. for ye sd
Thirty pounds Sterl: to be paid with cost of suit
                - Capt. BATTAILE, absent
        - Mr. MARTIN JOHNSON brought his accon agt: Capt. EDWD. THOMAS and declar'd
that ye said Capt. THOMAS stood indebted to him by Bill thirteen hundred & fifty pounds
of tobo: and caske and denied paymt., Wherefore he pray'd Judgmt. for ye same with
costs &c., But the Defendt. makeing it appeare that ye ballance due of the said Debts was
but Eight hundred & twenty pounds of tobo: & caske, this Court have therefore granted
Judgmt. against ye said Capt. EDWARD THOMAS to ye sd Mr. MARTIN JOHNSON for ye said

sum of Eight hundred and seventy pounds of tobo: and caske to be paid with costs of suit
als Exo.

                    - Mr. JOHN TALIAFERRO, present

p.   Essex County Court 11th of April 1693
70   - RICHARD FRYER of this County Complaineth against HENRY PICKETT of the
        same County in a Plea of Trespasse for that, that is to say, he said HENRY did by
force & armes &c. and against the peace & on the (blank) day of Janry: last past upon
the land of the Plt. he, the said Plt., being then and there in peaceable and quiet possession, by force & arms as aforesaid, enter and stopp molest hinder and breake ye
Chaine of the Surveyr: of the County thereunto lawfully called and ye Plt. Imployed and
ordered to lay out ye said land aforesaid of the Plts. as aforesaid; and ye Plantiff in fact
saith that by reason of such ye Defts. entry and force &c. as aforesaid &c., the aforesd.
Survayr: was hindered and impeded by the Defts. aforesaid in the lawfull and just
proceeding in his business &c., & other enormities to him hath done to ye Plts. damage
Three thousand pounds of tobacco wherefore he hath brought his accon and prayes
Judgmt. &c. for his damages so unjustly susteyned wth: cost of suit &c.
        To which ye Defendt. by Mr. JAMES BAUGHAN, his Attorney, appear'd in Febry:
Court last & pleaded not guilty; Whereupon the Court then ordered ye Sheriff of this
County or his Deputy to impannell an able Jury of the Neighbourhood who were nowise
concern'd by affinity, consanguinity or otherwise (being first sworn) were in ye com-
pany of the Surveyor of that precinct to goe upon ye land in difference on ye 23rd day
of February last (if fair, if not ye next fair day) and lay

p.   Essex County Court 11th of April 1693
71   out the same according to ye Plts. Patent of which they were to return an acct:
        of their proceedings to ye next Court then following; And it was further ordered
that they should have regard to all evidences that should be produced by either Plt. or
Defendt. and Capt. ANTHONY SMITH was by ye sd Court requested to swear ye said Jury
and evidences
        Which said Jury now appearing by name WM. YOUNG, EDWD. ADCOCK, DANLL.
DOBYNS, JOHN WEBB. JNO: GRIFFING, PHILL PARR, JOHN GATEWOOD, RAPH WHITTON,
ANDREW DUDDIN, HENRY WOODNUT, WM. COVINGTON and JOHN MICHELL, drew up and
delivered into ye Court this following verdt: under their hands & seales together with a
draught or plott of ye land protracted by the Surveyr: vist.
  In Obedience to an order of Essex County Court bearing date ye 11th: day of Febry:
1692/3, wee Jurors whose names are here underwritten, being summoned & sworn to
goe upon the land in difference between RICHD. FRYER Plt. and HENRY PICKETT Deft.,
have in company of EDWIN THACKER, Surveyr:, laid out a Patent of Land formerly
granted unto RANDOLPH CHAMBLY dated ye 10th day of May 1654 and since granted by
Patent to DAVID THOMAS & RICHARD MAUSBIN dated ye 28th: of July 1662, according to
ye ancient reputed bounds thereof haveing regard to all evidence produced by Plt. &
Defendt., and wee find that ye sd Defendt. hath not committed any Trespasse upon ye
Plts. sd land, in Witness wee have hereunto sett our hands & seales this 23d day of Febry:
1692/3; Whereupon ye Defendt. by his Attorney, humbly pray'd that ye sd Verdt. might
be confirm'd & moved for a nonsuit against ye Plt., upon wch: this Court have
confirmed ye same and granted ye Defendt. a nonsuit agt: ye Plt. to be paid with costs als
Exo.

p.   **Essex County Court 11th of April 1693**
72   - Ordered that WM. ACRES, who was subpena'd as an evidence in the difference
        between RICHD. FRYER Plt. and HENRY PICKETT, Defendt., be paid by the said
FRYER for six dayes attendance according to Law with cost als Exo.

    - Ordered that JOHN MITCHELL, who was subpena'd as an evidence in the dif-
ference between RICHARD FRYER Plantiff and HENRY PICKETT Defendt., be paid by the
Plt. for four dayes attendance according to Law with costs als Exo.

    - FRANCIS BROWNE being subpena'd as an evidence in the difference between
RICHARD FRYER Plt. & HENRY PICKETT Defendt. and attending two dayes, this Court have
therefore ordered that he be paid for ye same according to Law by ye sd FRYER with
costs als Exo.

    - Ordered that ANNE DRILL, who was subpena'd as an evidence in ye difference
between RICHARD FRYER Plt. and HENRY PICKETT Defendt., be paid by the said FRYER
for three dayes attendance according to Law wth costs als Exo.

    - Ordered that THOMAS GAINES who was subpena'd as an evidence in the dif-
ference between RICHARD FRYER and HENRY PICKETT Defts., be paid by the said FRYER
for two dayes attendance according to Law with costs als Exo.
                        - Capt. JNO. BATTAILE, present

p.   **Essex County Court 11th of April 1693**
73   - ROBERT DEPUTY brought his accon against WM. FITZ JEFFRIES and declar'd that
        the said FITZ JEFFRIES stood indebted to him in ye sum of Fifteen hundred &
twenty pounds of tobo: and cask & two pounds three shillings money sterlin by Acct.
and refused paymt: Wherefore he pray'd order for ye same with cost of suit &c.; Whereupon ye Court ordered Mr. ROBT: PLEY & Mr. JOHN ALMOND to audit, examine, state and
settle all accounts in difference between ye Plt. & Defendt. and return an account
thereof to this Court

    - WM. HUDSON brought his accon against JOHN WEBB SENR. and declar'd that he
obtained a nonsuit 8br: ye 8th: 1691 against ye said WEBB with costs, but ye same being
out of date humbly pray'd that it might be renewed by Scire facias with former and
present costs; which this Court have granted and ordered that ye sd WEBB pay ye same
to ye sd HUDSON with former & present costs

    - Judmt. is granted to JOHN POWELL against ye Estate of Mr. GEORGE HASLEWOOD
deced for Two thousand & fifty pounds of tobo: and cask by Bill and Seven hundred
pounds of tobo: by account; to be paid wth: cost of suit

    - At the request of Mr. FRA: THORNTON, Mr. ROBERT COLEMAN is recorded his
Attorney

    - Judgmt. is granted to Capt. JOHN CATLETT agt: ye Estate of Mr. GEORGE deced for
six hundred pounds of tobo: and cask by Bill, to be paid with costs of suit als Exo.

    - Judgmt. is granted to Mr. FRA: THORNTON against the Estate of Mr. GEORGE
HASLEWOOD deced for Two thousand five hundred pounds of tobo: and caske by Bill, to
be paid with cost of suit als Exo.

p.   **Essex County Court 11th of April 1693**
74   - RICHARD KING brought his accon agt: GEO: GROVE and declar'd that ye said
        GROVE stood indebted to him by Bill seven hundred pounds of tobo: and deny'd
paymt; Wherefore he pray'd Judgmt. for ye same with cost &c. but ye sd KING not appearing to prosecute his suit, this Court have dismist ye same

    - Judgmt. by scire facias is granted to WM. HUDSON agt: JNO. WEBB for a nonsuit
which is ordered to be paid with former & prsent costs

- PHILLIP PARR brought his accon of Trespasse to this Court against JOHN BRAISIER and in his Declaracon declar'd against JOHN BRAZIER to which the Defendant appear'd by Capt. ARTHUR SPICER and Mr. JOHN EVERET, his Attorneys, and pleaded to the insufficiency of ye Declaracon as not agreeing with the accon and moved for a nonsuit against the said PARR, which this Court have granted and ordered that the same be paid with costs

p.   Essex County Court 11th of April 1693
75   - Ordered that MARY HEWIT be bound up an Apprentice to FRANCIS BROWNE
        untill she shall attaine to Lawfull age, And that the Clerk accordingly draw In-
dentures
        - WM. PRICE brought his accon agt: HENRY LONG and declar'd that the said LONG stood indebted to him Four hundred and fifteen pounds of tobo: by acct: and denyed paymt; Wherefore he pray'd Judgmt., for ye same with costs &c., wch: sd LONG being by ye Sheriff return'd arrested was called to come forth and answer ye same made noe appearance. Judgmt. is therefore granted to ye said PRICE against the Sheriff for ye above said sum of Four hundred & fifteen pounds of tobo: with costs; provided ye said LONG do not appear at ye next Court and answer ye same
        - Judgmt. haveing this day past against ye Sheriff for Four hundred and fifteen pounds of tobo: and costs for the non appearance of HENRY LONG at the suit of WM. PRICE, Wherefore ye said Sheriff moved for an attachmt: agt: ye sd LONGs Estate for ye said sum & costs wch: is granted him returnable to ye next Court for Judgmt.
        - A nonsuit is granted to WM. LEAKE Defendt., agt: MARTHA STOPFORD Plt., ye Plt. not appearing to prosecute her accon; And ordered that ye same be paid with costs
        - Judgmt. on an Audit is granted to ROBERT DEPUTY agt: WM: FITZ JEFFRIES for thirty one shillings & nine pence to be paid with cost of suit als Exo.

p.   Essex County Court 11th of April 1693
76   - The difference depending betweeen WM. JEFFRIES and ROBERT DEPUTY is
        dismist, noe cause of accon appearing
        - Mr. ROBERT BROOKE prsent; Mr. FRAN: TALIAFERRO, Mr. BER: GAINES, Capt
            JOHN BATTAILE absent
        - An Indenture between HENRY PIGOTT, Son of HENRY PIGOTT of this County and NICHOLAS WARD of ye Citty of DUBLIN, Merchant, was at ye request of SARAH PIGOTT, Wife of ye above named HENRY PIGOTT, admitted to record
        - WM. CHENEY brought his accon to this Court against JAMES FUGEET and declar'd that ye said FUGEET stood indebted to him three hundred and fifty pounds of tobacco by Bill and deny'd paymt., Wherefore he pray'd Judgmt. for ye same with costs &c; To which the Defendt., by Mr. JOHN EVERITT, his Attorney, appear'd and pleaded Act of Limitacon, which plea this Court over rul'd for that ye sd FUGEET had absented himselfe out of this Colony after he contracted ye said Debt; And therefore have granted Judgmt. agt: ye said FUGEET to ye said CHENEY for ye sd sum of Three hundred & fifty pounds of tobo: to be paid with costs of suit
        - Mr. WM: LOCKETT appeared Attorney for Mr. HUGH MATHER agt: JOHN GATEWOOD
        - HUGH MATHER complaineth agt: JOHN GATEWOOD in an accon of the Case for that, that is to say, he ye Complt. haveing a hogshead of tobo: (under ye marke of his cargoe) brought to

p.   Essex County Court 11th of April 1693
77   ye House of the said GATEWOOD accordingly but his Boat with three men to
        fetch the same away the said GATEWOOD refused to deliver and still doth detain

the same from the Complt. under ye pretence (as ye Complt. conjectures for Storeage)
notwithstanding he was by the Complt. fore warned from takeing any of the Complts.
tobacco into his Store House; And ye Complt. further saith that by the said GATEWOOD
deteining the said hhd. of tobo: from him and ye Demurrage of the said meentime, he is
damnified and damage hath to ye value of Five thousand pounds of tobo: and caske;
Wherefore he hath brought this accon now humbly prays Judgmt. for ye same with
costs &c.; Whereupon ye Court have ordered that ye Sheriff impannell a Jury to try ye
truth of the premisses who vizt. Mr. WM. JOHNSON, Mr. ROBT. PLEY, PHILL. PARR, WM.
HUDSON, THOMAS GAINES, DAVID WILSON, JOHN HARPER, WM. BALL, WM. JEFFRIES,,
FRA: BROWNE, JOHN HOLT, RICHARD COVINGTON, return'd their Verdt. in these words;
Wee of the Jury do find for the Plt. ye hdd. of tobo: with ten pounds of tobo: damage; WM.
JOHNSON; which verdict (upon ye Plts. mocon) this Court have confirmed and ordered
that the Defendt. deliver ye Plt. sd hhd. of tobo: and pay ye said ten pds. of tobo: damage
with costs of suit

     - Mr. EDWIN THACKER brought his accon against JNO. DICK & declar'd that ye
said DICK stands indebted to him fifteen hundred eighty five pounds of sweet sented
tobo: by Bill & denies paymt: Wherefore he prayes Judgmt. for ye samd with costs &c.,
which said DICK being by the Sheriff return'd non est inventus was call'd to come forth
and answer ye same, but not appearing, an attachmt. is granted to ye sd THACKER agt:
ye Estate of y sd DICKs for ye above said sum & costs returnable to ye next Court for
Judgmt.

p.   Essex County Court 11th of April 1693
78   - HUGH MATHER complaineth against WM. PRICE in an accon of the Case for
      that, that is to say, he ye Complainant haveing a hogshead of tobacco (under the
marke of his Cargoe) brought to ye House of the said PRICE accordingly sent his Boat
with three men to fetch ye same away, but the said PRICE refused to deliver and still
doth detain the same from ye Complt. under the pretence (as ye Complt. conjectures) for
Storeage, notwithstanding he was by ye Complt. forewarned from takeing any of the
Complts. tobacco into his Store House; And ye Complainant further saith that by the
said PRICEs deteining the said Hogshead of tobo: from him and the demurrage of ye said
meentime, he is damnified and damage hath sustained to the value of Five thousand
pounds of tobo: and caske; Wherefore he hath brought his accon and humbly prayes
Judgmt. for the same with costs &c. Whereupon ye Court have ordered that the Sheriff
impannell a Jury to try the truth of the premisses who vizt. Mr. WM. JOHNSON, Mr.
ROBERT PLEY, PHILL PARR, WM. HUDSON, THOMAS GAINES, DAVID WILSON, JOHN HAR-
PER, WM. BALL, WM. JEFFRIES, FRA: BROWNE, JNO. SCOTT, RICHARD COVINGTON, returned their verdt: in these words; Wee of the Jury do find for ye Plt. ye hdd. of tobo: in
dispute with ten pounds of tobo: damage; WM. JOHNSON, wch: verdt: (upon ye Plts.
mocon) this court have comfirm'd and ordered that the Defendt. deliver to ye Plt. ye sd
Hogshead of tobo: and apy ye sd ten pds. of tobo: damage wth: cost of suit
  (On the margin: May ye 8th 1692: Then leveyed ye within Exo. on ye body of WM.
PRICE & the debt with costs satisfied to GEO: PARKE, S:S:E:C: Vera Recordatr FRANCIS
MERRIWETHER Cl. Cur)

p.   Essex County Court 11th of April 1693
79   - GEORGE DOBYNS brought his accon against Mr. ROBERT BROOKE and declar'd
      that ye said Mr. BROOKE stands indebted to him four hundred & ninety pounds of
tobo: and one pound nineteen Shill: & eleven pence Sterl, by Acct. and denies paymt.,
he therefore prayes Judgmt. for ye same with costs &c., but upon examining ye sd Accts.

there remaines but Six pounds & a halfe of tobo: due to ye said DOBYNS, wch: this Court have ordered to be paid with cost of suit

     - Mr. ROBERT PLEY brought his accon agt: Mr. ROBT. COLEMAN and declar'd that ye said COLEMAN stood indebted to him six hundred pounds of sweet sented tobo: by Note under his hand and denied paymt; Wherefore he pray'd Judgmt. for the same with costs &c., to which ye said COLEMAN appear'd but offering nothing materiall in barr thereof, this Court have therefore granted Judgmt. agt: ye said Mr. ROBT. COLEMAN to ye sd Mr. ROBT: PLEY for ye sd sum of Six hundred pounds of sweet sented tobacco to be paid with costs of suit

     - JAMES SMITH complaineth against DAVID MERRIDAY and ANN his Wife, in a plea of the Case. Whereas ANN MERRIDAY, Wife of DAVID MERRIDAY, did on or about ye 25th day of November last at ye Plantacon of Doctr: ROBERT DEPUTY in this County where yor: Complainant then lived, and your Complainant not being at home, she did take up your Complts. Hose contrary to Law or Right and did ride him away at her own will and pleasure untill he was all in a foame of heatt and almost dead, to yor: Complts. great damage of two thousand pounds of sweet sented tobo: and caske, wherefore your Complt. humbly

p.   **Essex County Court 11th of April 1693**
80   prayes yor: Worps: order against DAVID MERRIDAY and ANN his Wife for pre-
     sent paymt: of ye above said Two thousand pounds of sweet sented tobacco and caske and all cost of suit &c., To which the Defendt., by Mr. JOHN EVERITT, his Attorney, appear'd and pleaded that whereas they had in Febry: Court last nonsuited ye Plt. in his accon humbly conceiv'd that they were not enjoyn'd to answer thereto now unless that ye Plt. would imediately pay down ye same at the barr, wch: accordingly was done by ye Plt., Upon wch: the Defendts. further pleaded that they were not the psons. whom ye Plt. declar'd against for that their names were MERRIDITH wch: plea was over rul'd, Where-upon ye Court refer'd ye matter to a Jury who vizt: Mr. WM. JOHNSON, Mr. ROBT. PLEY, PHILL PARR, WM. HUDSON, THOMAS GAINES, DAVID WILSON, JOHN HARPER, WM. BALL, WM. JEFFRIES, FRA: BROWNE, JOHN SCOTT, RICHARD COVINGTON, being first sworn returned their verdt: in these words; Wee of the Jury do find for ye Plt. fifty pounds of tobo damage; WILLIAM JOHNSON, wch: verdict this Court have confirmed and ordered that ye Defendts. pay ye said Fifty pounds of tobo: damage to ye Plantiff with cost of suit als Exo.

     - FRANCIS MARRINER, assignee of ROBT. BEAVER, brought his accon against THOMAS ST. JOHN & declar'd yt: ye sd ST. JOHN stood indebted to him Two hundred and fifty pounds of sweet sented tobo: by Bill and denyed paymt. Wherefore he pray'd Judgmt. for ye same with costs &c., but ye sd MARRINR: not appearing to prosecute his accon, this Court have therefore dismist ye same

p.   **Essex County Court 11th of April 1693**
91   - MOSES ARMITAGE brought his accon against Mrs. ANNE HASLEWOOD, Admx. of
     Mr. GEORGE HASLEWOOD deced, and declared that ye said Mr. ANNE HASLEWOOD quallifed as aforesaid stands indebted to him Fifteen barrells of Indian Corne by Bill and three barrells ditto, Five hilling hoes, fifteen shillings & three pence and one thousand and eighty pounds of tobacco by Acct., and denyed paymt. Wherefore he pray'd Judgmt. for the same with costs &c., which said   ANNE HASLEWOOD being by the Sheriff returned non est inventus was call'd to come forth and answer the same but not appearing, an attachmt. is granted to ye said MOSES ARMITAGE against ye Estate of the said Mr. GEORGE HASLEWOOD for ye above sd sums & costs returnable to ye next Court for Judgmt.

- DAVID WILSON brought his accon agt: Mr. WM. TOMLIN and declar'd that above four yeares since ye said TOMLIN. receiver for Mr. THOMAS COOPER, received a hogshead of tobo: of the Plt. at ye House of Mr. ANTHONY NORTH containing Four hundred and thirty pounds neat for wch: sd hogshead of tobo: ye Plt. never received any satisfacon therefore humbly pray'd Judgment against ye said Mr. WM. TOMLIN for four hundred and thirty pounds of tobo and cask with costs &c.

To wch: ye Defendt. appear'd by Mr. JOHN EVERITT his Attorney and pleaded that the Plt. had noe cause for accon against him and therefore pray'd tht ye suit might be dismist. Whereupon ye Court on consideracon thereof have dismist ye same

p   Essex County Court 11th of April 1693
82   - Mr. FRANCIS GOULDMAN brought his accon agt: PETER HUDSON and declar'd
       that the said HUDSON stood indebted to him for the non performance of a Contract under the said HUDSONs hand and seale dated ye 15th of 9br: 1692 four thousand pounds of tobo: and caske and deny'd paymt., Wherefore he pray'd Judgmt. for ye same with costs To which the Defendt. by Mr. JOHN EVERITT. his Attorney. appear'd and pleaded that ye Plt. had not filed his Declaracon according to Law, and therefore moved for a nonsuit, which this Court have granted against ye Plt. to be paid with costs als Exo.
       - Mr. HENRY AWBREY, Sheriff, brought his accon agt: EDWARD DRACUS and declar d that last October Court. WM. LEAKE obtained a Judgmt. against him for six hundred pounds of sweet sented tobo: and caske with costs for the non appearance of EDWARD DRACUS at ye said LEAKEs suit: provided ye sd DRACUS should not appear at ye then following Court and answer lye same, which said DRACUS being call'd to answer ye same Febry: Court last made noe appearance. Whereupon ye Court (on ye said LEAKEs mocon) confirm'd ye said Judgmt. agt: ye Plt. wherefore he humbly prayes Judgmt. agt: ye said DRACUS for six hundred pounds of sweet sented tobo: and cask with costs &c., but ye Plt. not appearing to prosecute ye sd accon, this Court have dismist the same

p.   Essex County Court 11th of April 1693
83   - JAMES NEWBELL brought his accon agt: JOHN DAVIS & declar'd that the said
       DAVIS stands indebted to him Six hundred and ten pounds of sweet sented tobo. & cask by Acct. and denyes paymt:. he therefore prayes Judgmt. for the same with costs &c., but the Plt. not appearing to prosecute his said accon, this Court have therefore dismist the same
       - The difference between RALPH WHITTON Plt. and JERE: SHEPHERD Deft. is dismist for want of prosecution
       - Capt. GEO. TAYLER upon bringing his accon to this Court agt: JAMES GREDIT declares that the said GREDIT stands indebted to him by Bill four hundred and fifty pounds of tobo. & caske & denyes paymt:, wherefore he prayes Judgmt: for the same with costs: Whereupon this Court have granted Judgmt. to ye said Capt. GEORGE TAYLER against the said JAMES GREDIT for ye sd four hundred and fifty pounds of tobo: & cask to be paid with cost of suit
       - Mr. THOMAS HUCKLESCOTT brought his accon against ABRAHAM NORTH and declared that ye said NORTH stood indebted to him as Marrying Mrs. SARAH ROWZEE Nine hundred and thirty pounds of tobo. for medicines administered for wch: sum he hath brought his accon against the said ABRAHAM NORTH and prayes Judgmt. for ye same with cost of suit &c; But the Plt. not appearing to prosecute his said accon, this Court have dismist the same

p   <u>Essex County Court 11th of April 1693</u>
84   - DAVID WILSON complaineth against Mrs. ALICE FORBES, Exx. of Mr. ARTHUR
        FORBES deced in a plea on ye case for that, that is to say, he ye said Mr. ARTHUR
FORBES did amongst other things contained in his last Will and Testament in writing
bearing date ye 3d day of Aprill 1691, will as followeth vizt., It: It is my will that DAVID
WILSON do dwell and seat upon the said land Six yeares if he will, meaning ye seat of
land joyning upon SAMUEL THACKER which will appear by the said Will and Testamt:
relacon being thereunto had, not withstanding which ye Defendt. hath and doth deny
the Plt. possession thereof whereby he is damnified and damage hath to ye value of One
thousand pounds of tobo: and caske: Wherefore he hath brought his accon agt: ye Defendt., qualified as aforesaid, & humbly prayes Judgmt. for his said damage with all
costs of suit: And that ye Plt. may be by order of this Worpll. Court possest of ye sd Land
according to ye sd deceds last Will & Testament &c., Whereupon this Court have ordered
that ye Plantiff be possest of ye sd land according to ye sd deceds last Will and Testamt. &
that ye Deft. pay cost of suit
        - Ordered that Mr. JOHN ALMOND and Mr. FRA: GOULDMAN audit & examine the
accounts &c. of the Estate of JOHN SEARLE exhibited to this Court by Mr. ROBT: BROOKE &
return an acct: thereof under their hands to this Court

p.   <u>Essex County Court 11th of April 1693</u>
85   - The difference between JOHN RACKLY, assignee of CORNELIUS FRANSOM, Plt.
        & BARTHO: VANDERCRUIT Defendt., is at ye Defendts. request refer'd till next
Court
        - JOHN SCOTT, assignee of MARTIN MAZY brought his accon to this Court agt:
THOMAS PAINE and declar'd that the said PAINE stood indebted to him by Bill One thousand and eighty pounds of sweet sented tobo: and cask and denied paymt:, wherefore he
pray'd Judgmt: for the same with costs &s., wch: sd THO: PAINE being by the Sheriff return'd non est inventus was call'd to come forth and answer ye same but not appearing,
an Attachmt. is therefore granted to ye sd Plt. against ye Estate of ye said PAINE for ye
sd sum and costs returnable to ye next Court for Judgmt.
        - MOSES ARMITAGE brought his accon to this Court against JOHN ALMOND and
declar'd that he was Indebted to Mr. RICHARD ROBINSON Two pounds ten shillings and
ten pence, wch: debt ye said ROBINSON put into ye hands of the said ALMOND to receive
for his use, upon demand of which ye Plt. paid ye same to ye sd ALMOND by a Bill of sd
GEORGE HASLEWOODs as may appear by the said ALMONDs receipt, notwithstanding wch:
ye said ALMOND has fraudulently and unjustly compelled ye Plt. to pay ye sd Debt
againe to his prejudice & great damage of Two thousand pounds of tobo: and caske;
Wherefore he hath brought his accon and humbly prayes Judgmt. agt: ye sd ALMOND
for ye sd damage with cost of suit; To wch: ye Deft. appear'd and pleades that ye Plt. had
noe cause of accon agt: him & therefore moved for a nonsuit wch: this Court have
granted and ordered that ye Plt. pay ye same to ye Deft. wth: costs

p.   <u>Essex County Court 11th of April 1693</u>
86   - A nonsuit is granted to GEORGE PARKE Deft. agt: JNO: ALMOND Plt. he ye Plt.
        not fileing his Declaracon, to be paid with costs
        - The difference intr: Mr. PHILL PARR Plt. & DAVID LOYD Deft. is dismist for
want of prosecution
        - The difference intr: DAVID LOYD Plt. and Mr. PHILL PARR Deft. is dismist for
want of prosecution
        - THO: COVINGTON Defendt., non suit RALPH WHITTON Plt. he ye Plt. not fileing
Declaracon wch: this Court have ordered to be pd: with costs als Exo.

- THOMAS COOPER SENR. brought his accon to this Court against RICHARD
BRISENDEN and declares that the sd BRISENDEN standeth indebted to him in ye sum of
Three hundred pounds of sweet sented tobo: & caske to contain ye same and refuses
paymt: as may appear by Bill under his hand bearing date ye 10th day of 7br: 1691 &
therefore prayes Judgmt. for ye same with cost of suit &c., wch: said RICHD. BRISENDEN
being by ye Sheriff return'd non est inventus was call'd to come forth & answer ye
same but not appearing, an attachmt. is granted ye sd COOPER agt: ye Estate of ye sd
BRISENDEN for ye sd sum & costs returnable to ye next Court for Judgmt.
- The difference inter RICHD: HOLT JUNR. Plt. & ROGER LOVELESS Deft. is dismist
for want of prosecution

p.   Essex County Court 11th of April 1693
87   - The difference between THOMAS RADLY Plt. & Mr. ROBT: COLEMAN Defendt., in
        an accon of Slander is dismist for want of prosecution
- WM. BALL appear'd in Court and acknowledged a Deed of Sale to his three Children viz: SARAH, EDWARD and JOHN BALL. to be his act & deed, ye same is ordered to be
recorded
- The difference between JOHN HARPER Plt. and WM. BALL Defendt. is dismist
- WM. BALL brought his accon to this Court against JOHN HARPER and declar'd
that ye said HARPER stood indebted to him Forty shillings by Acct. & denyed paymt:.
wherefore he pray'd Judgmt. for ye same with costs &c., This Court have therefore
granted Judgmt. to ye said BALL against the said HARPER for ye sd Forty shillings (ye
said BALLs Wife hveing made Oath in Court that ye same was justly due) to be paid with
costs of suit als Exo.
- Ordered that ALEXANDR: DENAIN, who was subpena'd as an evidence in ye difference between WM. BALL Plt. and JOHN HARPER Defendt., be paid by ye Plt. for two
dayes attendance according to Law
- ROBERT DEPUTY brought his accon to this Court against JAMES NEWBELL and
declar'd that ye said NEWBALL standeth indebted unto him in ye sum of Eight hundred
pounds of sweet sented tobo: & caske to contain the same by Bill under his hand bearing
date ye 18 day of Aprill 1692 and refuseth paymt:, Therefore he humbly pray'd Judgmt.
for the same with cost of suit &c., wch: said NEWBELL being by ye Sheriff return'd
arrested was call'd to come forth and answer ye same but not appearing, Judgmt. (at ye
Plts. request) is granted him against ye Sheriff for ye sd sum & costs, provided ye Deft.
doe not appear at the next Court and answer the same

p.   Essex County Court 11th of April 1693
88   - Judgmt. haveing this day past against ye Sheriff for Eight hundred pounds of
        sweet sented tobacco and caske with costs for ye non appearance of JAMES NEW-
BELL at ye suit of ROBERT DEPUTY, the said Sheriff therefore moved for an Attachmt:
against ye said NEWBALLs Estate for ye said sum and costs, which is granted him
returnable to the next Court
- ROBERT DEPUTY brought his accon against JOSHUA NASON and declar'd that ye
said NASON standeth indebted to him by Acct. Six hundred pounds of tobo: and caske And
refuses paymt., wherefore he humbly pray'd Judgmt. for ye same wth: costs of suit &c.,
wch: said NASON being by the Sheriff return'd non est inventus was call'd to come forth
and answer ye same but makeing noe appearance, an Attachmt. is granted to ye sd
DEPUTY agt. ye Estate of the sd NASON for ye sd sum and costs returnable to ye next
Court for Judgmt: he having made Oath that ye same is justly due
- Mr. ROBERT PLEY brought his accon against RICHARD LEIGHTON and declar'd
tht ye said LEIGHTON stands indebted to him Thirty shillings in money and denies pay-

mt., wherefore he pray'd Judgmt. for ye same with costs &c., wch: sum said LEIGHTON
being by the Sheriff return'd arrested was call'd to come forth and answer ye same but
not appearing, Judgmt. (upon ye Plts. request) is granted him against the Sheriff for ye
sd sum & costs provided the said LEIGHTON do not appear at the next Court and answer ye
same

p.   Essex County Court 11th of April 1693
89   - Judgmt. haveing this day past against the Sheriff for Thirty shillings and
        costs for the non appearance of RICHARD LEIGHTON at ye suit of Mr. ROBERT
PLEY, ye said Sheriff therefore moved for an Attachment against the said LEIGHTONs
Estate for ye sd sum & costs, wch: is granted him returnable to ye next Court for Judgmt.
        - Ordered that Mr. ROBT: DEPUTY who was subpena'd as an evidence in the dif-
ference between JONAS SMITH Plt. and DAVID MERRIDAY & ANN his Wife Defts., be paid
by ye Plt. for three dayes attendance according to Law wth: costs
        - Ordered that ELIZABETH DEPUTY who was subpena'd as an evidence in ye dif-
ference between JONAS SMITH Plt. and DAVID MERRIDAY and ANN his Wife Defendts.,
be paid by ye Plt. for three dayes attendance according to Law with costs
        - Ordered that WM. HALL who was subpena'd as an evidence in ye difference
between JONAS SMITH Plt. and DAVID MERRIDAY & ANN his Wife Defendts., be paid by
ye Plt. for three dayes attendance according to Law with costs
        - Mr. HUGH MATHER and Mr. PETER HALL of LIVERPOOLE, Merchts., in Court
acknowledged Mr. WM. PECKETT to be their Attorney at Law
        - The Court is adjourn'd till the 10th day of May next

DEED and WILL BOOK of
ESSEX COUNTY, VIRGINIA
July 1692 - April 1693

(Pages 1 through 16 are missing)

pp. To all Christian People to whome these presents shall come, Capt. SAMUEL BLOM-
17- FEILD and Mr. THOMAS PARKER sendeth Greeting: Whereas divers controver-
18   seyes and debates heretofore have been had and is now depending between
HUMPHREY BOOTH of ye one part and JEREMYA WHITE of ye County of NEW KENT
of ye other part concerning a peice or parcell of land situate lying and being in ye
County of RAPPA: and on ye South side of ye River formerly belonging to Mr. THOMAS
PRICE, for the appeasing and determining whereof, ye said parties have submitted
themselves & are to become bound each of them to ye other by their severall obligacons
bearing date ye third day of October 1687 in ye sum of Forty thousand pounds of good
sound merchantable tobacco and caske to be paid convenient on demand with condicons on the obligacons endorsed for the performance of all & every ye award, arbitrament determinacon and Judgment of ye above said Capt. SAMUEL BLOMFEILD and Mr.
THOMAS PARKER, both of ye County of RAPPAHANNOCK (Arbitratrs: indifferently
elected and chosen) as well on ye part and behalfe of HUMPHREY BOOTH of ye one party
as on ye part and behalfe of ye said JEREMY WHITE of ye other party to award arbitrate
determine and judge of and considerating all and all manner of accons, strifes, various
quarrells, controverseyes, doubts and demands whatsoever had made & moved, stired or
depending between ye said HUMPHREY BOOTH of ye one part and JEREMYA WHITE of ye
other part from ye beginning of ye world untill ye day of ye date of these presents; So
as the award of Judgment of us, SAMUEL BLOMFEILD and THOMAS PARKER, Arbitras: for
and concerning ye premisses being One thousand acres of land lying and being as
abovesaid, made and putt in writing indented under our hands and seales this 3d day of
October 1687 as by ye said severall obligacons and their severall condicons more
plainly doth appear. Now Know yee that wee ye said Arbitrators as aforesaid, taking
upon in ye charge of ye said award and arbitrament, haveing veiwd and heard and examined ye (torn) and allegacons and rights of each party concerning ye One thousand
acres of land as abovesaid, minded to sett at unity and freindship concerning ye same,
do shew upon, make and put in writing this our award, arbitrament, determinacon and
Judgment between ye said parties for & concerning ye premisses in manner and form
following, that is to say, wee do award arbitrate determine and judge that ye right to
and in ye abovesaid land doth wholly and solely belong to ye said HUMPHREY BOOTH his
heires and assignes forever as Witness our hands and seales this (torn) day of October
1687 Signed sealed and delivered
 in ye presence of us
    RICHARD LEIGHTON   SAMLL. BLOMFEILD
    JOHN I H HINE   THO: PARKER
Vere Recordatr. p F. MERIWETHER, Cl. Cur

pp. KNOW ALL MEN by these presents that I JEREMYA WHITE of ye County of NEW
18- KENT do acknowledge my selfe to owe and stand justly indebted unto HUMPH-
19   REY BOOTH his heires Exrs. or assignes ye full and just sume of Forty thousand
     pounds of good sound merchantable tobacco & caske to be paid on demand con-
venient to content, for which payment well and truly to be made, I bind myselfe my
heirs Exrs. or Admrs. firmly by these presents this 3d day of October 1687

- The Condicion of this obligacon is such that if ye above bounden JEREMYA WHITE do and shall for his and every of his part and behalfe in all things well and truly stand to, observe, pforme, fullfill and keep ye Arbitraments, order, rule, determinacon & (torn) of Capt. SAMLL. BLOMFEILD and Mr. THOMAS PARKER, Arbitrators indifferently chosen elected and named, as well on the part & behalfe of ye said HUMPHREY BOOTH as ye within named JEREMYA WHITE to arbitrate, award, rule, decree and judge for ye touching or concerning all accons, suits, doubts & variences concerning a peece or parcell of land containing One thousand acres situate lying and being in the Parish of Sittingbourne in ye County of RAPPAHANNOCK now in ye possession and sole Custody of HUMPHREY BOOTH aforesaid now in question and controversy between ye said parties, & it is firmly concluded and agreed on by the said parties by these presents so as the award, arbitramt: or determinacon and Judgment of ye parties in and upon ye said premisses be made and given up in Writeing indented under their hands and seals shall for ever stand firme and Irrevokeable, in consideracon of ye full and true pformance of this condicon is this my obligation void and of none effect, otherwise in full force and vertue, against my selfe my heires Exrs. or Admrs. In Witness whereof both parties have hereunto set their hands and seales Interchangeably this 3d day of October 1687 Signed sealed & delivered in ye presence of us

    HEN: AWBREY   JEREMIAH WHITE
    JOHN *H HINE
Vere Recordatr: p F. MERIWETHER, Cl. Cur

pp.   KNOW ALL MEN by these presents that I JOHN PROSSER of ye Parish of Saint
19-   Maries in ye County of RAPPA: Planter, for a valuable consideracon to me in
21   hand paid by WILLIAM SMITH and THO: HILLIARD, both of ye Parish and County aforesaid, Planters, the receipt and payment whereof I hereby acknowledge and my selfe therewith fully satisfied, by these presents hath given granted bargained sold and confirmed unto ye said WILLIAM SMITH and THOMAS HILLIARD their heires and assignes all that peece or parcell of land lying between Mr. JOHN BUCKNERs land and ye land of Mr. JOHN HASLEWOOD, formerly JOHN PAINEs, and extends as followeth: beginning at a Stake by a Hickory at ye head of a branch of MUZENSEEN thence South East to ye Maine Run of GOLDEN VALE CREEKE, thence down ye run to a Hickory, thence up a branch to a marked white Oak in ye line of Mr. JOHN HASLEWOOD by Estimacon Fifty acres more or less, situate lying and being in ye Parish of St. Maryes and in ye County of RAPPAHANNOCK on ye South side thereof being part of a Patent of ye said PROSSERs bearing date ye 21th: of October 1684; To have and to hold ye said 50 acres of land more or less with all rights, titles, priviledges and profits whatsoever to them ye said SMITH and HILLIARD their heires and assignes for ever in as full and ample manner as may be collected out of ye said Patent, and ye said JOHN PROSSER for him selfe his heires Exrs. and Admrs. doth further covenant and grant that he will from time to time and at all times defend and keep indemnified ye said SMITH and HILLIARD their heires and assignes from all manner of persons claiming under him his heires or assignes or any persons whatsoever any right or interest to ye premisses or any part thereof aforesaid, And that said PROSSER and ELIZA: his Wife shall and will make acknowledgmt: in ye County Court of their act and deed. In Witness whereof I have to these presents sett my hand and seale this 30th: of December Ano Dom 1689 Signed sealed & delivered in ye presence of us

    JOHN CATLETT   JOHN PROSSER
    WILLIAM CATLETT
Recognitr. in Cur Com Rappa: 5 die 9br: ano 1690
Recordatr. 12th die   WM. COLSTON, Cl. Cur.

pp.   KNOW ALL MEN by these presents that I THOMAS HILLIARD of ye County of
21-   RAPPA: and Parish of St. Maryes, Planter, for a valuable consideracon to me in
22   hand paid and fully satisfied by WILLIAM SMITH of ye said County & Parish,
Planter, have bargained, sold and confirmed to WILLIAM SMITH his heires and
assignes for ever all my right title and interest of a parcell of land bought from JOHN
PROSSER by myselfe and ye said SMITH, as by a Deed of Sale appeares more at large ye
other side bearing date Xbr: 30th 1689; To have and to hold all that parcell or moyety of
land belonging to me being by estimacon 25 acres more or less with all rights, titles,
profits and priviledges wt:soever to ye said SMITH his heires and assignes forever, And
further ye said HILLIARD doth covenant & grant to keep, save, defend and Indemnified
ye said SMITH from any claim or claimes of any persons wt:soever from by under him
his heires or assignes. In Witness whereof I have hereunto sett my hand and seal this
second day of October 1691
   Signed sealed & delivered in ye presence of us
      ROBERT WAIGHT   THOMAS T HILLIARD
      REES EVANS
   Recognitr. 6 die May Ano 1692   JOHN CATLETT, FRAN: TALIAFERRO
  At a Court held for Essex County July ye 11th: 1692, The above and within Deeds were
by WM. SMITH produced in Court and at his request admitted to Record
                       Test F. MERIWETHER, Cl Cur
Vere Recordatr: Test F. MERIWETHER, Cl Cur

pp.   TO ALL CHRISTIAN PEOPLE to whom these presents shall come that I THOMAS
22-   GAINES of PISCATAWAY in ye County of RAPPA: send Greeting in our Lord God
23   Everlasting. Now know yee that I ye said THOMAS GAINES for diverse good
        causes and valuable consideracons me thereunto moveing hath given granted
bargained sold and confirmed unto JOHN BURNETT of ye above said CREEK, Planter, his
heires and assignes for ever all my right, title, claime and demand which I ye said THO-
MAS GAINES now have heretofore had or hereafter may have unto three hundred sixty
and five acres of land beginning at ye Cross line of RICHARD HOULT running along the
Pocoson as is by draught and Patent specified as being ye part of a devident of Seven
hundred and thirty acres, with all woods, underwoods, waters and water courses,
fishings, fowlings, wares, liberties, royalties, profits and hereditaments to ye said land
& premisses or to every or any part thereof belonging; To have and to hold the above
demised premisses with its appurtenances unto ye said JOHN BURNETT his heirs and
assignes for ever, and ye said THOMAS GAINES doth by these presents for him selfe his
heires or assignes promise and agree with ye sd JOHN BURNETT to warrant & defend
save and keep harmless ye said JOHN BURNETT of and from all manner of persons
whomsoever unto ye above demised land from laying any claime or claiming any right
title interest or estate wt:soever unto the above demised land and premisses by from or
under him ye said THOMAS GAINES his heires or assignes. In Witness whereof I ye said
THOMAS GAINES hereunto put my hand and seale ye 28th day of December 1668
Signed sealed & delivered in ye presence of us
      JOHN HEYWARD   THO: GAINES
      ROBT: ARMSTRONGE   MARGT: + GAINES
   Recognitr 3d Febris 1668 Test R. P. Clr.
      KNOW ALL MEN by these presents that I MARGRETT GAINES, Wife of THOMAS
GAINES, make my very good freind, RICHARD HOLT, to be my true and lawfull Attorney
for me to acknowledge a parcell of land which was sold to JOHN BURNETT by THOMAS
GAINES as Witness my hand ye 29th: of December 1668
Test JOHN HEYWARD   MARGRETT + GAINES

Recognitr in Cur Com Rappa 3d die Feb: 1668.
Record: 5 die   Test ROBT: PAYNE Cl Cur
                Copa: Test WM: COLSTON Cl Cur
At a Court held for Essex County July ye 11th 1692,
   Then ye within Deed was at ye request of JNO. BURNETT, Son to the within named JNO.
BURNETT, admitted to Record   Test F. MERIWETHER, Cl Cur
            Then Surveyed for JOHN BURNETT three hundred sixty five acres of land situate
in RAPPA: County on ye South side Rappa: River, being part of One thousand and thirty
acres granted unto THOMAS GAINES by Patent dated ye 27th: of Febry: 1665, beginning
at a great leaning Red Oake above ye land of HOLT by ye Maine Pocoson of PISCATTA-
WAY CREEKE being the beginning of ye said Patent, and runing thence North 11d. E.
220 poles to a red and white Oak on ye North side a branch, thence S. 88 d. E. 190 poles to
a red Oake by a PATH; thence N. W. 287 poles to two Cornr: red Oakes on a levell; thence
South West 128 poles to ye two white Oakes by a PATH; thence S. 21 d. 15m. W. 268 poles to
ye said Pocoson to three Maples, and thence down alongst ye said Pocoson its severall
courses to ye place it began; Surveyed according to ye ancient lines of sd Patent, dated
this 15th of May 1691.   p   EDWIN THACKER, Survayr:
   At a Court held for Essex County July ye 11th: 1692
Then ye within Survey was at ye request of JNO. BURNETT, Son of ye within named JOHN
BURNETT admitted to Record   Test F. MERIWETHER Cl Cur

p.   KNOW ALL MEN by these presents that wee HENRY AWBREY, WILLIAM MOSELEY,
24   EDWARD THOMAS & JOHN BATTAILE of ye County of Essex, Gent., are held and
        firmly bound unto our Sovereigne Lord and Lady, King William and Queen Mary,
in ye sum of One hundred thousand pounds of merchantable tobo: and cask, to ye true
paymt: thereof unto our said Sovereigne Lord and Lady their heires and successors
convenient on demand in ye County aforesaid; wee bind our selves and every of us, our
and every of our heires, Exrs. and Admrs. joyntly and severally firmly by these presents. Witness our hands and seales this 11th day of July Ano Dom 1692
            The Condicon of this Obligacon is such that Whereas the above bound HENRY
AWBREY is by the Rt. Honble. FRA: NICHOLSON Esqr., their Mats. Lt. Governr: of Virga:
appointed HIGH SHERIFF of Essex County for this ensueing year. Now if the said HENRY
AWBREY shall well and truely duly and faithfully by himselfe and such officers as shall
be by him nominated and thereunto sworn, execute all warrants, proclamacons and
precepts which have or shall come unto him, or them from the Right Honble: ye Lt.
Governr: and Councill, the Governr: or Commander in Cheife or any of the Councill, and
dilligently enquire & find out ye true quantity of land held in ye abovesd County by
any persons whatsoever and return a true and perfect list or Rent Roll of ye same unto
their Mats: Auditr: of this Colony upon oath, at such time and place as he shall appoint
and also render unto him a perticular perfect and full account of all their Mats: Revenues & dues in ye sd County dureing ye time of his Sherivalty and also that he shall due
payment make of all such publick dues as shall be levyed in ye aforesd. County of Essex
unto ye severall persons that shall be appointed to receive ye same, & do and performe
all such matters and things as belong & appertaine to ye office of SHERIFF of ye sd
County, then this obligacon to be void otherwise to stand & remaine of full force power
& vertue
Signed seal'd & delivered in presence of
    F. MERRIWETHER   HEN: AWBREY
          JAMES BAUGHAN   WILL: MOSELEY
                                                EDWARD THOMAS
Vere Recordatr. F. MERRIWETHER Cl Cur   JNO: BATTAILE

pp.   KNOW ALL MEN by these presents that I HENRY AWBREY of Essex County Gent.
25-   am held and firmly bound unto WILLIAM MOSELEY, EDWARD THOMAS and JOHN
26   BATTAILE of ye said County, Gent., in ye sum of Two hundred thousand pounds of
        merchantable tobo: and cask to ye true payment whereof unto ye said their
heires, Exrs. or Admrs. on demand convenient in ye aforesaid County, I bind my selfe
my heires and Admrs. firmly by these presents. Witness my hand and seale this 11th
day of July Ano Dom 1692
        The Condicon of this obligacon is such that whereas ye above bound HENRY
AWBREY is by ye Rt. Honble. FRANCIS NICHOLSON Esqr., their Maties. Lt. Governr: of
Virginia appointed SHERIFF of Essex County for this ensueing year and whereas ye
above named WILLIAM MOSELEY, EDWARD THOMAS and JOHN BATTAILE became bound
with ye said HENRY AWBREY in ye sum of One hundred thousand pounds of merchantable tobo: and cask unto their sacred Maties; their heires and successors that ye said
HENRY AWBREY shall well and truely duly & faithfully by himselfe and such as shall be
by him nominated and thereunto sworne execute all warrants, proclamacions and
precepts which have or shall come unto him or them from ye Govr. and Councill, and
dilligently enquire and find out ye true quantity of land held in ye abovesaid County of
Essex by any persons whatsoever & return a true and perfect list or Rent Roll of ye
same unto their Maties. Auditr: of this Colony upon Oath, as at such time & place as he
shall point, and also render unto him a perticular and full account of all their Maties:
Revenues and dues in ye said County dureing ye time of his Sherivallty And also tht due
payment make of all such publique dues as shall be levyed in ye aforesaid County of
Essex unto ye severall persons that shall be appointed to receive the same, & do and
perform all such matters & things as belong and apperteyne unto ye office of SHERIFF
of ye said County
  Now if ye above bound HENRY AWBREY his heires and Admrs. shall at all times hereafter for ever save keep harmless and indemnified ye sd WM. MOSELEY, EDWARD THO-
MAS and JOHN BATTAIALE their heires and Admrs. for and by reason of their being become bound as abovesaid, and of and from all accons, suits, troubles, pleas, Judgments,
executions and demands which may or shall happen by or concerning the same, That
then this obligacon to be void, otherwise to stand and remaine of full force power and
virtue
Signed sealed & delivered in ye presence of us
        JOHN CATLETT   HEN: AWBREY
        BERNARD GAINES
  Vere Recordr: Test F. MERRIWETHER Cl Cur

pp.   KNOW ALL MEN by these presents that wee GEORGE PARKE, EDWARD THOMAS and
26-   ANTHONY SMITH of ye County of Essex, Gent., are held and firmly bound unto
27   HENRY AWBREY, Sheriff of ye said County, Gent., his heires and Admrs., in ye
        sum of One hundred thousand pounds of merchantable tobo: and cask, to ye true
payment whereof convenient in ye abovesaid County on demand wee bind our selves
and every of us our and every of our heires and Admrs., joyntly and severally firmely
by these presents. Witenss our hands and seales this 11th day of July Ano Dom 1692
        The Condicon of this obligacon is such that whereas ye above named HENRY
AWBREY, Sheriff of the abovesaid County of Essex, hath assigned and deputed ye above
bound GEORGE PARKE his UNDER SHERIFF of ye said County, if therefore ye said GEORGE
PARKE & ye above bound EDWARD THOMAS and ANTHONY SMITH their heires and every
of them do at all times save keep harmless and indemnified as well ye said HENRY AW-
BREY his heires and every of them as also his goods and chattles of for and concerning
the returns and executions of all such process, writts of what nature soever, as are or

shall be hereafter directed to ye said Sheriff, and shall be brought and delivered to ye said GEORGE PARKE dureing the terme of said HENRY AWBREY shall be Sheriff of ye said County, And of and from all fines and amerciaments which may happen to be imposed upon ye said HENRY AWBREY for & concerning ye non executing, wrongfull executing or deteyning and any writts or warrants by ye said GEORGE PARKE and for and concerning any escape of any person that shall be arrested or apprehended by ye said GEORGE PARKE by virtue of any such process, writt or warrant, dureing the time that ye said HENRY AWBREY shall continue Sheriff of ye said County of Essex, and if the said GEORGE PARKE shall at all times upon demand render a full perfect and perticular account to ye said HENRY AWBREY his heires or Admrs., of all such accounts of Quit-rents, levyes, Officers fees and other things as he ye said HENRY AWBREY shall put into his hands to collect and shall faithfully do and performe all such matters and things as aopperteyne and belong to ye office of an UNDER SHERIFF for ye said County of Essex, Then ye above obligacon to be void, otherwise to stand and remaine of full force power and virtue

Signed sealed and delivered in prsence of

JOHN CATLETT	GEO: PARKE
F. MERIWETHER	EDWARD THOMAS
Vere Recordr Test. F. MERIWETHER, Cl Cur	ANTH: SMITH

pp.
27-
28
KNOW ALL MEN by these presents that I GEORGE PARKE of ye County of Essex am held and firmly bound unto EDWARD THOMAS and ANTHONY SMITH, Gent., of ye said County in ye sum of Two hundred thousand pounds of merchantable tobo: and caske to ye true payment whereof convenient in ye said County on demand I bind my self my heires firmely by these presents. Witness my hand and seale this 11th: day of July Ano Dom 1692

The Condicon of this obligacon is such that whereas the above named EDWARD THOMAS and ANTHONY SMITH became bound with ye said GEORGE PARKE to HENRY AW-BREY, Sheriff of the above sd County of Essex, for this ensueing year in the sum of One hundred thousand pounds of merchantable tobacco and caske for his true and faithfull p:formance of all such matters as belong and appertaine unto the Office of UNDER SHERIFF of ye said County of Essex, to which place and office ye said HENRY AWBREY hath assigned and deputed ye said GEORGE PARKE as by a Bond bearing date ye 11th day of July Ano Dom 1692 more fully appeares, If therefore ye said GEORGE PARKE shall from time to time and at all times forever hereafter save defend keep harmless and indemnified ye said EDWARD THOMAS and ANTHONY SMITH their heires from all accons suits troubles incumbrances pleas Judgments executions & demands whatsoever for ever concerning their become bound with him ye said GEO: PARKE in ye above men-coned Bond and of & from all matters and things in any wise thereunto relating, That then this obligacon to be void, otherwise to stand and remaine in full force power and virtue

Signed sealed & delivered in prsence of

RO: BROOKE,	GEO: PARKE
BERNARD GAINES	
Vere Recordatr. Test F. MERIWETHER, Cl Cur	

pp.
28-
29
At a Councill held at JAMES CITTY Aprill 2d 1692
              Present
The Rt. Honble. FRANCIS NICHOLSON Esqr. their Maties. Lt. Governr: of Virginia and Councill

It is the opinion of this Board that it is not for their Maties. service nor ye good of this

Country that ye Clerkes of the County Courts of this Colony should be impowered in their Commissions from Mr. Secretary to appoint Deputies; It is therefore ordered that Mr. Secretary COLE if he have granted any such commission forthwith call them in, but that ye business of ye Country may be dispatched without delay if any Clerke of a County Court shall be sick, or otherwise incapacitated, to give his attendance at ye Court, it is thought fitt and accordingly ordered that ye Court of such County appoint a Clerke to officiate during the sickness &c. of such Clerke, giving Mr. Secretary an account thereof forthwith but if any Clerke of a County Court shall be chosen a BURGESS that he have power and power is hereby given him to appoint a Deputy to officiate during his attendance on ye Genll. Assembly, but noe longer

                          Copa: vera Test   W. EDWARDS Cl Con

At a Court held for Essex County July ye 11th: 1692
Then ye above Order of ye Councill was published in Court and comitted to Record
                         Test F. MERIWETHER Cl Cur

pp.   At a Councill held at JAMES CITTY Aprill 27th: 1692   P:sent
29-   The Rt. Honble: FRANCIS NICHOLSON Esqr., their Maties. Lt. Governr. of
30   Virginia and Councill

      This Board takeing into their consideracon that ye POWDER their Maties have been graciously pleased to send to this Colony for the defence thereof, being dispost in ye severall Counties may give some persons occasion to think it is sent to ye said Counties to be used at MUSTERINGS and to excuse them from being provided as the Law directs; To ye end therefore that noe persons may be so deceived, It is hereby declared that ye said POWDER is only for ye defence of the Country, and not to be used but when ye Commanders or Deputy Commanders in Cheife shall find Emergent occasion requires and doth not excuse any person from being providers according to Law, And that ye said POWDER may be well secured in convenient places in ye respective Counties the Commander in Cheife are ordered to take care therein, and not to put above two barrells at one place, also to cause receipts to be taken of the persons where it shall be put, And to return an account of the severall places to ye Secretaries Office at JAMES CITTY forthwith and ye Commanders and Deputy Commanders in Cheife are ordered, if at any time they shall cause any of ye said POWDER to be used, imediately to give an account thereof to ye Rt. Honble. ye Lieut. Governr: or Commander in Cheife of the Country, and the respective Sheriffs of this Colony are hereby ordered at ye next Courts to be held for their Counties tó publish this Order and to cause it to be published at all ye Churches and Chappells in their sid Counties

                     Copa Vera Test   W. EDWARDS Cl Con

At a Court held for Essex County July ye 11th: 1692
Then ye above Order of Councill was published in Court and committed to Record
                       Test F. MERIWETHER Cl Cur

p.   THE DEPOSITION of JOHN RICHARDS aged Forty nine or thereabouts Saith that
30   MARY LAWRENCE did leave her two Children, ANN and EDWARD LAWRENCE,
      all alone in her House severall times for four or five dayes together with very little or no victualls, so long that there was great notice taken by the Neighbours of ye Children, and DANLL. TAYLOR liveing just by did releive them what he could but at last did tell me of it, and I did advise him for to goe to WM. COVINGTONs and see if he would take care after ye Boy for he was his Godfather, and if he would not then ye Parish might take care of them and farther your Depont: saith not

                  Vere Recordatr Test F. MERIWETHER Cl Cur

p.   Mr. FRANCIS MERIWETHER
31   Sr. I would desire you not to lett Mr. JOHN WATERS have a Certificate for his
       going out of ye Country untill you receive a Note from me yr: Subscriber for he
is my Debtor a considerable sum of money and tobacco
July ye 30th: 1692   THO: WHEELER
To Mr. FRAN: MERIWETHER, Clerke Essex County
                         Vere Recordatr: Test F. MERIWETHER Cl Cur

p.   Essex County ss: Whereas Complaint hath been made to me this day by
31   EVAN JONES that JOHN SORRILL stands justly indebted to him ye full sum of
       Eleven hundred twenty four pounds tobo: and he ye said SORRILL absenting
himselfe out of said County when it went under ye denominacon of RAPPA. COUNTY
  These are therefore in their Maties. names to will and require you to attach so much of
the Estate of ye sd SORRILL in ye hands of Mr. ROBT: BROOK as will satisfie ye said Debt
or you will answer ye Contrary, given under my hand this 29th of June 1692
To ye High Sheriff or his Deputy or instead to
  ye Constable to execute and make return   WILL: MOSELEY 1692/3
  July ye 9th: 1692. Then executed and attacht. ye within menconed sum of Tobo: in ye
hands of Mr. ROBT. BROOKES for ye use and acct: of EVAN JONES
                         p. GEO: PARKE S. Sh. E. C.
  Vere Recordatr Test F. MERIWETHER, Cl Cur

p.   October 10th: 1691   JOHN SORLE is Debt to EVAN JONES
31   To Sawyers Work done for you as p Agreement   624 lbs. tobo.
       To fetching in your man from GLOCESTER as pr Agreemt: 500
Sworn to in Court   EVAN JONES   sum   1124
  July ye 11th: 1692
  Vere Recordatr. Test F. MERIWETHER Cl Cur

p.   KNOW ALL MEN by these presents that wee JOHN SMITH and SAMLL. THACKER
32   are held and firmly bound unto HENRY AWBREY Gent. first in Commission for
       Essex County in ye sum of Twenty thousand pounds of merchantable Tobo: and
cask to ye true payment whereof on demand convenient in ye said County wee bind
ourselves and either of us, our and either of our heires, Exrs. and Admrs., joyntly &
severally firmly by these presents. Witness our hands and seales this 29th day of July
Ano Dom 1692
       The Condicon of this Obligacon is such that whereas the above bound JOHN
SMITH hath obtained a Licence for his MARRIAGE with JANE DOHHODY, Now if there
shall be noe lawfull cause to obstruct ye sd Marriage, then ye above obligacon to be
void,. otherwise to stand and remaine of full force & virtue
Signed seald and delivered in presence of
       WILLIAM BENDERY   JOHN SMITH
       F. MERIWETHER   SAM: THACKER
  Vere Recordatr: Test F. MERIWETHER Cl Cur.

p.   I the Subscriber do intend God willing for England in the *RICHARD and MARY,*
32   Capt. DANIEL BRADLEY, Commander
       July ye 10th: 1692   JOHN WATERS
             undr: writt   p. WM. COLSTON
                            ROBT: HALSEY
  Vere Recordatr. Test F. MERIWETHER Cl Cur

pp. TO ALL CHRISTIAN PEOPLE to whom these presents shall come Greeting in our
32- Lord God Everlasting. Know yee that I WILLIAM CLAIBORNE of ye Parish of St.
34 John in P:MONKEY NECK in KING & QUEEN County in ye Colony of Virginia, Gent.,
for a valuable consideracon being ye sum of Fifty pounds Sterl., to me in hand
paid by RICHARD COVINGTON of the Parish of South Farnham in ye County of Essex.
ye above said Colony of Virga: Planter, do by these presents give grant assigne and set
over unto him ye said RICHARD COVINGTON all my right title claime and interest to all
that Plantacon containing by estimacon Two hundred & fifty acres be it more or less
scituate & being in ye Parish of South Farnham and County of Essex commonly called &
known by the name of the BEST LAND and now in ye Tennecy or occupacon of the said
RICHARD COVINGTON and bounding as followeth to witt: West upon OLD ASSUAMAN-
SOCKEK FOOT PATH, South upon ye land of JNO: FORTH; East upon ye Main Swamp, so upon
ye land of WM. COVINGTON SENR., and THOMAS HAYWARTON, together with all and
singular ye houeings, fences, buildings, barnes, stables, orchards, woods or appurtenances whatsoever to ye same belonging with all reversion or reverserions, rents &
services thereof, and all ye Estate right & demands whatsoever claiming of him ye said
WM. CLAIBORNE to ye same; To have and to hold unto him ye said RICHARD COVINGTON
his heires or assignes for ever with all privilidges thereunto belonging in as large &
effectual manner as it was granted by ye Rt. Honble. ye Governr: ingageing myselfe my
heires that ye said RICHARD COVINGTON his heires shall have & enjoy every part of ye
aforesaid Plantacon & land with its appurtenances peaceably and quietly without ye
molstation of any persons whatsoever that may lay any claime thereunto with warranty from all persons and to acknowledge this my act and deed in Court being at any
time thereunto required, In Testimony of ye same, I have hereunto put my hand and
seale this tenth day of August in ye year of our Lord One thousand six hundred ninety &
two 1692
Signed sealed & delivered in ye presence of
WILLIAM /— COVINGTON SENR. his marke   W. CLAIBORNE
JAMES I SMITH; SAM: COATS
At a Court held for Essex County August ye 10th: ano 1692
Ye within named WILLIAM CLAIBORNE appeared and acknowledged ye within specified
contents to be his real act and deed, ye same was admitted to Record
Test Vere Recordatr: F. MERIWETHER, Cl Cur

pp. KNOW ALL MEN by these presents that I WILLIAM CLAIBORNE of ye Parish of
34- St. John in PAMUNKEY NECK in KING and QUEEN County and Colony of Virga:
35 Gent., am firmly bound unto RICHARD COVINGTON of the Parish of South Farnham in ye County of Esses in ye aforesaid Colony in Virga: Planter, in ye full
sum and just quantity of Two hundred pounds Sterling to be paid unto the said RICHARD
COVINGTON his heires I do bind myselfe firmly by these presents. Sealed with my seale
dated this tenth day of August Anno Dom 1692
The Condicon of this above written obligacon is that if the above bound WM. CLAI-
BORNE his heires shall for his and their part well and truely performe and keep all and
singular ye covenants and agreements which on ye prt of ye said WILLIAM CLAI-
BORNE are to be fullfilled contained in a certaine Deed of Sale drawn between ye said
WM. CLAIBORNE ye one partie and ye above named RICHARD COVINGTON on ye other
part for a certaine Plantacon and land with the appurtenances being in the County of
Essex and commonly cal'd and knowne by the name of BESTLANDS, ye said WM. CLAI-
BORNE his heires do warrant defend ye said RICHARD COVINGTON in the said Tract of
land to give any further assurance or title to ye said land as he shall think fitt, Than

EssEX COUNTY DEEDS & WILLS 1692-1693   -59-

this obligacon to be void, or else to remaine in full force and vertue
Signed sealed and delivered in presence of
     WILLIAM ⊢ COVINGTON SENR. his marke   W. CLAIBORNE
     JAMES ⊥ SMITH, SAM: COATS
  Vere Recordatr. Test F. MERIWETHER Cl Cur

pp.   TO ALL &c. Whereas &c. Now know yee that I ye said NATHANIEL BACON Esqr.
35-   Prsdt. &c. do with ye advice and consent of ye Councill of State accordingly give
36   and grante unto Mr. HUGH OWEN Two hundred and twenty acres of land in
      RAPPA: County, lying on both sides of the River on ye branches of OCCOPACE
beginning at a marked tree in ye line of WM. MOSELEY on ye North West side of ye
Maine Branch and extendeth thence North North West one hundred and thirty poles to
a red Oak on a levell, thence West to certaine branches of the said Swamp to red Oak
thirty seven poles and by or nigh ye same North West by North thirty four poles to a
small red Oak, thence West seventy poles to a white Oak on a Barren Ridge, thence North
West by North six degrees fifteen minutes North one hundred and seventy poles to red
Oak in COGHILLs Line, thence bounding on ye same North two degrees 1/2 East twenty
pole and a halfe to corner red Oake standing at the head of a small branch, thence to a
corner tree in ye line of WM. GRAY. North East five degrees forty five East thirty poles
& bounding on ye same to ye Maine Swamp, South East by East four hundred and two
poles to a marked corner tree of ye said GRAYes land and finally on ye land of WIL-
LIAM MOSELEY to the first menconed stacon, ye said Land being previously granted to
RICHARD GOOD by Pattent dated 29th: day of September 1674 and by him deserted for
want of seating according to Law and was since granted to Mr. THOMAS VICARIS by
Order of the Genll. Court dated in JAMES CITTY ye thirtieth day of October One thousand
six hundred eighty five and by him never Patented and is since granted to Mr. HUGH
OWEN by Order of the Genll. Court bearing date the 19th day of Aprill Ano Dom 1690, And
is further due by and for ye Importacon of Five persons &c.; To have and to hold &c. To
be held &c., yeilding and paying &c. Provided &c. dated ye 21st: day of Aprill 1690
Record WILLIAM COLE, Secr: NATHANIEL BACON Pr.

pp.   TO ALL TO WHOM these presents shall come Greeting. Know yee that I HUGH
36-   OWEN of the County of NEW KENT for and in consideracon of One thousand
37   pounds of tobo: to me in hand paid by ROBERT BEVERLEY of KING and QUEEN
      County, the receipt whereof I do hereby acknowledge and myselfe therewith to
be fully satisfied and paid, have bargained sold and sett over unto ye said ROBERT
BEVERLEY and his heires for ever all that my land in this within written Patent menconed and all my right and title thereto hereby warranting ye same to ye said ROBERT
his heires & against ye lawfull claim of me ye said HUGH my heires and all persons
whatsoever claiming by from or under me. In Witness whereof I have hereunto sett
my hand and seale this thirtieth day of May Ano Dom 1692 and do hereby impower and
appoint my good freind, Mr. FRANCIS MERIWETHER, to acknowledge this my Deed at any
Court held for Essex County, And what my said Attorney shall lawfully do in ye precincts by vertue thereof I do hereby ratifie and confirm as good and effectuall as if I
myselfe were personally pr:sent Given under my hand ye day and year above written
Signed seal'd & delivered in pr:sence of
     W. CLAIBORNE   HUGH OWEN
     JOSUE NORMENT
  At a Court held for Essex County August ye 10th: ano 1692
FRANCIS MERIWETHER by vertue of a power from ye above named HUGH OWEN acknow-

ledged ye above specified contents to be his ye said OWENs real act & deed and it was
admitted to Record

                                    Test F. MERIWETHER, Cl Cur

p.   ROBERT BEVERLEY of KING and QUEEN County, Yeoman, do hereby constitute
38   and appoint my loveing freind, Mr. RICHARD GREGORY of ye said County to take
        ye acknowledgmt. of a Deed for Two hundred and twenty acres of land lying in
RAPPA: County now called Essex made by Mr. HUGH OWEN to me, and what my said
Attorney shall lawfully act and do by vertue hereof, I do hereby ratifie and confirm as
good and effectuall as I myselfe were p:sonally pr:sent In Witness whereof I have
hereunto sett my hand this Eighth day of August Ano Dom 1692
Test JOSHUA STORY   R. BEVERLEY
      JOHN HALFORD
  Vere Recordatr. Test F. MERIWETHER, Cl Cur

pp.   THIS INDENTURE made this ninth day of August in ye year of our Lord One
38-   thousand six hundred and ninety two Between JOHN SMITH of the Parish of Ware
41   and County of GLOCESTER, Gent., of ye one parte, and JNO: TALIAFERRO of ye
        Parish of St. Maries and County of Essex of ye other parte. Witnesseth that ye
said JOHN SMITH for sum of Fifty pounds of good and lawfull money of England to him
before ye ensealing of these presents by ye said JOHN TALIAFERRO well and truely contented and paid, whereof and wherewith he acknowledged himselfe satisfied, and
thereof hath sold unto ye said JNO. TALIAFERRO and to his heires and assignes forever
all that tract of land being in ye Parish of Saint Maries and County of Essex containing
Three hundred acres bounded as followeth, (Videlt.) begining at a Pocoson over agt: ye
DOEGS LAND and running its severall courses it being the one half moiety of a certaine
tract of land taken up and patented by CHARLES GRIMES & bequeathed to MARY
DEBNAM bearing date 11th: of 9br: 61; it may appear, with all appurtenances thereunto
belonging as houses orchards fencing &c., To have and to hold ye said Plantacon with
all rights whatsoever from ye said JOHN SMITH his heires for ever to ye said JNO.
TALIAFERRO his heires and assignes for ever, And ye said SMITH for him his heires
covenanteth with ye said TALIAFERRO in manner following, that he ye said SMITH is
now the very true and lawfull owner of all the premisses in fee, and that ye said JNO.
SMITH hath full power to sell ye premisses and also that ye said JNO. SMITH and his
heires will at any time at ye cost of said JNO. TALIAFERRO or his heires make and execute a good sure perfect estate in ye Law in fee simple as by said JOHN TALIAFERRO his
heires shall be reasonably devised, And that JOHN TALIAFERRO shall from henceforth
for ever lawfully and quietly have and enjoy all ye said tract of land without any hindrance of ye sd JOHN SMITH his heires or any other persons whatsoever And farther ye
said SMITH doth agree to acknowledge this Instrumt: in Essex Court next. In Witness
whereof ye said SMITH hath put his hand and affixed his seale ye date above said
Signed sealed and delivered in ye presence of
      JNO: BATTAILE   JOHN SMITH
      KATH: K BATTAILE, DAVID GITTINGS
  At a Court held for Essex County Augt: ye 10th: ano 1692
The wthin named JOHN SMITH appeared in Court and acknowledged ye within contents
to be his real act and ded, ye same was admitted to Record
                                    Test F. MERIWETHER Cl Cur
  Also Capt. JNO: BATTAILE appeared in Court & did by vertue of a Power from ELIZA:
SMITH, Wife to ye within named JOHN SMITH, relinquish her ye sd ELIZABETHs right of

Dower of in & to ye within granted land & premisses ye same was admitted to Record
Test F. MERIWETHER Cl Cur
(The first part of JOHN SMITH's Bond to JOHN TALIAFERRO is in Latin.)
The Condicon of this obligacon is such that if ye above bounden JOHN SMITH his heires
and every of them shall for his part in all things keep all and singular ye agreements
which are or ought to be observed in one Instrumt: of writeing bearing even date with
these presents made between ye said JOHN SMITH of ye one part and JOHN TALIAFERRO
of other part WITHOUT fraud or covin, Then this present obligacon to be void or else to
be and remaine in full force
Signed sealed and delivered in ye presence of

    JNO: BATTAILE   JOHN SMITH
    DAVID GITTINS
Vere Recordatr: Test F. MERIWETHER, Cl Cur
        KNOW ALL MEN by these presents that I ELIZA: SMITH of ye Parish of Ware and
County of GLOUR: do authorize and appoint Mr. JOHN BATTAILE of ye Parish of St. Maries
and County of Essex my true and lawfull Attorney for me and in my name to make ack-
nowledgment of a certain parcell sould by my Husband, JNO. SMITH, unto Mr. JOHN
TALIAFERRO, of the Parish and County aforesaid; it being the land whereon ye said
JOHN TALIAFERRO now liveth and what my said Attorney shall lawfully act and do in ye
premisses I do hereby confirm as Witness my hand and seale this (blank) day of (blank)
Ano 1692
Test WILLI: JOURNEY   ELIZABETH SMITH
    FRAN: TALIAFERRO
Vere Recordatr: Test F. MERIWETHER Cl Cur

pp.   THIS INDENTURE made ye 30d. day of May 1692 and in ye 4th year of ye Reigne
42-   of our Sovereign Lord and Lady, William and Mary, Between ROBERT CADE of the
47   County of Essex of ye one party and RICH: STEEVENS of MIDDX. County of ye
       other party. Witnesseth that ye said ROBERT CADE for and in consideracon of ye
sum of Four thousand eight hundred pounds of good sweet sented tobacco and cask to
him in hand already received before ye ensealing and delivery of these presents, to the
said ROBERT CADE well and truely paid, by these presents hath given and sold unto ye
said RICHARD STEEVENS his heires and assignes for ever One hundred acres of land
situate and being in Farnham Parish in Essex County which said hundred acres of land
is part of a greater devident formerly granted to THOMAS HARPER and containing by
estimation Two hundred acres for which One hundred acres being part thereof conveyed by the said HARPER unto ye said CADE by sale dated ye Seventh day of March
1672, and the other hundred acres conveyed by JOHN HARPER, Son and heire of the
aforesaid THO: HARPER, unto said ROBERT CADE and ye said CADE doth oblige himselfe to
ye said STEEVENS that ye aforesaid hundred acres of land shall be bounded as followeth:
viz. beginning at a marked Hickory on a point of the Maine Swamp of PESCATAWAY
CREEK at ye mouth of the Middle Branch in ye Fork between them, from thence running up ye sd Branch to a Branch called ye BRIDGE BRANCH to ye Corner wight Oake of
Mr. FREMANs standing in ye mouth of ye said branch, so running up ye sd branch to ye
head, from thence by a line of marked trees to ye head of CRUMPLE QUARTER BRANCH,
from thence by the back line to a corner red Oak of WILLIAM FREMANs, standing near
ye head of ye said Branch by the PATH side and running North by a line of marked
trees to a corner wight Oak standing by ye Maine Swamp side, from thence down ye said
Swamp to a marked Hickory where first began and containing by estemacon One hundred acres of land be it more or lss together with all houses buildings orchards gardens
feeding pastures woods mines quaries waters hereditaments belonging to ye aforesaid

premisses which said lands with their appurtenances by these pr:sents intended to be granted are being in ye County and Parish aforesaid and now in ye tenure and occupation of him ye said ROBERT CADE or his assigns and also all his estate right title claime and demands of him ye said ROBERT CADE in or to ye same; To have and to hold ye said messuage or Tenement and all and singular other ye premisses hereby granted with every of their rights to ye said RICHARD STEEVES his heires or assignes for ever and the said ROBERT CADE for himselfe his heires doth warrant ye sd messuage and all the other premisses before granted with ye appurtenances unto ye said RICHD. STEEVENS his heires or assignes for ever against him ye said ROBERT CADE his heires or assignes and all and every other persons claiming by from or under him and that he the said RICHD: STEEVENS his heires or assignes and every of them shall by vertue of these presents at all times for ever hereafter lawfully peaceably and quietly possess & enjoy ye said messuage and all & singular ye before granted premisses and kept harmless by ye said ROBERT CADE his heires of and from all former and other gifts grants judgments and arrearages of Rent fines and from all other troubles and in respect of ye premisses shall grown due and payable to ye Cheife Lord or Lords of ye Fee or Fees of ye premisses only excepted & foreprized, and ye said ROBERT CADE upon reasonable request & at ye cost & charges of ye said RICH: STEEVENS his heires or assignes do acknowledge every such further lawfull & reasonable acts and assurances and conveyances in ye Law whatsoever for ye further better and more perfect assurance the before hereby granted premisses unto ye said RICH: STEEVENS In Witness whereof wee have hereunto sett our hands and fixed our seals this 30th: day of May 1692
Signed sealed and delivered in ye presence of us

    WILLIAM FREEMAN   ROB: R CADE
    EDWARD FREEMAN   LETTISIA L CADE

At a Court held for Essex County August 10th: ano 1692
The within named ROBERT CADE appeared in Court and acknowledged ye within specified contents to be his real act and deed, ye same was admitted to Record
                Test F. MERIWETHER, Cl Cur

  Also LETTISIA, Wife to ye within named ROBT. CADE, appeared in Court and freely and voluntarily relinquished her right of Dower of in & to ye within granted land and premisses, ye same was admitted to record
                Test F. MERIWETHER, Cl Cur

pp.   TO ALL CHRISTIAN PEOPLE to whome these pr:sents shall come, JNO. HARPER of
47-   ye County of Essex in Virga: send Greetings. And now know yee that I ye said
49   JOHN HARPER for a valuable consideracon already in hand received or secured
       to be paid, have sold unto ALEXANDER DONAIN of the Parish of Farnham &
County aforesaid in Virga: and unto his heires or assignes all that parcell of land containing by estimacon Two hundred and three acres of land being part of that portion of land left me by my deceased Father, THOMAS HARPER, and bounded as followeth: Begining at a corner white Oak by the Maine Pocoson being the begining of ye said Patten & running South eighty two poles, thence South seven degrees East seventy six poles, thence South twelve degrees East one hundred thirty two poles to a red Oak by the head of a small branch, thence South West eighty seven pole to a live Oak and white Oak, thence West by North halfe One hundred & seventeen pole to a red Oak on a Hill, thence North two degrees East sixteen poles to a white Oak, thence up ye said branch fifty eight poles to a great white Oak on ye Westward side thereof to two white Oaks at ye head of a branch, thence down and alongst ye said branch one hundred and fifty two poles to a white Oake on a point of high land on ye lower side on ye mouth thereof, by

the White Marsh. thence North forty three degrees East through ye said White Marsh to
a Stake by the Maine Run of sd Pocoson, and thence by the said Run to ye place it begun; To have and to hold ye above said Two hundred and three acres of land according
as it is bounded in manner aforesd. in all its rights with all privilidges of what nature
or kind soever thereunto belonging unto him ye said ALEXANDR: DENAM & unto his
heires for ever, he ye said ALEXANDER DENAM his heires and assignes yeilding and
paying unto our Sovereign Lord the King his heires and Successors all such rights
duties and service as shall hereafter become due for ye same; And I ye said JOHN HAR-
PER do hereby further covenant for my heires and every of them ye said ALEXANDER
DENAM his heires and assignes and every of them shall & may at all times for ever
hereafter peaceably and quietly hold ye Two hundred and three acres of land & every
part thereof without ye hindrance of me ye said JNO: HARPER or any claiming from or
under us & will also warrant & defend this present sale from ye claime of all other
persons and also that I ye said JNO: HARPER will either by myselfe or lawfull attorney
acknowledge this present sale as my act & deed together with my wives free and volun-
tary consent to be procured in ye County Court of Essex. In Witness whereof I ye sd JNO:
HARPER have hereunto sett my hand & affixed my seale this nineth day of June in ye
year of our Lord 1692
Signed sealed and delivered in ye presence of us
        WILLIAM CONSTANTINE   JOHN HARPER
        WM. C   COX   LEDY HAR ⟋ PER her marke
   At a Court held for Essex County August ye 10th: 1692
The within named JOHN HARPER appeared in Court and acknowledged ye within speci-
fied contents to be his real act and deed, ye same was admitted to Record
   Also LYDIA, Wife of ye within named JNO: HARPER appeared in Court and freely and
voluntarily relinquished her right of dower of in and to ye within granted lands &
premisses, ye same was admitted to Record
                Test F. MERIWETHER, Cl Cur

pp.   Virga: ss   By ye Rt. Honblr: ye Lt. Governr.
50-   A Proclamacon appointed places for SHIPS
51   Whereas by an Act of Assembly made ye 23d. of 7br: 1667, its provided that all
           Ships & Vessells shall ryde in such places as ye Governr: shall think most con-
venient for their security and preservacon from other Enemies in time of Warr: Know
yee therefore that I FRANCIS NICHOLSON Esqr., their Maties Lt. Govr: of this their Dominion by and with the advice of ye Councill of State for ye greater security of Ships
and vessells trading to this their Maties Country in this Time of Warr, do hereby in
their Maties. names order & appoint that all ye Ships and vessells that now are or shall
come into this County shall ride in ye Harbours & places hereafter appointed, vizt., in
ye Upper Precincts of JAMES RIVER above SANDY POINT, in ye Lower Precincts of
JAMES RIVER in ELIZA: RIVER above ye Town; in NANSEMOND RIVER above ye FORT in
PAGAN CREEK as high as they can conveniently goe; in WARWICK RIVER above SANDY
POINT in YORKE RIVER as high as Coll. NATH. BACON lately lived, in ye River in
MOEJACK BAY as high as they can conveniently, in RAPPA. RIVER above ye FORT in
CORATOMEN RIVER and as high as they can conveniently goe in RAPPA. RIVER and in
PEAMKETANCK RIVER as high as they can conveniently, in POTOMACK RIVER in
WICOCOMICO and LOWER MACHOTINCK as high as they can and as high as APAMATRIX
CREEK at ye EASTERNE SHORE as high as they can goe in ye usuall places Ships &
vessells ride
   And Whereas by an Act of Assembly made 7br: ye 24th 1672, it is provided that in time
of Warr no person or persons shall goe on board any Shipp or Vessell comeing into

their Maties. Countrys either in Sloop boate or Canoe before ye said Ship or Vessell hath
sent on shore and thereby is knwon what she is, upon certaine penalties and forfei-
tures in ye said Act presented, I do therefore hereby with ye advice & consent of ye
Councill aforesaid, strictly charge & command all person and persons whatsoever that
from henceforth they doe not presume to goe on board any Ship or vessell by any
means whatsoever untill ye said Ship or vessell hath performed wht by ye before recited Act of Assembly is directed and appointed upon penalty of paying ye severall sums
of Tobo: menconed in ye before said Act, given under my hand and ye Seale of ye
Colony this 5th day of July in ye 4th year of ye Reigne of our Sovereign Lord and Lady,
Wm. and Mary, by ye Grace of God of England Scotland France & Ireland, King & Queen
Defenders of ye faith Ano Dom 1692

To ye Sheriff of Essex County   FR: NICHOLSON
   or his Deputy   GOD SAVE THE KING & QUEEN
   At a Court held for Essex County August ye 10th: ano dom 1692
The within Proclamacon was published in Court & committed to Record
               Test F. MERIWETHER Cl Cur

pp.   IN OBEDIENCE to an Order of Essex County Court dated ye 11th: day of July 1692;
51-   have been in Company of an able Jury upon ye Land in difference between
52   JAMES FULLERTON Plt. and JOHN PRICE Deft., and have surveyed and layd out a
         Patent of Seven hundred acres granted unto JAMES FULLERTON, ye Plts. Father,
bearing date ye 20th: of September 1667; according to ye findings and directions of ye
Jury, but I find Fourteen hundred and eighty acres wth:in ye said Survey as my appear
by the Plott above said, I found ye first four Courses given in said Patent to agree with
ye ancient lines in Course and distance as near as is common in our practice upon old
surveyes ye severall old lines leading to Corner trees, and ye fifth Course I do found to
agree with ye Course given in ye Patent. I followed said antient line untill it brought
into ye Maine Pocoson of PESCATAWAY CREEK (which is so reputed) as did appear by
two sufficient evidences, but wee mett with it at ye end of One hundred and ninety
poles, when ye Patent give Three hundred and Twenty, but by reason we wanted of our
distance, ye Jury ordered me to continue alongst ye old line untill we had run out Three
hundred and twenty poles which wee found to end on a levell, & wee still continued
alongst said old line and crost two branches, and at ye third branch at ye end of six
hundred thirty two poles wee found an antient Corner white Oak, which WM. ACRES
upon his Oath did say that he markt. that very tree by ye order of Majr. GEORGE MORRIS
Surveyr: for a Corner of JAMES FULLERTONs land, and WM. ACRES did further say that
that old line which brot. us to that white Oak containes a mile or two further untill they
mett with an INDIAN PATH, and that FULLERTON would not corner there, but he and
Majr. MORRIS returned to tht branch and there ordered that white Oak to be markt for
his Corner. Now it appears to me that if Majr: GEORGE MORRIS did order that tree to be
markt. for a corner of JAMES FULLERTONs land that he was in a great Error and did not
know in what part of ye line it was by reason of his running so far and so comeing
back now, whether a single Oath is sufficient to prove that white Oak a Corner of ye
Patent when it gives near a mile more measure then is exprest in ye Patent, or whether
it ought to end at ye main Pocoson by reason ye Patent expressly sayes ye main Pocoson to ye beginning, there being more than seven hundred acres of land on ye North
side of ye main Pocoson, I leave to yor: Worspps. to Judge
       The above Pltt surveyed this 2d of August 1692
                                        p EDWIN THACKER, Surveyr:
   Vere recordatr. Test F. MERIWETHER, Cl Cur

pp.   THIS INDENTURE made ye twenty forth day of March in ye third year of ye
53-   Reign of William and Mary by ye grace of God King and Queen of &c., and in ye
55   year of our Lord One thousand six hundred ninety and one Between JOHN
WATERS JUNR. of ye Parish of South Farnham in ye County of RAPPA. Gent., on
ye one part, and PHILL PARR of ye aforesaid Parish and County, Gent., on ye other part,
Witnesseth that ye above named JOHN WATERS JUNR. for and in consideracon of Five
thousand pounds of every way well condiconed sweet sented Tobo: and cask in hand
paid by ye within named PHILLIP PARR, before ye ensealing & delivery hereof, and by
these presents have granted unto ye said PHILLIP PARR to his heires and assignes for
ever, all ye Plantacon and tract of land lying and being on ye South side of PISCADA-
WAY CREEKE in GLOVERS NECK in South Farnham Parish and County of RAPPA: being
part or parcell of a tract of land formerly granted by Sr. WILLIAM BARKLEY Knt. to Mr.
THOMAS PATTISON and since given by Mr. GEORGE BROOKES, who is lately deceased, to
JOHN WATERS JUNR., bounded as followeth, beginning at ye Northerwest Corner of JOHN
SAVAGEs back line being a red Oak standing on ye North side of said BROOKES SPRING
BRANCH and runing thence forth Eighty five degrees West one hundred & ninety poles
to a Stake by two marked red Oakes and thence forth Twenty four degrees East One hundred eighty two poles to a marked Hickory, corner tree of JOHN WEBSTERs land, thence
North Eighty five degrees East one hundred and ninety poles along ye said WEBSTERs
line to a stake between a red Oak and a white Oak standing in ye aforesd. SAVAGEs line
and thence North Twenty four degrees West one hundred eighty two poles along the
said SAVAGEs line to ye first menconed red Oake, ye place it first began, conteyning by
estimacon Two hundred acres together with all & singular ye rights profits houses
buildings orchards gardens and other hereditaments unto ye said parcell of land and
premisses belonging & also all Patents, Charters & evidences touching anywaise concerning ye same; To have and to hold ye sd parcell of land & bargained premisses to ye
said PHILL. PARR his heires and assignes for ever, And ye said JOHN WATERS ye sd
Plantacon & land wth: ye appertenances before by ye present bargained & sold unto
him by ye said PHILLIP PARR do for ever freely discharge of ye said JOHN WATERS
JUNR. his heires and assignes agt: all other titles whatsoever and that ye said JOHN
WATERS JUNR. at ye time of ye deliverey of these pr:sents is and standeth seized of ye sd
land & premisses of a firm sure and indefeazable estate of Inheritance of fee simple and
ye said JOHN WATERS JUNR. for himselfe his heires do farther promise at all times hereafter for and dureing ye space of seven yeares next ensueing ye date hereof upon ye
reasonable request and at ye costs and charges in Law of him ye sd PHILLIP PARR his
heires make do performe or cause to be made and acknowledged every such further
acts & conveyances in ye Law for ye more better conveying of ye sd premisses as shall
be reasonably devised or required. In Witness whereof ye said JNO: WATERS JUNR.
have to this present Indenture sett his hand and seale, giveing deed & state with full
and peaceable possession by Livery of seizin of & in ye above menconed premisses with
ye appurtenances thereunto belonging ye day & year above written
Signed sealed and delivered in ye presence of
     THO: HARWAR, THO: EDMONDSON   JOHN WATERS JUNR.
     ROBT: COLEMAN, WILLIAM JOHNSON
  At a Court held for Essex County Augt: ye 10th: Ano 1692
The within named JNO: WATERS JUNR. appeared in Court and acknowledged ye within
specified Contract to be his real act and deed, ye same was admitted to Record
                Test Vere Recordatr: F. MERIWETHER, Cl Cur

p.   Plott
56   The Table of the figure
            A is the begining wt: Oake ye upper Corner tree of ye land granted to WM. ACRES
B is a red Oake of ACRES
C is a red Oake
D is a red Oake & Hickory
E is three corner trees in a valley
E. is the Maine Pococon
G is ye antient corner white Oake by a great branch
                    Vere Recordatr. Test F. MERIWETHER, Cl Cur
            See Report & Survey on page 41 (marked out - 51 inserted)

p.   The Deposition of JOSEPH BECKLEY aged about 42 yeares or thereabouts saith
57   that EBEDMELOCK POTTER did in ye year 1682 promise your Depont. a Cow for
            part satisfacion of a Debt due from ye sd POTTER to ye Depont., & your Depont.
staying longar then ordinary when he came to demand ye said Cow he said he had sold
ye Cow to JNO. BATES and further yor: Depont. saith not
Sworn before me this first day of April 1692   JOSEPH BECKLEY
        WM. MOSELEY 1692
    Vere Recordatr. Test F. MERIWETHER, Cl Cur Com Essex

p.   The Deposition of ROBERT RUDDERFORD aged fivety eight yeares or thereabouts
57   & MARGT: his Wife aged forty eight yeares or thereabouts saith that Mr. ROBERT
            SYNOCK did threaten ABIM: POTTER for a Debt to seize his Cow and Calfe for fear
of which & to prevent ye seizure of his Cow and Calfe under Couler did make over ye
said Cow and Calfe to JOHN BATES, and further yor: Deponts. did hear ye said JOHN BATES
say if were called in question by the said SYNOCK abut ye saile of ye Cow & Calfe that he
would to have his Oath pay to ye sd POTTER a bushell or halfe a bushell of Corne, and
further your Deponts. say that ye said POTTER did afterwards come to composicon with
ye said SYNOCK and receive his Cow and Calfe again of ye said BATES and at ye fall did
kill ye Cow, ye Calfe whereof did live and encrease to ye number of ten head of Cattle
and farther your Deponts. saith not
Augt: 10th: 1692 Sworne to in Court   ROBT: R RUDDERFORD
        Test FM Cl Cur Com Essex   MARGT: ✳ RUDDERFORD
    Vere Recordatr: Test F. MERIWETHER Cl Cur Essex

p.   Essex County. These are to certifie that WM. COLEMAN intendeth out of ye
57   County this imediate Shiping out of Rappa: River. In Testimony whereof I
            have put my hand this 28th: July 1692
                                                    WILL: COLLMAN
    Vere Recordatr: F. MERIWETHER, Cl Cur

p.   Essex County July 28th: 1692: These are to give notice to all people that THOMAS
58   BUTLER of the present County is bound out of the Country by this present
            Shipping now in Rappa: River as witness my hand
                                                    THOMAS + BUTLER
    Vere Recordatr. Test F. MERIWETHER, Cl Cur

p.   On the back of an Attachment granted to WM. LEAKE against RICHARD GREGORY
58   was writt, vizt.
            August the 3d: 1692. Then Executed the within menconed Attachment on a

Black Steer and a Cow and Calfe marked with a swallow forke on each ear it being part of the Estate of RICHARD GREGORY and seized for a Debt due to WM: LEAKE.

p. GEO: PARKE, Sub Sher: Essex Co.

Vere Recordatr: Teste F. MERIWETHER, Cl Cur

p.   On back of an Attachment granted to Mr. JNO. TAVERNER against the Estate of
58   JOHN SORRELL for Five hundred pounds of tobo: and cask and costs was writt
          vizt., September the 9th: 1692. Then executed the within Precept and attacht. so much of the Estate of JNO: SORRILLs in the hands of Mr. ROBT. BROOKE as will satisfie the within contents for the use of Mr. JNO. TAVERNER

p. GEO: PARKE Sub Sher: Essex Co.

Vere Recordatr. Teste F. MERIWETHER, Cl Cur

p.   On ye back of an attachmt. granted to HENRY PICKETT agt: ye Estate of DAVID
58   LOYD for Three hundred and forty pounds of tobo: & caske & costs was writt
          vizt., July ye 30th: 1692. Then Executed ye within attachmt: on a Gray Gelding it being part of ye Estate of DAVID LOYD & attacht: for a Debt due to HENRY PICKETT

p. GEO: PARKE, Sub Sher: Essex Co.

Vere Recordatr. Test F. MERIWETHER, Cl Cur

pp.   Virginis ss. By the Rt. Honble. the Lt. Governr:
59-   A PROCLAMACON
61   Whereas in my seeing the Fleet made up and goeing about the Country to
          exercise the Malitia, Complaints have been made unto me that severall Idle desolute SEAMAN have run from on board their Mats: Shipps of War and Merchant Ships that have come to this Country and lye Sculking up and downe which may be of evil consequence unless care be taken for the timely prevention thereof and to the end the same may be prevented and the said persons put to work thereby to gett them an honest livelyhood and prevent the evil courses they might otherwise necessarily take to get a Liveing, I FRANCIS NICHOLSON Esqr. their Mats: Lt. Governr: of this their Colony and Dominion of Virginia by and with the advice and consent of their Mats: Councill of this Colony do hereby in their Mats. names strictly charge required and command all and every their Mats. Officers Civill and Military within this Government to cause to be seized all stragling Seamen that shall be found in their respective Counties and them safely to convey to the Guner of the Platform at TYNDALLS POINT who is hereby in their Mats. names commanded safely to secure all such Seamen as shall be delivered into his possession till they be sent for by Capt. RICHD. FINCH, Commander of their Mats: Ship, *HENRY PRISE,* who is already ordered to send thither every weeke or as often as conveniently he can receive all shall be there and enter such and so many of them into Pay on board their Mats: Shipp under his Command as he shall have occasion for; for their Mats. Service in the said Shipp and give those he shall not judg fitt for their Mats: service a Certificate that he hath refused them that they may not be taken up againe, And I do hereby further require and command the Justices of the Peace of the severall Counties in this Colony that they bind over to the Genll. Court all persons who have harboared or entertained any of the aforesaid Seamen there to be proceeded against for their contempt of my Proclamacon in that behalfe heretofore sett forth to the Contrary makeing return of all persons to them bound over together with their recognizances in convenient time to ye Secretaries Office, And I charge and command all FERRY MEN to be carefull not to lett any Seamen over their Ferries who have not lawfull papers; Forasmuch as it is supposed severall persons have taken up anchors, cables and boats left in ye Rivers or Bays belonging to this Governmt., & ignorantly keep the same not

knowing but that they may do soe, to ye end therefore that noe person may be so deceived, I do hereby with ye advice of their Mats: Councill aforesaid make known that all anchors cables and boats left in ye water belong properly and only to their Mats: ye finders and takers up to be allowed a certain proportionable allowance for thier encouragmt. and trouble, And I do therefore hereby charge and comand all & every person whatsoever who already hath or hereafter shall take up any anchors, cables or boats that he forthwith give an account thereof to ye Sheriff of ye County where he dwells, who is imediately to return ye same to ye Secretaries Office, And all due care shall be taken for ye taker up his pay.

And whereas it is thought fitt that LYCENSES for MARRIAGES be only directed to ye Minister of ye Parish where ye woman to be marryed dwells, if he be duely quallified, but if he be not or their be no Minister in ye Parish, then to ye next Orthodox Minister by name I do hereby in their Mats. names by & with the advice of ye Councill aforesaid hereby charge and command all persons herein concerned not to act contrary hereto as they will anser the contrary

And to ye end ye good Law made at an Assembly begun in Aprill 1691 Entituled an Act for ye more Effectual Suppressing the severall Sins and Offences of SWEARING, CURSSING, PROPHANING Gods Holy name, SABBATH abusing, DRUNKENNESS, FORNICATION and ADULTERY may by often being made publique kept in remembrance and some persons thereby deter'd committing the abominable sins therein menconed & other minded of ye said Law, I do hereby command that ye said Law be once every TWO MONETHS published in every respective CHURCH and CHAPPELL of Ease in this Governmt: and to ye end it may not faile of being performed I do hereby require ye Courts of ye severall Counties in this Colony to put it into ye Grand Juries charge and that ye Ministers put ye Vestrys in minde of it and I do further command that ye order of Councill requireing ye Publishing his Mats. most gracious Letter to ye Right Reverend Father in God ye Bishop of London be duly observed

And that all and whatsoever is herein commanded may be duely and fully observed and obeyed I do hereby in their Mats: names strictly charge and require ye severall persons herein concerned not to faile of giving ready and due obedience thereto as they will answer ye contrary at their utmost perills.

Given under my hand & ye seale of ye Colony ye 18th: of August in ye fourth year of ye Reign of our Sovereign Lord and Lady, William and Mary, by ye grace of God of England, Scotland, France & Ireland, King and Queen defenders of ye faith Anno Domini 1692

To the Sheriff of Essex County or his Deputy   FR: NICHOLSON
                         GOD SAVE YE KING & QUEEN
At a Court held for Essex County 7br: ye 10th 1692
The above Proclamacon was published in Court and committed to Record
                Test F. MERIWETHER, Cl Cur

pp.   At a Councill held at JAMES CITTY July 5th: 1692
61-   Present
62   The Rt. Honble FRANCIS NICHOLSON Esqr. their Mats. Lt. Govr. of Virginia
           The Honble Councill
               On ye Rt. Honble: ye Lt. Govr: Informing that he understands ye Govrs: of
CHRIST CHURCH HOSPITAL in England Complaine that they never near from y Boyes
they bind Apprentices to ye Inhabitants of this Colony, It is ordered that ye severall
Masters of ye Boyes cause them to write at least twice a year to ye Governr: of ye said
HOSPITALL & fully performe what by their Indentures they are bound to do for them,
And it is further ordered that if any of ye said Boyes Masters shall dye, their Exrs. or

Admrs. comply with this Order, And ye respective Justices of ye Peace in this Colony are ordered to take care that this Order be fully performed ye same lending greatly to ye reputacon and credit of ye Country

      Copa vera Test   W. EDWARDS, Cl Con:

 At a Court held for Essex County 7br: 10th: 1692
The within Order of Councill was published in Court and commited to Record

      Test F. MERIWETHER, Cl Cur

pp. KNOW ALL MEN by these presents that I THOMAS PARKER of ye County of Essex
62- for divers good causes & consideracons me at this present especially thereunto
63   moveing have given granted and confirmed and do hereby give unto JEREMIAH
    PARKER my Son a certaine parcell of land being part of that land that I bought
of LODOWICK ROWZIE & JOHN ROWZIE lying on OCCUPACON CREEK in ye said County
beginning at a marked white Oake by a Marsh side called ye ROTTEN MARSH, standing
in ye line of ye said Land of mine and running along ye said line to marked white Oak
by ye treate Marsh side leaning over ye said Marsh from thence across a small neck or
poynt of ye sd land of mine by a line of marked trees to a marked red Oak by ye branch
side that falleth into ye said ROTTEN MARSH, and finally down ye said branch to ye first
menconed stacon: To have and to hold ye said parcell of land to him ye said JEREMIAH
PARKER and to ye heires of his body lawfully begotten for ever and in default of such
heires, unto my Son, JNO: PARKER, after ye decease of ye said JEREMIAH PARKER and to
ye heires of ye said JNO. PARKER for ever; provided alwaies and be it hereby provided
and excepted that ye said JEREMIAH PARKER shall be and it is hereby debarred from
selling giveing leaseing or morgageing ye said land or any part thereof, And if at any
time or times ye said JEREMIAH PARKER shall sell, give, sett to lease, or morgage ye said
land or any part thereof, then ye said land so sold given leased or morgaged shall
imediately revert to me ye Doner and my heires for ever, anything in this Deed of Gift
to ye contrary notwithstanding, Know yee that I have put ye said JEREMIAH PARKER in
possession of ye said Land according to ye tenour of this Deed. Witness my hand and
seal July ye tenth ano Dom 1692

Witness GEO: PARKE   THO: PARKER SENR.
   MARTINE JOHNSON

 At a Court held for Essex County 7br: ye 10th ano 1692
The within named THO: PARKER appeared in Court & acknowledged the within specified
content to be his real act & deed

     Test F. MERIWETHER, Cl Cur

p.   Two cropps a slitt of each ear & an under keele of each ear. F. MERIWETHER
63   The above marke being mine both in hogs & Cattle I request you will upon ye
    record   Yor: Servant JOHN LOVEN

 Vere Recordatr: ye 28th: day of September Ano 1692; Test F. MERIWETHER Cl Cur

p.   On the back side of an Attachment granted to THO: GRIFFEN against ye Estate of
64   JOHN SEARLE for his Cloaths and costs was made this following return. Septem-
    ber ye 19th: 1691. Then executed ye within attachment soe much of the Estate of
JOHN SORRILS in the hands of Mr. ROBERT BROOKES as will satisfie ye within contents

      p GEO: PARKE S.S.E. C.

 Vere Recordatr Test F. MERIWETHER Cl Cur

p.   Sr: Herewith I send you Mr. BENJAMIN MARSHes Bill and do desire you to use
64   your utmost endeavour in the recovery thereof, And this shall be your warrant
        of Attorney from Sr. yor: humble Servt.
    To Mr. JOHN TAVERNER or to DENIS CARTY   STEVEN WELLS
        Attorney at Law these pr:sent
    Vere Recordatr: Test F. MERIWETHER Cl Cur

p.   THOMAS WOOD aged 64 yeares or thereabouts saith that Twenty seven yeares
64   agoe to his knowledge the Streight Swamp was reputed to be ye Maine Swamp
        of PISCATAWAY CREEKE by THOMAS HARPER, THOMAS COOPER and FRANCIS
BROWN SENIOR and JAMES BOUGHEN SENIOR who ware ye first seaters on that CREEKE &
further saith not
Sworn to in Essex Court 7br: 29th: 1692   Signed THOMAS WOOD
Test F. MERIWETHER Cl Cur
        The within named THOMAS WOOD gave in this Depo: to the last Court in ye dif-
ference between JAMES FULLERTON Plt. and JNO. PRICE Defendt., which said Depo: being
delivered to ye Jury to use miscarryed and ye Court & Foreman of the Jury being
sensible thereof, the Court have admitted ye within Depo: to be taken this Court in ye
presence of ye Plt. & Deft., 7br: 29th 1692
                        Test F. MERIWETHER, Cl Cur

p.   The Deposicon of NICH: COPELAND aged about 50 yeares saith he saw Corne
65   growing in the land claimed by Capt. JOHN BATTAILE as Garding to MARY COG-
        WELL of Mr. THOMAS VICARIS above twenty yeares since & further saith that he
knew a man & his Wife & family live on the said land since that time which were put
there by JAMES COGWELL & that the Depont. saw fruit trees growing on ye said Land &
further saith not
Sworn to in Essex County Court 8br: 10th: 1692   NICHOLAS 𝓝 COPELAND
    Test F: MERIWETHER   Vere Recordatr. Test F. MERIWETHER, Cl Cur

p.   Essex County. Whereas Complaint hath been made this day to me by the Church
65   Wardens of South Farnham Parish in ye County abovesaid that MARY OUGLEY,
        late of the aforesaid Parish and County haveing committed ye sin of fornication
with a Negro in which a bastard Child was begotten, And shee ye said MARY haveing
illegally absented herselfe out of the aforesaid Pish: & County without makeing such
satisfacon as ye Law in such cases enjoynes, These are therefore in their Mats: names to
will and require you forthwith in light hereof to attache so much of ye Estate of sd
OUGLEY in this County as will pay & satisfie One thousand pounds of tobo: with costs soe
much being due to ye sd Parish as a fine for committing ye aforesaid sin and make due
return thereof to ye next Court hereof you may not faile as you will answer ye contrary
Given under my hand this last day of Augt: 1692
To ye HIgh Sherr: of Essex County or   ANTHO: SMITH
 his Deputy Septr: 2d 1692
    Then executed the within attachmt: in ye hands of Capt. EDWARD THOMAS on three
barrells of Indian Corne   p GEO: PARKE, Sub Sher: Essex Co.
    Vere Recordatr: Test F. MERIWETHER, Cl Cur

pp.   THIS INDENTURE made this fourth day of July Anno Dom 1692 and in ye 3d year
66-   of our Sovereign Lord and Lady, William and Mary, King and Queen over Eng-
67   land Scotland France Ireland and Virginia &c., between GEORGE WARD of ye
        County of Essex, Planter, and in ye Collony of Virga: of ye one part and JOHN

MOODIE of ye same County and Collony, Planter, of the other part; Witnesseth that ye said GEORGE WARD for a valuable consideracon in hand already received have given and confirmed unto ye said JOHN MOODYE his heires or assignes for ever all his right estate claime and demand into a certaine parcell of land conteyning a hundred acres more or less, the said land situate lying and being in the County of Essex aforesaid, beginning at a corner white Oake standing upon ye ROAD side and so along the said ROAD downward to a Corner red Oake being a corner tree to ye said land of JOHN EVANS Land and to ye Land of WALTER JONES, then along the line of THOMAS ROSON over a Swamp and along the said line to a corner red Oake on the toppe of the Hill & thence following the Inward line of THOMAS SADLER over the said Swamp and along the said line to the first corner white Oake; To have and to hold th said land with all woods, waters and appurtenances thereunto belonging to ye said JOHN MOODIE his heires or assignes subject nevertheless to ye Qutt rents that shall from henceforth grow due for the same to our Sovereign Lord & Lady, the King and Queen, their heires and Successors, And ye said GEORGE WARD for ye said valuble consideracon th said Land with ye premisses & appurtenances hereby granted and sold will warrant and defend unto ye said JOHN MOODIE his heires and assignes from him and any other person wt:soever and the said GEORGE WARD doth farther gree due acknowledgment to make of all and singular the before menconed granted premisses before the Justices holding Court for ye County of Essex and there to be enrolled according to ye Statute in that case provided, And further ye said GEORGE WARD do hereby agree at the reasonble request cost & charge of him ye said JNO: MOODIE to make and suffer to be made very such acts as by Councill in ye Law learned shall be required for better and more perfect assurance of the hereby granted with rights thereunto belonging. In Witness whereof ye said GEORGE WARD have hereunto sett his hand & fixed his seale the day and year first above written
Signed sealed & delivered in pr:sence of
    THO: HUCKLESCOTT   GEORGE X WARD
    THOMAS LAMBERT
  At an adjourned Court held for Essex County 7br: ye 29tH; 1692
The abovesaid GEORGE WARD appear'd and acknowledged ye within and above specified contents to be his real act and deed, ye same was admitted to Record
                    Vere Recordatr: Test F. MERIWETHER, Cl Cur

pp.   TO ALL CHRISTIAN PEOPLE to whome these presents shall come, I DAVID COGHILL
68-   of RAPPA: County in Virginia am possessed of a parcell of land containing Two
71   hundred & fifty acres of land being part of a Pattent of One thousand and fifty
       acres of land as by ye said Pattns: relation being thereunto had may more at
large appeare, Now Know yee yt: I the said DAVID COGHILL for a valuable consideration ye sume of Eighteen pounds Sterling by me in hand already received, I DAVID COGHILL thereinto moveing have granted sold and confirm unto RICHARD BOOKER of GLOCESTR: COUNTY his heires or assignes Two hundred and fifty acres of land sittuate & lying at the had of PORT TOBACCO CREEKE in RAPPAHANNOCK County in ye Collony of Virginia which said Two hundred and fifty acres adjoyneing with ye Plantation commonly known or called by the name of JAMES COGHILLs Plantation wch: is now in the tenure and occupation of the said RICHARD BOOKER, together with all houseing, fenceing, orchards, gardings, and all other ye appurtenances whatsoever belonging, together wth: all profitts & comodities granted by vertue of the said Pattnt: or by any other wayes or meanes whatsoever To have and to hold the said Land togeather with all and singular the aforesaid appurtenances and comodities belonging unto ye said RICHARD BOOKER his heires and assignes for ever; And the said DAVID COGHILL for himselfe his

heires doth promise with ye said RICHARD BOOKER that he ye said DAVID COGHILL shall for ever renounce & disdaine all right and interest that ever he had or ever may have unto ye said Two hundred and fifty acres of land, and do warrant and confirme ye sd Land from me ye said DAVID COGHILL my heires and assignes forever in as full manner as any p:son doth or may enjoy his land by vertue of any Patts: granted in this Collony and from henceforth forever peaceably and quietly occupie and enjoy the aforesaid land without any molestation of me DAVID COGHILL my heires or assignes, And I do further covenant that if at any time hereafter it shall happen there shall arise concerning ye said land any molestation or interruption whatsoever, and do hereby most fully and absolutely warrant and assure the said land from me my heires unto ye said RICHARD BOOKER his heires and will by my selfe or certaine attorney acknowledge these present Deed of Sale in RAPPA: County Court in ye said County aforesaid when thereunto required In Witness whereof I have sett my hand and seale this Twentieth day of July One thousand six hundred Ninety two 1692
Signed & delivered in ye pr:sence of us
          CHILION WHITE   DAVID COGHILL
          WILLIAM LOBB, WILLIAM W R RYDER,
          WILL: SMITH, ROBB: MYNNE
    Memorandum yt: I DAVID COGHILL doe redeliver this within menconed Bill of Sale to RICHARD BOOKER as Witness my hand and seale this 5th day of September Ano Dom 1692
Wittness JOHN SCOTT,   DAVID COGHILL
          WILLIAM LOBB
    At a Court held for Essex County October ye 10th: 1692
ROBERT MYNNE by vertue of a Power from ye wth:in named DAVID COGHILL appeared and acknowledged the within specified contents to be his ye sd COGHILLs real act and deed, ye same was admitted to Record   Test FRAN: MERIWETHER, Cl Cur
          KNOW ALL MEN by these presents that I DAVID COGHILL of RAPPAHANNOCK County do acknowledge and confess ourselves to owe and to stand indebted unto RICHARD BOOKER of GLOUCESTER County in Virginia in ye full and just sum of Thirty six pounds of good and lawfull mony of England, due to be paid unto ye said RICHARD BOOKER his heires & assignes upon demand for which payment truely to be paid I do bind myselfe as wittness my hand and seale this twentieth day of July Anno Domini 1692
    The Condicon of this obligacon is such that if the above bounden DAVID COGHILL his heires do at all time hereafter keep all the covenants which on his part ought to be kept menconed in a Bill of Sale bearing equall date between ye said DAVID COGHILL of the one part and RICHARD BOOKER of the other part for a tract of land in RAPPAHANNOCK County according to ye true meaning of the said Bill of Sale then this present obligacon to be void or else to be in full force and vertue
Signed & delivered in ye pr:sence of us
          CHILION WHITE, WILLIAM LOBB,   DAVID COGHILL
          WILLIAM W R RYDER, ROBT: MYNNE
    Memorand: that I doe redeliver ye abovemenconed Bond to RICHARD BOOKER or his heires as wittness my hand & seale this 5th: day of September Ano Dom 1692
    At a Court held for Essex County October ye 10th: 1692
The within bond was at ye request of the wth:in named RICHARD BOOKER admitted to Record   Test F. MERIWETHER Cl Cur

p.   KNOW ALL MEN by these presents that I JOHN VERGITT do acknowledge & confess
72   myselfe indebted unto RICHARD BOOKER of GLOUCESTER County the true and just
          sume of Thirty six pounds of good and lawfull money of England due to be paid

for which payment I do bind myselfe my heires as witness my hand this twentieth day
of July 1692

The Consideration of this obligacon is such that if DAVID COGHILL his heires shall at
all times hereafter keep all agreements in a Bill of Saile bearing equall date betweene
DAVID COGHILL and RICHARD BOOKER for a tract of land in RAPPAHANNOCK County as
by Deed may appear without fraud or further delay, then this present obligation to be
void or else to stand in full force

Signed sealed & delivered in presence of us

    CHILION WHITE, WILLIAM LOBB,   JOHN S VIRGITT
    WILLIAM W R RYDER, ROBT: MYNNE

 At a Court held for Essex County October ye 10th: 1692
The within Bond was at ye request of ye within named RICHARD BOOKER admitted to
Record   Vere Recordtr: Test F. MERIWETHER, Cl Cur

p.   KNOW ALL MEN by these presents that I DAVID COGHILL of RAPPAHANNOCK
73   County in Virginia have made in my steade & place Mr. ROBERT MYNES or
        CHILION WHITE, them or either of them my true and lawfull Attorneys for me
and in my name to acknowledge bargaine & sayle of all and singular ye premisses
hereby sould unto ye said RICHARD BOOKER his heires and assignes in any Corte or
Cortes to be holden for & within the County of RAPPA:, and to doe all acts necessary to
be done in the premisses hereby ratefieing and allowing all they or either of my said
Attorneys shall doe in the premisses, to be as good & effectual as if he ye said DAVID
COGHILL had been then & there personally present and had done ye same in his owne
proper person. In Witness whereof I have hereunto sett my hand and seale ye 20th day
of July 1692

Signed sealed & delivered in ye presence of us

    WILLIAM LOBB,   DAVID COGHILL
    WILLIAM W R RYDER, WILL: SMITH

 Memoranda: That I do againe authorize & impower my Attorneys to acknowledge ye
sale to RICHARD BOOKER or his heires as witness my hand this 5th: day of September
Anno Dom 1692

Signed sealed & delivered in ye pr:sence of us

    JOHN SCOTT,   DAVID COGHILL
    WILLIAM LOBB

 At a Court held for Essex County 8br: ye 10th 1692
The within power was proved by ye Oaths of WM. LOBB and WM. RYDER and admitted to
Record   Vere Recordatr. Test F. MERIWETHER, Cl Cur

pp.   TO ALL CHRISTIAN PEOPLE to whom these presents shall come, WILLIAM FREE-
74-   MAN of ye County of Essex in Virginia send Greeting And now know yee that I
75   ye said WILLIAM FREEMAN for a valuable consideracon already in hand
       received have given and confirmed unto FRANCIS BROWNE of the County above
said in Virginia and unto his heires for ever, all that parcell of land containing by estimation fifty acres of land being part of three hundred acres of land formerly sould &
made over unto EDWARD FREEMAN by THOMAS HARPER, sale bearing date ye nineteenth
day of November 1689 and so sould and made over unto WILLIAM FREEMAN by RICHARD
FREEMAN, Son and heire to EDWARD FREEMAN abovesd., sale bearing date ye first day of
October 1688; and bounded as followeth; beginning at a corner white Oake standing by
or nye a branch side called ye LONG BRANCH, thence up the said Branch to a corner

white Oake by or ny the line of the above sd. FRANCIS BROWNE, thence alongst ye said
line to a corner white Oake standing by the MIDLE BRANCH, thence down the said
Branch to ye place first begun, To have and to hold the above said Fifty acres of land
according as it is bounded in manner aforesd. in all its rights together with all privilidges of what nature kind or quallity sovever belonging unto him ye said FRANCIS
BROWNE & unto his heires for ever; he ye said FRANCIS BROWNE his heires yealding and
paying unto our Sovereign Lord ye King his heires and Successors all such right dutyes
as shall hereafter become due for the same; And I the said WILLIAM FREEMAN do hereby further covenant for me my heires the said FRANCIS BROWNE his heires may at all
times for ever hereafter peaceably and quietly have injoy ye Fifty acres of land in
manner aforesd: without the hindrance of me the said WILLIAM FREEMAN my heires or
any persons claiming from or under me and will alsoe warrant this present sale from
the claime of all other persons whatsoever for ever; And that I covenant to give such
further assurance of the premisses as shall hereafter be required for ye more sure
confirming of ye same unto him. In Witness whereof I ye said WILLIAM FREEMAN
have hereunto sett my hand and affixed my seale this 7th: day of September in the year
of our Lord God Ano Dom 1692
Signed sealed and delivered in the presence of us
    EDWARD FREEMAN   WILLIAM FREEMAN
    JOHN BURNETT, ROBERT R CADE
  Recognitr. in Cur Com Essex 10 die Novembr: Ano 1692 et Recordatr.
             Test F. MERIWETHER, Cl Cur

p.   KNOW ALL MEN by these presents that I JOHN WATERS of the County of Essex of
76   Rappahannock River in Virginia, Planter, doe by these presents constitute and
       appoint my beloved Friend, Mr. JAMES BAUGHAN, of the aforesaid County and
River, for me and in my name and steade to ask shew for and demand all such sums of
money or tobacco that I have oweing or due to me in Virginia, and withall to use all
lawfull meanes for the recovery of all just such sumes of money or tobacco as aforesaid
and likewise to make one or more attorneys as he shall think fitt or necessary, And
further do by these presents authorize and impower my said Attorney to answer for me
all such actions that shall be commenced against me and whatsoever my said Attorney
shall lawfully act and doe in and about the premisses I doe ratefie and allow of as if I
myselfe were personally present. In Testimony whereof I have hereunto sett my hand
and seale this 27th: day of August 1692
Signed sealed & delivered in the presence of us
    ROBT: COLEMAN,   JOHN WATERS
    DAVID LOYDE, WALTER ᒲ PAVEALE
  At a Court held for Essex County October ye 11th: 1692
The within power was proved by the Oath of ROBT: COLEMAN & admitted to Record
        Vere Recordatr: Test F. MERIWETHER Cl Cur

pp.   THIS INDENTURE made the seventh day of March Ano Dom 1691 Between BRYAN
77- WARD of RAPPAHANNOCK County, Plantr:, and MARY his Wife of the one part
79   and JOHN ALMOND of the same County, Plantr: of the other part; Witnesseth
       that the said BRYAN WARD and MARY his Wife for a valuable consideraton to
them in hand at & before the ensealing and delivery hereof by the said JOHN ALMOND
well and truely paid the receipt whereof they do hereby acknowledge, have granted
unto the said JOHN ALMOND his heires and assignes, all that tract or dividend of Land
conteyning Two hundred ninety nine acres and one halfe acre situate & being on the

South side of the said County about six miles back in the woods upon or near the branches of OCCUPACON RUN & MATTAPONY PATH, beginning at a white Oake & a corner tree to Mr. THOMAS BUTTON and extending thence So. W. one hundred and ninety perches to a double tree vizt. a white Oake and a red Oake standing by MATTAPONY PATH thence along the said PATH its severall courses being brought into a straight line is No. 12 degr. 30 mts. Wt. One hundred eighty nine perches to a red Oake corner tree to NICHOLAS COPELAND, thence along the said COPELANDs line W. No. 79 degr. Et. four hundred thirty one perches to a Hickory in ye line of the said BUTTON, thence along the said BUTTONs line So. 48 degr. 30 mts., Wt. two hundred seventy seven perches to the first menconed white Oake, all which before bargained land was granted to ye said BRYAN WARD by Patent dated the 23th of October 1690 as in and by ye said Patent may appear and all woods timber & trees standing growing or being in upon the said land or any part thereof, Also all wayes passages, waters, profitts, priviledges and herediata-mts. whatsoever to the said land belonging and all the Estate, right and demand whatso-ever of the said BRYAN and MARY of in & to ye same, And all Deeds, Charters & Writings concerning the before bargained premisses; To have and to hld with the appurte-nances unto the said JOHN ALMOND his heires and assignes from the day of the date and delivery of these presents to the onely use and behoofe of him said JOHN ALMOND his heires and assignes for ever, and the said BRYAN WARD for himselfe his heires grant in manner following vizt., that he the said JOHN ALMOND at all times for ever hereafter lawfully and quietly have all the sd tract or dividend of land & premisses with the ap-purtenances before granted without the lawfull let or interruption of the said BRYAN & MARY his Wife or any other persons lawfully claiming any right to the land bargained thereof (the yearly rents & levies which shall from henceforth grow due to be paid to the Chief Lord or Lords of the Fee or Fees of the pr:misses only excepted) and that he the said BRYAN WARD and MARY his Wife shall at the next Court held for the said County of RAPPAHANNOCK before their Mats: Justices of ye Peace acknowledge these presents according to the Law and that he ye said BRYAN WARD will at any time here-after at the reasonable request cost and charges in the Law for the further more abso-lute conveying & assuring of all the before bargained premisses unto ye said JOHN ALMOND as by his or their Councill learned in the Law shall be required In Witness whereof the said parties to these presents have set their hands and seales the day and yeare first above written

Signed Sealed and delivered in the presence of us

  CORNELIUS NOELL   BRYAN ☩ WARD

  DANIEL NOELL, EMOND E C CONNELLEY   MARY M WARD

 At a Court held for Essex County November ye 10th: Ano Dom 1692

The within named BRYAN WARD appeared & acknowledged the within specified con-tents to ye within named JOHN ALMOND to be his the said BRYAN WARDs real act & deed, ye same is admitted to record

   Recorded ye 27th: day of December Ano Dom 1692 Test F. MERIWETHER Cl Cur

pp. KNOW ALL MEN by these presents that I JOHN BAKER of the County of GLOSTER

80- doe for & in consideration of a valuable sume of Four thousand pounds of good

81   lawfull tobacco by me in hand already received the receipt whereof I the said

   JOHN BAKER do hereby acknowledge, have granted unto WILLIAM MOSELEY of the County of Essex his heires and assignes forever a certaine parsell of land con-taining Two hundred acres being part of a Pattent granted to Mr. THOMAS BUTTON (deceast) for Three thousand six hundred & fifty acres bearing date the nineteenth day of July One thousand six hundred Sixty six; which sd land is commonly known by ye name of BUTTONS RANGE, And was by the said BUTTON given & bequeathed to his Brother, ROBT. BUTTON in England, and by him the said ROBT. BUTTON sold and assigned to him the said Mr. JOHN BAKER as will at large appear by the Generall Court Records the said land lying and being in the County of Essex (which formerly went under the name of RAPPAHANNOCK County) and on the branches of OCCUPACON and GILSONS about some five miles back in the woods, beginning at a white Oake on ye South side of a branch of OCCUPACON & extending thence South West two hundred and sixty five perches to a Maple & an Ash in a small branch of GILSONS being in ye line of a parcell of land Mr. MATRUM WRIGHT had of the said BAKER, thence along the said land North West One hundred twenty six perches to an Hickory saplin with three red Okes saplins marked triangle about it being near the RANGE PATH, thence North East two hundres sixty five perches between two Hicorys & two red Okes in the line of the whole devident thence along ye same South East One hundred twenty six perches to first menconed white Oke being well bounded on all sides with marked trees, I the said JOHN BAKER do hereby sell unto WILLIAM MOSELEY his heires and assignes for ever; To have and enjoy the same with all its rites and priviledges of all woods, water courses and whatsoever els peaceably and quietly without any hindrance or disturbance of me ye said JOHN BAKER my heires or any other persons claiming any part thereof; Also I the said JOHN BAKER do oblige myselfe my heires to make what further assurance he ye said WILLIAM MOSELEY or his Councell in Law shall require in that case, And do farther engage my selfe lto acknowledge this my Deed of Land before the Court of Essex (there to be enroaled) when thereunto lawfully called by the said WILLIAM MOSELEY or his heires, he or they yeilding & paying all dues or impositions which are or shall be charged and for farther confirmation hereof I have hereunto sett my hand and seale this Tenth day of November 1692

Signed sealed & delivered in the presence of us
    GEO: PARKE,   JOHN BAKER
    JAMES BOUGHAN, F. MERIWETHER
  At a Court held for Essex County November ye 10th: Ano 1692
The above named JOHN BAKER appeared & acknowledged the above specified contents to the abovenamed WILLIAM MOSELEY to be his the said BAKERs act & deed, ye same was admitted to Record
          Recordatr: xvi die 10bris: Ano Dom 1692   Test F. MERIWETHER, Cl Cur

p.   Virginia ss   By his Excellency
82   A Proclamacon
        Whereas their sacred Mats: have by their Royall comission bearing date at Westminster ye first day of March in the fourth year of their Mats. Reign constitute and appointed me, Sr. EDMOND ANDROS, Knt., Lt. & Governr: Genll. of this their Mats. Colony & Dominion of Virga: thereby giveing and granting unto me full power to exercise all and all manner of Jurisdicons & authorities to the same belonging, Now to ye end that ye Peace of their Mats. Dominions may be the better securied and all proceedings in Law continued and that the Ordinary Course of Justice may not be interrupted, I have thought fitt by and with the advice of their Mats: Councill of this Colony in their Mats. names to publish and declare all Magistrates and Officers Civill & Military to continue and remaine in all and singular their powers authorities and jurisdicons untill further order be taken therein, hereby requireing them to proceed in the Execution of their severall dutyes and all their Mats. subjects within this Colony are to be aiding and abetting to them therein and to yeild all due obedience to this Proclamacon Given under my hand & the Seale of the Colony the 21th day of September in the fourth year

of the Reign of our Sovereign Lord & Lady, William and Mary, by the Grace of God of England Scotland France & Ireland, King & Queen Defendrs: of the faith Anno Dom 1692
To the Sheriff of Essex County or his Deputy
A Proclamacon for Continueing all Officers &c.   E. ANDROS
     p. CHR: ROBINSON Sec.   GOD SAVE THE KING & QUEEN
  At a Court held for Essex County October ye 10th: Ano 1692
The within Proclamacon was published in Court & committed to Record
           Test F. MERIWETHER, Cl Cur

p.   Virga: ss   By his Excellency
83   A Proclamacon
     Whereas according to news lately reced here it hath pleased God to give great success and Victory to their Mats. force by Sea agt: the forces and Fleet of the FRENCH KING whereby many of their Capitoll Ships and others were destroyed. I Sr. EDMOND ANDROS Knt. their Mats. Lt. & Govr: Genll. of this Colony with the advice of the Councill of State do hereby in their Mats: names require and command that Sunday next being ye 25th: of this Instant 7br: be observed and kept by all & every ye inhabitants of JAMES CITTY & the parts adjacent & that Sunday the nineth day of October next be kept & observed in all other parts of this Governmt: as a day of PUBLICK THANKSGIVING to Almighty God for ye same and to pray for the continuance of his Blessings, And ye Ministers in their respective Parishes are desired to do what belongs to their duty on the occasion. Given under my hand and the Seale of the Colony the 21th day of September in the fourth yeare of the Reign of our Sovereign Lord and Lady, William and Mary, by the Grace of God of England Scotland France and Ireland, King & Queen Defendrs: of the faith Annoq Dom 1692
To the Sher: of Essex County or his Deputy   E. ANDROS
         GOD SAVE THE KING AND QUEEN
A Proclamation for a Publick Thanksgiving
       C: p CHR: ROBINSON Sec:
  At a Court held for Essex County October ye 10th Ano 1692
The within Proclamacon was published and committed to Record
           Test F. MERIWETHER, Cl Cur

pp.   THIS INDENTURE made ye xii day of September in the year of our Lord God One
84-   thousand six hundred ninety & two and in the fourth year of the Reign of or:
89   Sovraign Lord and Lady, King William and Queen Mary over England &c., Be-
       tweene JOHN BAKER of KINGSTON Pish in GLOCESTER County of the one pt: and
JOHN GARNETT of the above Parish & County, Planter, of the other parte; Witnesseth ye said JOHN BAKER for the sum of Nine thousand pounds of good sweet sented tobacco and cask to him in hand paid at & before the ensealing & delivery of these presents by the said JOHN GARNETT have given granted & confirmed unto the said JOHN GARNETT his heires and assignes for ever Six hundred acres of land being part of that tract of land commonly called by the name of BUTTONS RANG containing 3650 acres granted former-ly to Mr. THOMAS BUTTON deced by Pattent dated ye 19th: of July 1666 which said tract of land was given and bequeathed by the last Will and Testament of the said BUTTON to his Brother, ROBERT BUTTON, as by the said Will dated ye first day of March 1669 will more largely appeare & since by the said heire of the said THOMAS BUTTON duly conveyed unto the abovesd. JOHN BAKER as by an Order of the President & Councell to him granted at JAMES CITTY & dated ye 27th of Octobr: 1688 may & will appeare, which sd six hundred acres of land hereby sold and confirmed unto the said JOHN GARNETT by the sd

JOHN BAKER is bounded as followeth: Begining at a corner red Oake in the NNW line of
Mr. DANIELL GAINES his Dividend and running by his line NNW 300 perches to three
red Oakes near a small branch of OCCUPACON, thence NW 81 perches to a white Oake
neare another branch of OCCUPACON, thence SW 274 perches to a Maple and an Ash in a
small branch of GILSONs, thence SE thirty perches to a Spanish Oake & an Hickory,
thence SW 47 perches to an Hickory, thence SE 304 perches to a Maple in the Maine
Swamp of GILSONs, thence along an old Crooked line its severall courses being brought
into a straight line is N. 54 & halfe degrees Easterly 210 perches to the first menconed
Station; All which said six hundred acres of land bounded as aforesd. with all and singular ye rights togeather with all ye houses orchards woods rents profitts & appurtenances wt:soever to the same belonging or to any part thereof by these presents to be
granted and sold unto the said JOHN GARNETT by the said JOHN BAKER are scituate lying
and being in the Parish of Sittenburne in ye County of Essex lately called by the name
of RAPPAHANNOCK COUNTY, on ye South side of Rappahannock River about five miles
back into the woods as by the above BUTTONS Pattent doth fully appeare; To have and to
hold the said land bounded as abovesd. & all other the premisses with their rights unto
the said JOHN GARNETT his heires & assignes and the said JOHN BAKER for himselfe his
heires the said land with all & singular other ye premisses before sold with the appurtenances unto the said JOHN GARNETT against him the said JOHN BAKER his heires and
assignes and all other p:sons lawfully claiming from by or under him, and will fully
and absolutely warrant and forever defend by these pr:sents, the said JOHN BAKER at ye
time of the delivery of these presents is untill a good & absolute Estate of Inheritance of
all ye before granted premisses shall be vested in & upon the said JOHN GARNETT his
heires according to the meaning of these presents without any condicon and that the
said JOHN BAKER, at the time of the ensealing and delivery of these presents, hath full
power and lawfull authority to grant ye before menconed premisses unto the said JOHN
GARNETT in manner & forme aforesd. And that he ye said JOHN GARNETT his heires at
all tymes for ever hereafter lawfully & quietly have and injoy ye sd Six hundred acres
of land without any lawfull lett or disturbance of ye said JOHN BAKER his heires or any
other p:sons whatsoever and farther ye said JOHN BAKER doth bind himselfe p:sonally
to appear at ye next Court held for the County of Essex & before ye said Court (according
to ye usuall custome provided in such cases), will acknowledge by this Instrument of
Writing to ye onely use of the said JOHN GARNETT all the interest which he hath in ye
sd premisses, and also ye said JOHN BAKER doth hereby bind himselfe his heires that
ELIZABETH his Wife shall likewise within six months after her arivall into this Colony
of Virginia appear before ye above sd Court & accordingly relinquish her right of
Dower of in & to ye above said premisses with all the Interest which she hath or may
have to the same, I ye sd JOHN BAKER have by my hond dated with these pr:sents bound
myselfe my heires for ye p:fect p:formance of all & every ye articles menconed in these
pr:sents unto ye sd JNO: GARNETT his heires & assignes in ye full sum of Nine thousand
pounds of Principall sweet sented tobacco with cask; In Witness whereof I ye sd JNO.
BAKER have hereunto sett my hand & seale the day & year first above written &
delivered
Signed sealed & delivered in ye presence of us
        HENRY PRESSON   JOHN BAKER
        THOMAS HAYES, GEORGE AXE
At a Court held for Essex County November ye 10th: Ano. 1692
The above named JOHN BAKER appeared & acknowledged ye specified contents to ye
abovesaid JNO. GARNETT ye sd BAKERs real act & deed, ye same was admitted to Record
                        Vere Recordatr: Test F. MERIWETHER, Cl Cur

KNOW ALL MEN by these presents that I JOHN BAKER of Kingstone Pish in GLOSTR. County am holden & firmly bound unto JOHN GARNETT of the abovesd. Pish & County, Planter, the full sume of Eighteen thousand pounds of Principall sweet sented tobacco with cask to comaine ye same; to which payment well & truely to be p:formed I bind me my heires firmly by these pr:sents sealed with my seale and dated ye viith day of September in ye year of our Lord God One thousand six hundred Ninety & two & in ye Fourth year of the Reigne of our Sovereign Lord and Lady, King William & Queen Mary of England &c.

  The Condicon of this present obligacon is such that if the above named JOHN GARNETT his heires & assignes shall & may from henceforth peaceably & quietly have & injoy a certain parcell of land containing by Survey Six hundred acres being part of a greater tract granted by Patltent to Mr. THO: BUTTON deced called & known by ye name of BUTTONS RANGE being on ye South side of Rappahannock River in ye County of Essex lately known by ye name of RAPPAHANNOCK COUNTY to be sold by y above bounden JNO. BAKER to ye said JOHN GARNETT by a certaine Indenture of bargaine & sale bearing date with these pr:sents save harmless from all manner of Incumbrances suffered or done by ye sd JNO: BAKER or by his meanes & further if he JNO. BAKER and ELIZA: his Wife their heires do truly observe l& keep all condicons & agreemts. wch: on their part ought to be kept menconed in ye above specified Indenture, then this pr"sent obligacon to be void or else to stand & be in full force & vertue. Signed sealed & delivered in ye presence of us

  HENRY PRESSON,   JOHN BAKER
  THOMAS HAYES, GEORGE AXE
  At a Court held for Essex County November: 10th 1692
The within named JNO. BAKER appeared and acknowledged ye within bond to be his act and deed, ye same was committed to Record; The within bond is truely recorded in ye above County Courts Office   Test F. MERIWETHER Cl Cur

pp.   THIS INDENTURE made ye viith day of September in the year of our Lord God One
90-   thousand six hundred ninety & two and in the fourth year of the Reign of our
96   Sovereign Lord & Lady, William and Mary over England &c., Between JOHN
        BAKER of Kingstone Pish. in GLOSTR: County of the one pte: and ROBERT FOSTER
of the above Pish: & County, Planter, of the other pte: Witnesseth that the said JOHN BAKER for and in consideracon of the sum of Three thousand pounds of good sweet sented tobacco and cask to him in hand paid hath given and confirmed unto the said ROBT. FOSTER his heires & assignes for ever Two hundred acres of land being part of the tract of land commonly called by ye name of BUTTONS RANG containing 3650 acres granted formerly to Mr. THOMAS BUTTON deced by Pattent dated ye 19th: of July 1666 which sd Tract was given & bequeathed by ye last Will and Testament of the said BUTTON to his Brother, ROBT. BUTTON, as by the said Will dated ye first day of March 1669 will appear & since by the heirs of the said THOMAS BUTTON duely conveyed unto ye above JOHN BAKER by an Order of the President and Councill granted at JAMES CITTY dated the 27th: of October 1688 may and will appeare which said Two hundred acres of land hereby sold unto the said ROBT: FOSTER is bounded beginning at an Hickory tree to Mr. JNO. GARNETT in the line of Mr. WRIGHT extending thence SW 230 perches to a red Oke on a hill side neare a branch, thence SE 139 perches a red Oake corner tree to JOHN FOSTER, thence along said JNO: FOSTERs NE 230 perches to a Hickory, a red Oake corner to the said JOHN FOSTER, thence along the line of GARNETTs NW One hundred thirty nine perches to the first Stacon to the first specified place where it was begun first to be measured all which said Two hundred acres of land bounden as aforesaid with all and

singular the rights together with all the houses orchards woods rents profitts and appurtenances whatsoever to the same belonging unto the said ROBERT FOSTER by the said
JNO: BAKER are situate lying and being in the Pish of Sittingbourne in the County of
Essex lately called by the name of RAPPAHANNOCK County on the South side of Rappahannock River, about five miles back into the woods, as by the above BUTTONs Pattent
doth fully appeare; To have and to hold unto the said ROBERT FOSTER his heires and
assignes against him the said JNO. BAKER his heirs & assignes and all other persons
whatsoever lawfully claiming from by or under him shall & will fully absolutely warrant & forever defend by these presents and that ye said ROBERT FOSTER his heires shall
and may by force & vertue of these pr:sents at all tymes forever hereafter lawfully and
quietly hold and enjoy ye said land and have the rents and profitts thereof to his and
theire owne proper use without the lawfull disturbance of ye said JNO. BAKER by his
heires or any other person (ye quitt rents for ye same which shall hereafter become
due onely excepted) and further ye said JNO. BAKER doth bind himselfe his heirs personally to appeare at the next Court held for the County of Essex (& before the said Court
according to the usual custome provided in such cases) will acknowledge this Instrument of Writeing to the only use of the said ROBT: FOSTER his heris all the interest wch:
he hath in ye sd premisses according to the true intent & meaning of these presents
and also the said JOHN BAKER doth bind himselfe his heires that ELIZABETH his Wife
shall within six months of her arivall in this Colony of Virginia appeare before the
abovesd: Court & openly relinquish her right of Dower of in and to ye abovesd.
premisses with all the interest that she hath or may hve to the same; Lastly that he the
said JNO. BAKER doth for himselfe his heires promise that he will at the times upon
reasonble request and at the costs and charges in ye Law of ye said ROBERT FOSTER
make and execute all such further and lawfull acts and assurances in the Law wt:soever
for ye better assurance of the abovesd. pr:misses unto ye said ROBERT FOSTER be it by
Deed or confirmacons of Warranty or any wayes or meands as by said ROBERT FOSTER or
his Councill learned in the Law shall be reasonably advised for the better confirmacon
of ye sale I the said JNO: BAKER have by my Bond dated with these pr:sents bound me
dmy heires and assignes in the full sum of Three thousand pounds of principall sweet
sented tobacco with caske unto the said ROBERT FOSTER his heires & assignes for ye due
p:formance of all the articles menconed in the pr:sents In Witness whereof I the said
JOHN BAKER have hereunto sett my hand and seale
Signed sealed and delivered in the pr:sence of us
     HENRY. PRESSON,   JOHN BAKER
     THOMAS HAYES, GEORGE AXE
  At a Court held for Essex County November ye 10th Ano. 1692
The within named JNO. BAKER appear'd & acknowledged the within specified contents
to ye within named ROBT: FOSTER to be his ye sd BAKERs real act and deed, ye same was
admitted to Record
          Vere Recordatr: Test F. MERIWETHER, Cl Cur
     KNOW ALL MEN by these presents that I JOHN BAKER of Kingstone Parish in
GLOSTR: County am bound unto ROBERT FOSTER of the above Parish & County, Planter, in
the full sum of Six thousand pounds of principall sweet sented tobacco with cask for the
same to which payment I bind me and my heires dated the seventh day of September in
the year of our Lord One thousand six hundred & ninety and two and in the Fourth year
of the Reign of our Sovereign Lord and Lady, King William and Queen Mary over
England &c.
  The Condicon of this obligacon is that if the above named ROBERT FOSTER his heires
may forevermore peaceably and quietly hold and enjoy a certain parcell of land con-

taining Two hundred acres being on the South side of Rappahannock River in the
County of Essex lately known by the name of RAPPAHANNOCK County, and every part
thereof menconed in a certaine Indenture of Bargaine and Sale bearing date with these
presents made between JOHN BAKER of the one pte: and ROBERT FOSTER of the other pte:
and if the sd JOHN BAKER and ELIZABETH his Wife their heires truely fullfill & keep all
condicons which on their parts ought to be kept menconed in the above specified
Indenture Then this present obligacon to be voyd or else to stand in full force and
vertue
Signed sealed and delivered in ye presence of us
    HENRY PRESSON   JOHN BAKER
    THOMAS HAYES, GEORGE AXE
  At a Court held for Essex County November ye 10th: Ano 1692
The within named JNO: BAKER appear'd and acknowledged ye within Bond to be his act
and deed, ye same was admitted to Record   Vere Recordatr: Test F. MERIWETHER Cl Cur

pp.   THIS INDENTURE made ye vii day of September in the year of our Lord God One
97-   thousand six hundred ninety and two and in the Fourth year of the Reign of
103   our Sovereign Lord and Lady, King Will and Queen Mary over England &c. Be-
           tweene JOHN BAKER of Kingstone Pish. in GLOSTR: County of the one pte: and
WM. SMITHER of the above Pish. and County, Planter, of the other pte:, Witnesseth that
the said JOHN BAKER for the sum of Three thousand pounds of good sweet sented tobo:
and cask have sold unto the said WM. SMITH his heires & assignes Two hundred acres of
land being part of that tract of land commonly called by the name of BUTTONS RANG
containing 3650 acres granted formerly to Mr. THOMAS BUTTON deced by Patent dated ye
19th: of July 1666 which said tract of land was bequeathed by the last Will of the sd BUT-
TON to his Brother, ROBERT BUTTON, as by his said Will dated the first day of March 1669
will appeare, and since by the heires of the said THOMAS BUTTON conveyed unto the
above JOHN BAKER as by an order of the President and Councill granted at JAMES CITTY
dated the 27th of October 1688 may & will appeare which said Two hundred acres of land
is bounded Beginning at a red Oake neare a branch corner tree to a peice of land purchased by ROBERT FOSTER of the said BAKER and running thence SW 126 perches between two red Oakes and an Hickory, thence S. 41 and a halfe degrees E. 230 perches to a
white Oake thence N. 54 and a halfe degrees Easterly along the old line of the maine
Divident to a white Oake corner tree to a p:cell of land bought by JOHN FOSTER of the
said BAKER, thence along the said FOSTERs lines NW 264 perches to the first station, all
which said Two hundred acres of land bounded as aforesaid with all the rights together
with all the houses, orchards, woods, rents, priviledges and appurtenances to the same
belonging unto the said WM. SMITHER by the said JOHN BAKER are scituate and being in
the Pish of Sittingbourne in the County of Essex, lately called by the name of RAPPA:
County, on ye South side of Rappa: River above five miles back into the Woods as by the
above BUTTONs Pattent doth fully appeare; To have and to hold the said land unto the
said WM. SMITHER his heires & assignes and the said JOHN BAKER for himselfe the said
land before sold with the appurtenances against him the sd JOHN BAKER his heires and
every other persons whatsoever lawfully claiming under him absolutely warrant and
defend by these pr:sents and that the said WM. SMITHER his heires at all times for ever
hereafter lawfully and quietly hold and injoy the said land and all the premisses & take
the rents and profitts thereof to his and their own proper use without the lett or disturbance of said JOHN BAKER his heires or any other p:sons under him and further the
said JOHN BAKER doth bind himselfe to appeare at the next Court held for the County of
Essex and before the said Court (according to the usual custome provided in such cases)
will acknowledge by this Instrument of Writeing to the only use of the sd WM. SMITHER

his heires and assignes all the interesdt which he hath in the said premisses and also the said JOHN BAKER will bind himselfe that ELIZABETH his Wife shall within six months of her arivall into this Colony of Virginia appeare before the above said Court and openly relinquish her right of dower to ye aforesd. pr:misses with all the interest that she hath or may have to the same, Lastly he ye said JOHN BAKER doth promise that he will upon reasonable request and at the proper costs and charges in the Law of said WM. SMITHER make all lawfull acts for the better assurance of the above pr:misses as by sd WM. SMITHER his heires or his or their Counceill learned in ye Law shall be reasonably required; I the said JOHN BAKER have by my bond dated with these presents bound me my heires in the full sum of Six thousand pounds of principall sweet sented tobo: with cask unto ye sd WM. SMITHER his heires for the due performance of all the articles menconed in these presents. In Witness whereof, I the said JOHN BAKER have hereunto sett my hand & seale

Signed sealed & delivered in ye presence of us
Test   SALVATOR MUSCOE   JOHN BAKER
       JAMES MARWOOD, JNO: MILLER

  At a Court held for Essex County November ye 10th: Ano 1692
The within named JNO. BAKER appear'd & acknowledged ye within specified contents to be his real act & deed, ye same was admitted to Record
                      Vere Recordatr: Test F. MERIWETHER, Cl Cur

  KNOW ALL MEN by these presents that I JOHN BAKER am firmly bound unto WM. SMITHER in the full sume of Six thousand pounds of principall sweet sented Tobo: with caske to wch: payment to be truely performed I bind me my heires dated ye vii day of September in ye year of our Lord God One thousand six hundred ninety and two and in the Fourth year of the Reign of our Sovereign Lord and Lady, King Wm. and Queen Mary ovr: England &c.,
  The condicon of this pr:sent obligacon is that if WM. SMITHER his heires or assignes may forevermore peaceably and quietly hold and enjoy a certaine p:cell of land containing Two hundred acres menconed to be bargained and sold by the above bounden JNO: BAKER to sd WM. SMITHER by a certaine Indenture of Bargaine and Sale sufficiently saved harmless from all manner of Estates & incumbrances and further if said JNO. BAKER & ELIZABETH his Wife do well and truely observe all ye covenants wch: on their parts ought to be fulfilled this pr:sent obligacon to be voyd or else to stand in full force and vertue

Signed sealed and delivered in the pr:sence of us
Teste   SALVATOR MUSCOE   JOHN BAKER
        JAMES MARWOOD, JNO: MILLER

  At a Court held for Essex County November ye 10th: Ano 1692
The within named JNO. BAKER appear'd & acknowledged the within specified contents to be his act & deed, ye same is admitted to record
                      Vere Recordatr: Test F. MERIWETHER, Cl Cur

pp.   THIS INDENTURE made ye vii day of September in the year of our Lord God One
103-   thousand six hundred ninety and two and in the Fourth year of the Reign of
108   our Sovereing Lord and Lady, Wm: and Mary; King and Queen over England &c.
           Betweene JNO: BAKER of Kingstone Pish: in GLOSTR: County of the one pte: and
JNO: FOSTER of the above Pish: & County, Planter, of the other Witnesseth that the said
JNO. BAKER for the summe of Three thousand pounds of good sweet sented Tobo: and
caske to him in hand payd hath granted unto the sd JNO. FOSTER Two hundred acres of
land being part of that tract of land commonly called BUTTONS RANG containing 3650
acres granted formerly to Mr. THOMAS BUTTON deced by Pattent dated ye 19th day of

July 1666, which said tract was given & bequeathed by the last Will of the said BUTTON to
his Brother, ROBERT BUTTON, as by the said Will dated the first day of March 1669 will
appeare and since by the heires of the said THOMAS BUTTON duely convayed unto the
above JNO. BAKER as by an Order of the President and Councill granted at JAMES CITTY
dated the 27th: of October 1688 will appeare, which said Two hundred acres of land is
bounden Begining at a Maple corner tree to 600 acres of land belonging to Mr. JNO.
GARNETT which he purchased of the said BAKER; and standing in the Maine Swamp of
GILSONS RUN and extending thence along the said GARNETTs line N.W. 165 perches to
two Hickories & a red Oake in the sd line thence S.W. 234 perches to a red Oake, thence
SE 125 perches to a white Oake, thence along an old line of the Maine Divident N. 54 &
halfe degrees East 232 perches to the first station, all which said land with all houses
orchards, woods to the same belonging being in ye Pish of Sittingbourne in the County
of Essex lately called by the name of RAPPAHANNOCK County on the South side of
Rappahannock River about five miles back into the woods as by the above BUTTONs
Pattent doth appeare; To have and to hold unto the said JNO. FOSTER his heires and
assignes against him the sd JNO. BAKER his heires & all other p:sons claiming from by
or under him & will fully & absolutely warrant & that ye sd JNO: FOSTER his heires may
by vertue of these pr:sents forever hereafter lawfully & quietly hold ye said land & all
the before granted premisses & take ye profitts thereof to his own proper use without
ye lawfull trouble of ye sd JNO: BAKER or any claiming under him and further the sd
JNO. BAKER doth bind himselfe to appeare at the next Court held for ye County of Essex
& before ye sd Court (according to ye usuall custome provided in such cases) will
accordingly acknowledge by this Instrumt. of Writeing to the onely use of sd JNO.
FOSTER all the Interest which he hath in ye sd premisses & also ye sd JNO. BAKER doth
bind himselfe that ELIZA: his Wife shall within six months after he arival into this
Colony of Virginia appeare before ye abovesd. Court & openly relinquish her right of
dower in ye abovesd. premisses In Witness whereof I the said JNO: BAKER have here-
unto sett my hand & seale
Signed sealed & delivered in ye presence of us
        HENRY PRESSON   JOHN BAKER
        THOMAS HAYES, GEORGE AXE
  At a Court held for Essex County November ye 10th: Ano. 1692
The within named JNO. BAKER appear'd & acknowledged the within specified contents
to the within named JNO. FOSTER to be his real act & deed, the same was admitted to
Record   Vere Recordatr: Test F. MERIWETHER Cl Cur
        KNOW ALL MEN by these presents that JNO: BAKER is holden & firmly bound un-
to JNO. FOSTER in the full sume of Six thousand pounds of principle sweet sented tobacco
and cask dated ye vii day of September in ye yeare of our Lord God One thousand six
hundred ninety and two
        - The Condicon of these pr:sents is that if ye above named JNO. FOSTER his heires
from henceforth peaceably & quietly hold a certaine p:cell of land containing Two
hundred acres sold by the above bounden JNO: BAKER to ye sd JNO: FOSTER by Indenture
of Bargaine and Sale bearing date with these presents & saved harmless from all
manner of Estate & Incombrances done by ye sd JNO: BAKER and further if ye sd JNO:
BAKER & ELIZABETH his Wife, their heirs do truely observe all the covenants wch: on
their parts ought to be observed Then this present obligacon to be voyd or else to stand
in full force
Signed sealed & delivered in the pr:sence of us
        HENRY PRESSEN   JOHN BAKER
        THOMAS HAYES, GEORGE AXE

At a Court held for Essex County November ye 10th: 1692
The within named JNO: BAKER appear'd & acknowledged ye within contents to ye within
named JNO: FOSTER to be his ye sd BAKERs act & deed, ye same was admitted to Record
Vere Recordatr: Test F. MERIWETHER, Cl Cur

pp.   THIS INDENTURE made ye vii day of September in ye yeare of or: Lord God One
109-   thousand six hundred ninety & two & in the Fourth yeare of ye Raigne of or:
113   Soveraigne Lord & Lady, King Wm: and Queen Mary over England &c., Between
         JNO: BAKER of Kingstone Pish in GLOSTR. County of ye one pte: & WM. HOWLETT
of ye abovesd Pish and County, Planter, of ye other pte: Witnesseth that ye said JNO:
BAKER for Three thousand pounds of good sweet sented Tobacco & caske to him paid
have granted unto sd WM. HOWLETT his heires Two hundred acres of land being part of
yt: tract of land commonly called by the name of BUTTONS RANG containing 3650 acres
granted formerly to Mr. THOMAS BUTTON deced by Pattent dated ye 19th: of July 1666
wch: sd tract was given by ye last Will of ye sd BUTTON to his Brother, ROBT. BUTTON, as
by sd Will dated ye first of March 1669 will appeare & since the heires of ye sd THOMAS
BUTTON duely convayed unto ye abovesaid BAKER as by an Ordr: of ye President & Councill granted at JAMES CITTY dated ye 27th: of Octobr: 1688 may & will appeare wch: sd
Two hundred acres of land hereby sold to ye sd WM. HOWLETT is bounded beginning at
two Hickories & two red Oakes a corner to 200 acres yt: WM. MOSELEY purchased of ye sd
BAKER, and extending along his sd line SW 265 perches to three red Oakes standing
about an Hickory neare the RANG PATH & in the line of Mr. WRIGHTs 1200 acres, thence
along the said WRIGHTs line NW 144 perches to an Ash in ye sd line in the head of a
small branch oppositt to the RANG PLANTACON thence NE 190 perches to an Hickory in
the line of Coll. JNO. CATLETT, then along the line of the sd CATLETT (viz) S. 60 degrees E.
77 perches to a small Hickory, thence S. E. 39 perches to the first station, all wch: sd Two
hundred acres of land together with all the houses orchards rents priviledges to the
same belonging being in the Pish of Sittinburne in ye County of Essex lately called by
the name of RAPPAHANNOCK County on the South side of Rappahannock River about
five miles back into ye Woods, To have & to hold unto ye sd WM. HOWLETT his heirs &
assignes and the said JNO: BAKER the said Land against him the sd JNO. BAKER his heires
and all other p:sons lawfully claiming under him shall & will absolutely warrant & forever defend and that the sd. WM. HOWLETT by vertue of these pr:sents at all tymes hereafter lawfully & quietly occupy & enjoy the said land without ye lawfull lett or disturbance of ye sd JNO: BAKER his heires or any p:sons lawfully claiming under him and
further ye sd JNO; BAKER doth bind himselfe p:sonally to appeare at ye next Court held
for the County of Essex and acknowledge by this Instrumt: of writing to ye onely use of
ye sd WM. HOWLETT his heires & assignes all the interest wch: he hath in ye sd
pr:misses and alsoe the sd JNO. BAKER doth bind himselfe his heires that ELIZABETH his
Wife shall within six moneths after her arivall into this Colony of Virginia appeare
before the abovesd Court & openly relinquish her right of Dower In Witness whereof
ye sd JNO: BAKER have hereunto sett my hand & seale ye day & yeare first above written
Signed sealed & delivered in ye presence of us
        HENRY PRESSON   JOHN BAKER
        THOMAS HAYES, GEORGE AXE
  At a Court held for Essex County November ye 10th: ano 1692
The within named JNO: BAKER appear'd & acknowledged ye within specified contents to
the within named WM. HOWLETT, to be his ye sd BAKERs real act & deed the same was
admitted to Record
              Vere Recordtr: Test F. MERIWETHER Cl Cur

KNOW ALL MEN by these presents that I JOHN BAKER am firmly bound unto WM. HOW-
LETT in the full sume of Six thousand pounds of principle sweet sented tobo: with caske
to wch: paymt: to be truely performed I bind me my heires dated ye vii day of Septembr:
in the yeare of our Lord God One thousand six hundred ninety and two and in the
Fourth yeare of the Reign of or: Sovereigne Lord & Lady King Wm. and Queen Mary

The condicon of this pr:sent obligacon is that if WM. HOWLETT his heires and assignes
may forevermore peaceably and quietly hold and enjoy a certain p:cell of land containing Two hundred acres menconed to be bargained and sold by the above bounden
JNO: BAKER to sd WM: HOWLETT by a certaine Indenture of bargaine and sale sufficiently saved harmless from all manner of Estates & incumbrances and further if said JNO.
BAKER & ELIZABETH his Wife do well and truely observe all ye covenants wch: on their
parts ought to be observed, Then this pr:sent obligacon to be voyd or else stand in full
force and vertue

Signed sealed & delivered in the pr:sence of us
    HENRY PRESSON   JOHN BAKER
    THOMAS HAYES, GEORGE AXE
At a Court held for Essex County Novembr: ye 10th: Ano 1692
The within named JNO: BAKER appear'd & acknowledged the within specified contents
to be his real act & deed, ye same are admitted to Record
               Vere Recordatr: Test F. MERIWETHER Cl Cur

pp.   To all Experint Pepell to whom these shall com I RICHARD FREMAN Son & hare
114-   of EDWARD FREMAN deseased of the County of Esix, Planter, send Greting: Know
115   yee that I RICHARD FREMAN for diveries good cases and vallable considerasiones
        me thare unto moveing and espeselly for & in considerasion of Five thousand
pounds of swetsented tobacco and caske all redey in hand reseved ye resepate whareof I
doe hearebey acnoledge & of everey parte & parsell heareof doe by these presentes
acnoledge myselfe fulley satefied contented & payed have given granted bargained
soulde alened assured & confered & by these presents doe give grant bargine selle &
confirme unto my Brother, WILLIAM FREMAN, of ye abovesd Countey, Planter, aparte of
a parsell of land that my Father, EDWARD FREMAN, bought of THOMAS HARPER containg
Three hundred akres as more or less may apeare by a convance from undr the sd HAR-
PERs hand baring date ye ninetenth day of November One thousan six hundred sixty
nine lying & being in the aforesd County & on ye South side of Rappahanock River
beging at WILLIAM AKRES upon corner tree upon the mane Swamp of PESCATACON
CREKE & soe runing up the mane Swamp Westerly to ye MEDELL BRANCE & so up ye sd
BRANCE Southerly to a branch called ye LONG BRANCE to a corner white Oake standing
in the mouth of the brance & so up ye sd brance to a corner reded Oake & soe Easterley
by a line of marked trees to the line of ye above sd WM. AKRES & so along the said
AKRES line to ye place it furste begune for One hundred & fiftey akres of land be it
more or less To have & to holde ye sd bargined land & primieses unto ye sd WILLIAM
FREMAN & his hares & assynes for ever with all rites priliges & appertanementes thare
unto belonging with warrantey agaynst me RICHARD FREMAN my hares Exectors or
assignes or any other parson or parsones whatsoever claiming aney jutrite or estate in
ye primisies and fuder do bind me my hares for to give the abovesd WILLIAM FREMAN
his hares aney other fuder assurantly as the laned in the Law shall advise defise as
witness my hand and seale this 10th: day of Desember 1692

Signed sealed and delivered in the presentes of us
    JAMES BOUGHAN,   RICHARD ∫| FREMAN
    WILLIAM JOHNSON

At a Court held for Essex County Febry: ye 10th: anno 1692
The within named RICHARD FREMAN appear'd & acknowledged ye within specified
contents to the within named WILLIAM FREMAN to be his the sd RICHARD FREMANs real
act & deed, the same is ordered to be recorded
				Vere Recordatr: Test F. MERIWETHER, Cl Cur

pp.		THIS INDENTURE made the tenth day of Febry: in the yeare of our Lord One
115-		thousand six hundred ninety and two and in the Fourth yeare of the Reigne of
118		our Soveraigne Lord and Lady, William and Mary of England Scotland France
		and Ireland, King and Queen Defenders of the faith &c., Betweene VINCENT
VAUSE of the County of Essex in the Collony of Virginia, Planter, and ANNE his Wife of
the one party and EDWARD THOMAS of the same County and Collony, Mercht., of the
other party; Witnesseth that the said VINCENT VAUSE and ANNE his Wife for and in
consideracon of one Lusty Man Negro and one English Man Servt., to him in hand paid
or secured to be paid before the ensealing & delivery of these pr:sents by the sd
EDWARD THOMAS whereof the said VINCENT VAUSE and ANNE his Wife have sold unto
the sd EDWARD THOMAS his heires and assignes all that Plantacon & p:rcell of land
whereon the said VINCENT VAUSE and ANNE his Wife hath lately lived containing Two
hundred & fifty acres more or less it being the one moyety of a Devidend quantity Five
hundred acres bequeathed unto the said ANNE by the Last Will & Testament of JOHN
PENNE late of the aforesd. County deceased; & part of Two thousand acres formerly
granted to RICHARD BENNET Esqr., by Patten bearing date the 4th day of Novembr: 1642
scituate lyinge & beinge in Essex County bounded as followeth viz: beginninge at a corner Stake standinge in a Marsh dividinge this Land from the Land of Mr. HENRY WIL-
LIAMSON and running So. West alongst the said WILLIAMSONs line Three hundred and
twenty poles to a corner tree, thence parralell with Rappa: River North thirty one degrees West one hundred and Sixty poles to a corner Hickory, thence North East one
hundred and seventy poles to the head of ye Marsh of another Creeke to a corner Locust
and forked Chesnut a Oake, thence continuinge the same course to the Maine Run
issuinge into the said Creeke, thence down and alongst said Run and Creeke to Rappa:
River and lastly downe the said River to the sd Stake beinge the Corner of Mr. HENRY
WILLIAMSONs land, the place began at, includinge the aforesd. quantity of two hundred and fifty acres of land more or less togeather withall and singular ye houses edi-
fices, buildings, orchards and fences, with all woods timber and timber trees standinge
growinge lyinge or beinge To have and to hold the said Plantacon and p:cell of land and
every part thereof with all the comodities and advantages to ye same belonginge or any
wise appertaininge, unto the said EDWARD THOMAS his heires and assignes and the said
VINCENT VAUSE and ANNE his Wife for them selves their heires doe grant to & with the
said EDWARD THOMAS his heires in manner & forme followinge, that is to say, that the
said VINCENT VAUSE and ANNE his Wife now have full right and lawful authority to
grant and sell the pr:misses unto said EDWARD THOMAS and promise warrant and grant
that the Plantacon and pr:cell of land is free and cleare from all manner of former gifts
grants mortgages from all other charges done by the said VINCENT VAUSE and ANNE his
Wife & doth warrant and grant with the said EDWARD THOMAS lthat he shall and may
from henceforth forever peaceably and quietly hold every part thereof, against them
the said VINCENT VAUSE and ANNE his Wife, and all manner of persons lawfully
claiminge by or under him or them or either of them or under their meanes or any
other p:sons wt:soever In Witness whereof the said VINCENT VAUSE and ANNE his Wife
have hereunto sett their hands and fixed their seales the day and yeare first above
written

Signed sealed & delivered in pr:sents of us
    JNO. BATTAILE
    RO: BROOKE

VINCENT *Lu* VAUSE
ANNE *Ag* VAUSE

At a Court held for Essex County Febry: ye 10th: ano 1692
The within named VINCENT VAUSE appear'd & acknowledged the within specified contents to the within named EDWARD THOMAS to be his the said VAUSEs real act and deed, the same was ordered to be recorded
    Test F. MERIWETHER, Cl Cur
    Also the within named ANNE VAUSE appear'd and acknowledged the within specified contents to ye within named EDWARD THOMAS to be her ye said ANNEs real act & deed, the same was ordered to be recorded
    Test F. MERIWETHER Cl Cur
    Essex ss. Wee the Subscribers haveing privately examined ANN VAUSE, ye Wife of VINCENT VAUSE, whether she is willing & voluntarily doth of her own free will and intent without coertion compultion or constraint of her said Husband freely acknowledge a certaine Deed of Sale of a parcell of land to Capt. EDWARD THOMAS bearing date ye 10th: of Febry: 1692, and find it was her voluntary act and inclinacon without menasis or threats whereof have sett our hands his 10th: of Febry: 1692/3
        WILL: MOSELEY
        RO: BROOKS
At a Court held for Essex County Febrya: ye 10th: ano 1692
The within menconed Examinacon was at ye request of ye within named Capt. EDWARD THOMAS ordered to be recorded
    Test Vere Recordatr: F. MERIWETHER, Cl Cur

pp.   THIS INDENTURE made this Tenth day of January in ye yeare of our Lord God
119-   One thousand six hundred Ninety and two and in the third yeare of the Reigne
120   of our Sovereigne Lord & Lady, William and Mary over England Scotland France
       and Ireland and Virginia, King & Queen Defenders of the faith &c. Between
CORNELIUS NOELL of the Parish of Sittenbourne in ye County of Essex and Colonye of Virginia of the one aprt and THOMAS CLOUTSOME of the other part Witnesseth that the said CORNELIUS NOELL for a valuable consideracon in hand already reced the receipt whereof he do hereby acknowledge and to be therewith fully satisfied and contented hath and doth hereby give sell and confirm unto the said THOMAS CLOUTSOME his heires & assignes all his right title interest and claime whatsoever of in and to a certaine peice and parcell of land containing by estimacon Two hundred acres of land, being part of 390 acres of land granted to the said CORNELIUS NOELL by Patent bearing date ye 23d day of October 1690, ye said Land situate lying and being in the County of Essex aforesaid and bounded as followeth beginning at a small red Oke in the line of Mr. THOMAS PAGE corner tree to Mr. VICARS, and extending along the said VICARS line South three degrees Easterly two hundred forty three perches to a red Oake in the line of Majr. THOMAS HAWKINS, thence along ye sd line to a Spanish Oake corner tree standing by a branch side, thence up the branch to a corner Maple, thence Westerly to a white Oake corner tree, thence North to PAGEs line a white Oake corner tree, thence to the beginning tree; To have and to hold the said land with all woods water courses and appertenances thereunto belonging or any wise appertaining to the said THOMAS COUTSOM his heires and assignes forever subject nevertheless to the Quitrents that shall become due to our Sovereign Lord and Lady ye King & Queen, their heirs and Successors, And further the sd CORNELIUS NOELL doth covenant that the said THOMAS CLOUTSOME his heires &c., shall peaceably hold and enjoy the above granted Premisses

without the lett and molestation of him the said CORNELIUS NOELL his heires forever or
from any other person through or under him laying any claime to the same and that
he will make due acknowledgment of ye land in the County Court of Essex thre to be
enroled according to the Statute in that case made & provided; In Witness whereof the
said CORNELIUS NOELL hath hereunto sett his hand & seale lthe date first above written
Signed sealed & delivered in presence of us

     THOMAS HUCKLESCOTT,   CORNELIUS NOELL
     MARY HUCKLESCOTT

  At a Court held for Essex County Febry: ye 10th: ano 1692
The within named CORNELIUS NOELL appear'd & acknowledged ye within specified
contents to be his real act & deed, ye same was ordered to be recorded

       Test F. MERIWETHER, Cl Cur

pp.   THIS INDENTURE made this tenth day of January in ye yeare of our Lord God One
121- thousand six hundred ninety and two and in the third yeare of the Reigne of
122   our Sovereign Lord and Lady, William and Mary over England Scotland France
       Ireland and Virginia, King & Queen Defendrs: of the faith &c., Witness that COR-
NELIUS NOELL of the Parish of Sittenbourne in the County of Essex & Col. of Virginia out
of the Love he bears to EDMOND CONOLE as also divers other good causes & consideracons
him thereunto moveing hath and doth by these presents give and confirm unto the said
EDMOND CONOLE his heires & assignes all his right and claime whatsoever of in and to a
certaine peice or parcell of land conteyning by estimacon One hundred & ninety acres
of land being part of a greater tract of land granted by Patent to the said CORNELIUS
NOELL bearing date ye 23d day of October 1690; the said land scituate and being in the
aforesd. County of Essex and bounded as followeth; beginning at marked Spanish Oake
standing in the line of Majr. THOMAS HAWKINS, thence along the said line to a saplin
red Oake on the topp of a Hill near a small branch thence forty three degrees Easterly
to the line of PAGE aforesd. Sixty eight perches to a Stake between two Spanish Oakes
and a Hickory in a valye, thence along the said PAGEs line to a white Oake corner tree
of THOMAS COUTSOMEs, thence along the line of the said CLOUTSOMEs line to the sd
Spanish Oake; To have and to hold the said Land with all woods underwoods water
courses & appertlenances thereunto belonging to the said EDMOND CONOLE his heires or
assignes forever subject nevertheless to the Quitrents that shall grow due for ye same
to our Sovereign Lord and Lady, the King and Queen, their heires and Successors, And
further the said CORNELIUS NOELL doth covenant the said EDMOND CONELE his heires &c.
shall peaceably occupie and enjoy the above granted premisses without the lett or
molestation of him ye sd CORNELIUS NOELL his heires for ever or from any other persons that through or under him shall lay any claime to the sd premisses & that he will
duely acknowledge ye same in Essex County Court thereto be enroled according to ye
Law in that case provided; In Witness whereof ye sd CORNELIUS NOELL hath sett his
hand and seale ye date first above written
Signed sealed and delivered in pr:sence of us

     THOMAS HUCKLESCOTT   CORNELIUS NOELL
     MARY HUCKLESCOTT

  At a Court held for Essex County Febry: lye 10th ano 1692
The within named CORNELIUS NOELL appear'd & acknowledged the within specified
contents to be his real act & deed, ye same was ordered to be recorded

        Vere Recordatr: Test F. MERIWETHER, Cl Cur

pp.   THIS INDENTURE made this tenth day of January in the yeare of our Lord God
123-   One thousand six hundred ninety and two and in the third yeare of the Reigne
125   of our Sovereign Lord and Lady, William and Mary over England Scotland
France Ireland & Virginia, King and Queen Defendrs: of the faith &c., Between
THOMAS CLOUTSOME of the Parish of Sittenbourne in the County of Essex and Coll. of
Virginia of the one part and CORNELIUS NOELL of the same Parish and County and Coll.
of the other part Witnesseth that the said THOMAS CLOUTSOME and MARY his Wife for a
valuable consideracon in hand already received have sold unto the said CORNELIUS
NOELL his heires all their right and interest whatsoever to a certaine parcell of land
containing by estimacon two hundred acres being part of a greater tract of land by
Deed of Gift granted to the said MARY, Wife to the said THOMAS CLOUTSOME, bearingd ate
the (blank) the said land scituate & being in the County of Essex aforesaid & bounded as
followeth joyning to the land of JAMES BOWLER, NICHOLAS COPELAND and to the land of
the said CORNELIUS NOELL; To have and to hold ye said land with all woods underwoods
water courses & appertenances thereunto belonging to the said CORNELIUS NOELL his
heires & assignes forever subject nevertheless to the Quit rents that shall become due
for the same to our Sovereign Lord and Lady, King & Queene, their heires and Successors and further the said THOMAS CLOUTSOME and MARY his Wife doe covenant that
the said CORNELIUS NOELL his heires shall peaceably have & enjoy ye said above
granted premises without the hindrance or evasion of him the said THOMAS and MARY
his Wife, their heirs and assignes forever, or from any other persons under them
laying any claime to ye same and that they will make due acknowledgmt: of the same in
the County Court of Essex there to be enroled according to ye Statutes in that case made
and provided In Witness whereof the said THOMAS CLOUTSOME & MARY his Wife have
hereunto sett their hands and seales
Signed sealed & delivered in prsence of us
          DANIELL NOELL   THOMAS T CLOUTSOME
          THOMAS HUCKLESCOTT,   Ye marke of M MARY CLOUTSOME
          MARY HUCKLESCOTT, JOHN WEARE
     At a Court held for Essex County Febry: ye 10th: ano 1692
The within named THOMAS CLOUTSOME appear'd & acknowledged the within specified
contents to be his real act and deed, ye same ordered to be recorded
               Test F. MERIWETHER, Cl Cur
     Also EDMOND CONOLE by virtue of a Power from ye within named MARY CLOUT-
SOME appear'd & acknowledged her ye sd MARYs right &c., of ye within menconed land,
ye same was ordered to be recorded
               Vere Recordatr: Test F. MERIWETHER, Cl Cur
     KNOW ALL MEN by these presents that I MARY CLOUTSOME of Essex County and
Parish of Sittenbourne do make and appoint EDMUND CONOLE my true and lawfull Attorney for me to acknowledge all my right and claime of and to a certaine parcell of land
granted and sold to CORNELIUS NOELL of the same County and Parish and menconed in a
conveyance under ye hand & seale of THOMAS CLOUTSOME my Husband & me Constituant
bearing date with these presents warranting and confirming what my said Attorney
shall lawfully doe in ye premises as if I were personally present. In Witness whereof I
have hereunto sett my hand and seale this tenth day of January 1692
Signed sealed and delivered in pr:sence of us
          JOHN WEARE,   MARY M CLOUTSOME
          DANIELL NOELL
               Vere Recordatr: Test F. MERIWETHER, Cl Cur

pp.   THIS INDENTURE made this tenth day of Febry: 1692 and in the third year of
125-   the Reign of our Sovereign Lord and Lady, King Willm. & Queene Mary &c.
127   between RICHARD WILTON and MARY his Wife of the one part and WILLM:
         COMPTON of the other part Witnesseth that ye said RICHARD WILTON and MARY
his Wife for & in consideration of Two thousand foure hundred pounds of good sound
merchantable tobacco to them paid in hand before the sealing and delivery of these
pr:sents have demised leased bargained and sold unto ye said WILLIAM COMPTON al that
tract or parcell of land containing Fifty acres bounding upon the HORSE BRANCH upon
BATEs Land & upon BUTCHERs line ye said Land being in ye Parish of Sittingbourne in
the County of Essex & Colony of Virginia and all the right & interest whatsoever of him
the said RICHARD WILTON and MARY his Wife to ye same; To have and to hold all ye sd
demised premisses hereby granted to the said WILLIAM COMPTON his heirs &c., from the
day before ye date of these presents unto ye full end and terme of Eighty nine yeares
from henceforth next ensueing and fully to be compleat and ended yeilding and paying
therefore yearly and every yeare unto the said RICHARD WILTON his heires &c. one
Eare of Indian Corne upon the 25th day of December if demanded and also paying the
fines that shall become due to our Sovereign Lord and Lady, the King and Queen, their
heires and Successors; Further the said RICHARD WILTON & MARY his Wife do for
themselves, their heires, covenant and agree with the said WILLM: COMPTON his heires
to give further and better assurance of the said land and acknowledge ye same in the
County of Essex when thereunto required In Witness whereof the parties above mentioned have hereunto sett their hands and seales
Signed sealed and delviered in presence of us
        REES EVANS,   RICHD: R WILTON
        THO: HUCKLESCOTT   MARY WILTON M
    At a Court held for Essex County Febry: ye 10th: Ano 1692
The within menconed RICHD. WILTON appear'd & acknowledged ye within specified
contents to be his real act & deed, ye same was ordered to be recorded
                        Test F. MERIWETHER, Cl Cur
    Also ye within named MARY WILTON appear'd & acknowledged ye within con-
tents to be her real act and ded, ye same is ordered to be recorded
                        Test F. MERIWETHER, Cl Cur

pp.   KNOW ALL MEN by these presents that I JOHN HUTSON of County of RAPPA: of
128-   ye Parish of Sittingbourne have given and by these presents do for me my
129   heires give and confirm unto BARTHOLOMEW VAWTER of the County & Parrish
         aforesd. his heires or assignes, One hundred and fifty acres of land lying on the
South side of Rappa: River and bounded by JAMES BOWLER and DANIEL NOWEL being the
one halfe of a parcell of land formerly bequeathed to the said JOHN HUTSON & WM.
HUTSON by THO: PAGE, being likewise part of a Pattent formerly granted to the said THO:
PAGE, WM. HUTSON, SAMLL. WEILDING, the said One hundred and fifty acres of land
with all its rights and priviledges; To have and to hold from me the said JNO. HUTSON
my heires and assignes to him the said BARTHOLOMEW VAWTER his heires or assignes
in as large and ample manner as may be collected out of the Patent without ye lett and
deniall or interuption of me ye sd JNO: HUTSON my heires or assignes or any persons
claiming any part thereof from by or under me my heires or assignes, the said BARTHO:
VAWTER paying & discharging ye rights and services from hence forth to grow & become due and of right accustomed. In Witness whereof I have hereunto sett my hand
and seale this 5th of 9br: 1690

Signed sealed & delivered in the pr:sents of us
    FRA: SLAUGHTER,
    BERNARD GAINES
                        JNO:JN HUTSON

At a Court held for Essex County Febry: ye 10th Ano. 1692
The within named JNO. HUTSON appear'd & acknowledged the within specified contents
to be his real act and deed, the same was ordered to be recorded
                Test F. MERIWETHER, Cl Cur

pp.   KNOW ALL MEN by these presents that wee ANNE HASLEWOOD, ED: THOMAS &
129- JNO: BATTAILE are held and firmly bound unto the Worpll. their Mats: Justices
130   of the Peace for the County of Essex in the sum of Fifty thousand pounds of
       good sound merchantable tobacco and cask to ye true paymt. whereof unto the
said Justices their heires and assignes convenient in the abovesd County on demand,
wee bind us, our heires joyntly and severally firmly by these presents Witness our
hands & seales this 10th: day of Febry: Ano Dom 1692
   The Condicon of this Obligacon is such that if the abovesaid bound ANNE HASLEWOOD,
Admx. of the Estate of Mr. GEO: HASLEWOOD deced, do make or cause to be made a true and
perfect Inventory of all and singular the goods chattells & creditts of ye sd deceds wch:
have or shall come to her hands or possession of her ye said ANNE HASLEWOOD or in to
ye hands of any other p:son or p:sons for her and ye same so made do exhibit to ye next
Court to be held for the said County of Essex & make oath thereto, And well and truely
administer on all the said Estate according to Law & give a true and just account of her
administracon when she shall be thereunto lawfully required, and all ye rest & residue
of the sd goods chattells & creditts wch: shall be found remaining upon account of ye sd
Admrcon. ye same being first examined & allowed of by ye said Court, shall deliver &
pay unto such p:sons respectively as ye Court p:rsuant to Law shall appoint, then ye
above obligacon to be void, otherwise to stand & remaine in ful force power & vertue
Signed sealed & delivered in presence of us
    JOHN CATLETT   ANN HASLEWOOD
    F. MERIWETHER   EDWARD THOMAS
                                  JNO: BATTAILE
        Vere Recordatr: Test F. MERIWETHER, Cl Cur

pp.   IN THE NAME OF GOD Amen. I JOHN EVANS of Essex Countye and in the Parish
131- of South Farnham doe make and ordaine this my last Will & Testament in man-
133   ner and forme following; first I commend my Soule to God that gave it hopeing
       through ye merritorious death and passion of my blessed Lord and Saviour Jesus
Christ to receive full forgiveness and remission of all my sins and a joyfull resurrection at ye last day, And my body to be decently and Christian like buried at the dis-
cretion of my Executrix hereafter named, And as for my worldly Estate that God hath
benne pleased to bestow upon me, I dispose of in manner & forme following.
   I give unto my Sonne, HENRY, two cowes that formerly went in his name and all
my wearing Cloaths except a Kersie Coate & a pr: of Leather Breetches
   Item I give to my Sonne, JON:, a parcell of land lying on the other side of HOS-
KINS RUNNE conteyning a hundred twenty five acres
   Item I give to my Sonne, THOMAS, one part of the land I now live on lying on ye
same side of ye MAINE ROAD that I now live on
   Item I give to my Sonne, BENJAMIN, ye other part of the Land I now live on now
the ROADE to be ye division and it is my will that if either of my Sons: THOMAS or BEN-
JAMIN shall be willing to dispose of either part or all their respective portions of land,
they shall not make sale or: give it to any other then ye heires of their owne: bodies or

each to ye other

Item It is my will that if either my Sonne, JON:, THOMAS or BENJAMIN shall die without heires of their owne body that then their part of land shall descend upon their younger Brother and his heires

Item I give to my Daughter, SUSAN, two cowes that formerly went in her name wth: the female encrease

Item I give unto SARAH, my Daughter, one heifer

Item I give to my Daughter, ELIZABETH, a cow and a heifer

Item I give unto my Sonne, JON: one cow that formerly went by his name and ye heifer that came of that cow

Item I give to my Sonne, THOMAS, one red & white heifer

Item I give to my Sonne, BENJAMIN, a yearling heifer

Item It is my will that the cattle that I have herein willed to my seveall Children that the female encrease with the named Cattle shall forthwith goe on: to ye increasing of their Stock till they come to age severally but ye male increase to be my Executrixs.

Item I give to my Sonne, HENRY, my Pistolls Holsters and horse furniture and a Carbine and furniture

As for the rest of my Estate I give it to my loving Wife, SUSANNA EVANS, and make her ye Executrix of this my last Will and Testament hereby revokeing and makeing null all former Wills by me at any time made. Witness my hand and seale this 29th day of August 1692

Signed sealed & published in presents of us

DANIELL (H HARRISONS   JON:⊥ EVANS
THOMAS HUCKLESCOTT

Wee the Subscribers did see Mr. JON: EVANS signe seale and publish this as his last Will & Testament. Witness our hands Febry: ye 10th 1692

Sworne to in Court Febry: 10th: 1692   DANIELL (H+ HARRISONS
     F. M. Cl Cur   THO: HUCKLESCOTT

At a Court held for Essex County Febry: ye 10th: Ano 1692
The within and above written Will was proved by the Oaths of ye Witnesses and a Probat thereof granted to ye Executrix therein named

Vere Recordatr: Test F. MERIWETHER, Cl Cur

pp.   Virginia ss   By his Excellency   A PROCLAMACON
133-   Whereas I have by advice in Councill resolved that the Genll. Assembly which
134   was continued by Proragacon to meet at JAMES CITY upon the twentieth day of
        Aprill be declared by Proclamacon to be desolves

These are therefore to signifie and I do in their Mats: names hereby publish & declare that the said Assembly is desolved and ye sd Assembly is hereby declared to be desolved to all intents & purposes of wch: all members of the sd Assembly and all other persons are to take notice accordingly; Given under my hand & ye Seale of the Colony this first day of November in ye Fourth year of the Reign of our Sovereign Lord and Lady, William and Mary, by the Grace of God of England Scotland France and Ireland, King & Queen defenders of the faith &c. Annoq Dom 1692

To the Sheriff of Essex County or his Deputy   GOD SAVE YE KING & QUEEN
                                                                E. ANDROS

A Proclamacon for Disolveing Assembly Examined
     p MILES CARY

Vere Recordatr: Test F. MERIWETHER, Cl Cur

pp.   Virga: ss   A PROCLAMACON by his Excy:
134-   Whereas her Royall Majty. hath been graciously pleased by her Lettr: dated at
137   White-Hall May ye twenty sixth One thousand six hundred ninety two directed
        to me Sr. EDMD: ANDROS, Knt., their Mats. Lt: and Govr. Genll. of Virginia this
their Colony and Dominion of Virga: to signifie that by Lettrs: Patents under the Great
Seale of England bearing date ye seventeenth day of Febry: last past, their Mats. have
given unto THOMAS NEAL Esqr. his Exrs. Admrs. and assignes all power and authority to
Erect setle & establish within the Cheif Ports of their Mats. Islands, Colonies and Plantacons in America, an Office or Offices for the receiving and dispatching of Lettrs: &
Packetts and to receive same and deliver the same undr: such rates and sums of money
as the Plantrs: shall agree to give, or as shall be proportionable to the rates for ye
carryage of Lettrs: ascertained in the Act of Parliament for Erecting and Establishing a
Post Office, to hold & enjoy the same for ye terme of one & Twenty years with such
powers and clauses as are necessary in that behalfe, as by the said Lettrs: Pattents re-
lacon being thereunto had may more fully appear and tht for ROBERT COTTON and THO-
MAS FRANKLAND Esqr., Post Master Genll., have at the desire and nominacon of ye sd
THOMAS NEALE in pursuance of their Mats: comands in the sd Lettrs: Patents for an
Instrumt: under their hands and the Seale of that Post Office bearing date ye 17 day of
Febry: last deputed and constituted ANDREW HAMILTON of EAST JARSEY in America Esqr.
to govern and manage ye said Genll. Post Office for and through out all their Mats:
Plantacons and Colonyes upon the Maine Land or Continent of North America and for
and throughout the severall iles and islands in North America lying near or adjoyning
to ye sd Contint: or Maine Land for the said terme of one and twenty years & in and by
the said Instruments relacon being thereunto had may more fully appear and hath
thought fitt at the humble request of ye said THOMAS NEALE and for his encouragemt:
in this usefull undertakeing further to signifie their will and pleasure to see mee to
assist and countenance him ye sd ANDREW HAMILTON his Deputies Agents or Dirtr:
upon all occasions in ye Managemt: of the said Genll. Post Office and in the due execution of all and singular the powers and authorities contained in their Lettrs: Pattents
and in the Instrumt: above menconed under ye hand and Seale of the said Post Master
Genll. according to their true intent & meaning and to issue such Orders & directions
from time to time as shall be requisite and fitt for ye better p:formance of this service
pr:suant to ye powers in their sd Lettrs: Patents and Whereas PETER HEYMAN, Gent.,
hath applyed himselfe to me and produced a Deputacon from the said ANDREW HAMIL-
TON (by order of the sd THOMAS NEALE) under ye hand and Seale of ye sd ANDREW
HAMILTON bearing date ye Eighteenth day of Aprill last wherein he hath impowered ye
sd PETER HEYMAN to act as Deputy Post Master of & over all the Colonyes and Plantacons
within the Governmt: of Virga: and MARYLAND as by ye sd Deputacon may more fully
appear
        I therefore by advice in Council have ordered and by this Proclamacon do publish and
make known that the said PETER HEYMAN is appointed & authorised as Deputy Post
Mastr: to manage ye sd Post Office in this their Mats. Governmt. of Virga: of wch: all
Officers and p:rsons wt:soever are to take notice and to be aideing and assisting to him
ye sd PETER HEYMAN his Deputies & Servants in his due execution thereof accordingly
Given under my hand and the Seale of the Colony at JAMES CITY this Twelfth day of
Janry: in ye Fourth year of the Reign of their Mats: Anno Dom. 1692
To the Sheriff of Essex County or his Deputy   E. ANDROS
    to be published at ye next Court & in ye respective Parish Churches & Chapels of Ease
in ye sd County
                    A PROCLAMACON for a POST OFFICE   MILES CARY
                            GOD SAVE YE KING & QUEEN

At a Court held for Essex County Febry: ye 10th: Ano 1692
Ye within Proclamacon was published in open Court
Recordatr: Test F. MERIWETHER Cl Cur

p. 138 February 9th 1692. The derect marke & Collars of JOHN SOUTHURNs his Catell they being four of one marke derecting the right year cropt and a nick under and over ye left yere cropt and slet; the :1: a red Cowe with a yalla bluch on her left sholder the :2: Cowe all red and a red Bull, and a Black Ster with a twith talle and belly: and a black Cowe hir right yere cropt and a nick under & over ye left year only cropt and a red Cowe marked as followeth: a flourdeles and the right yere ye left swolee forke as witness my hand the date above written

Teste ANTONY RICHARDSON, THOMAS T TOSTLY JOHN SOUTHURN
ROBERT X GOVIRE; JOHN SMITH
Vere Recordatr: Test F. MERIWETHER Cl Cur

pp. 138-139 At a Court held for ye County of GLOUR: Xbr: ye 17th Ano 1691
Present their Mats. Justices
Judgment is this day granted unto RICHARD BALEY, assignee of JNO. BARNS and WILLIT ROBERTS against JNO. AUSTIN for ye present payment of Two thousand pounds of tobacco & caske due by bill with costs als Exo. deducting what ye sd AUSTIN can make appear to be justly due unto him by Accots: and no execution to issue untill next Court Vera Copia Test JOHN BUCKNER, Cl Cur

To accon petent	21
To Exet. Judmt. Copa	16
To file Bill & Cop costs	06
	13

J. B. CCur

These are to certifie that noe execution hath issued out of this Office on this Judgmt. May ye last 1692 Test JOHN BUCKNER, C Cur

These are therefore in their Mats. names to will & require you to arrest the body of the within named JNO. AUSTIN and him in ye safe custody to keep without Baile or Mainprise untill he hath fully satisfie and pay ye within written Judgmt. unto ye within named RICHARD BALEY or his order herein faile not, also make due return hereof. Given under my hand this 23d day of August Ano Dom 1692
To the Sheriff of Essex County or his Deputy WILL: MOSELEY 1692

Exo iss rec	28
Exo & ordr:	20
& bill costs	03
	51

F. MERIWETHER Cl Cur Com Essex

The within Rec. Precept executed and paid p GEO: PARKE SSEC

Dt.	1100
Cl fees	94
Sher: fees	106
	1300

Security Mr. WM. YOUNG
Vere Recordatr: Test F. MERIWETHER, Cl Cur

p. 140 KNOW ALL MEN by these presents that wee ABRAHAM NORTH and LODOWICK ROWZIE both of the County of Essex in Virga: are held and firmly bound unto our Sovereign Lord and Lady, King Wm: & Queen Mary, their heires and Successors in the sum of Twenty thousand pounds of good sound merchantable toba: and cask to ye true paymt. whereof wee bind ourselve our heires Joyntly & severally firmly by these presents Witness our hands and seales this 25th day of Janry: Ano Dom 1692

The Condicon of this obligacon is such that whereas ye above bound ABRAHAM NORTH
has obteyned a LYCENSE for his MARRIAGE with SARAH ROWZIE, Now if there shall not
be no lawfull cause to obstruct ye sd Marriage then the above obligacon to be void
otherwise to stand and remaine of full force and virtue
Signed sealed & delivered in the presence of us
    THOMAS STANDRIDGE,   ABRAHAM NORTH
    F. MERIWETHER   LODOWICK ROWZEE
        Vere Recordatr: Test F. MERIWETHER Cl Cur

p.   The marke of Mr. ABRAHAM BRADLEY, a Cropp on the right eare and a slitt in
141   ye Crop and under keel & upper keel, a crop on the left eare and an under keele
        Vere Recordatr: 20 die Febry: Ano 1692 Test F. MERIWETHER Cl Cur

p.   The marke of Mr. RICHARD COVINGTON a crop on the right ear and an under
141   under keele with an under keele on the left ear
        Vere Recordatr: 20th die Febry: ano 1692 Test F. MERIWETHER Cl Cur

p.   Xbr. ye 24th: 1692. I would request you to record ye ear marke of my Cattle and
141   Hoggs (vizt) on the right ear a crop & a slitt undr: ye crop cross wayes and on ye
    left ear a crop and two slitts in ye crop
To FRANCIS MERIWETHER   EDWARD E ALLISON
  Clerke of Essex County
        Vere Recordatr: 26th die Febry: ano 1692. F. MERIWETHER, Cl Cur

p.   Essex County ss. Febry. 25th 1692/3
141   I would request you to record ye marke of my Cattle and Hoggs as followeth
    (vizt) a hole in ye right ear & a crop and upper keele on ye left   Sign
To FRANCIS MERIWETHER   JAMES RICHARDSON
  Clk. of Essex County
        Vere Recordatr. 26th die Febry: ano 1692 Test F. MERIWETHER Cl Cur

p.   Janry: ye 10th 1692/3. I would request you to record ye marke of my Cattle and
142   Hoggs as followeth, vizt., on ye right ear a crop and a hole
    slitt out; & on the left
    ear a slitt right downe near the upper part cut off
To FRANCIS MERIWETHER   ROBT: THOMAS
  Clk. of Essex County
        Vere Recordatr. 26th die Febry: ano 1692 Test F. MERIWETHER Cl Cur

pp. Essex County: Whereas RALPH WHITTON hath made a Complaint to me that
142- JOSHUA NASON standeth justly indebted unto him One thousand thirty & three
143 pounds of good Tobo: due by Bill and Acct:, and he ye said NASON haveing
    illegally absented himselfe and the greatest part of his Estate out of this County
without makeing ye sd WHITTON satisfaction, these are therefore in their Mats. names
to will and require you forthwith on sight hereof to attach so much of the Estate of the
said JOSHUA NASON in this County as will fully satisfie ye aforesaid sum of One thousand
thirty and three pds. tobo: with costs of suit and make return thereof to the next Court
held for this County hereof, you may not faile as you will answer the contrary. Given
under my hand this fifth of Janry: 1692
To the Sheriff of Essex County   EDWARD THOMAS
  or his Deputy to execute Janry: ye 7th 1691/2

Executed the within precept on 2 hhds. of tobacco weighing nett 112, it being part of ye Estate of the said JOSHUA NASON and attachmt. for use of RALPH WHITTON for a Deed due to ye said WHITTON   p GEO: PARKE SSEC
          Vere Recordatr: Test F. MERIWETHER, Cl Cur

p.   KNOW ALL MEN by these presents that I ROBERT YARD of GLOCESTER County
143   Gent. do ordaine constitute and appoint Mr. ROBT. COLEMAN of Essex County my
         true & lawfull Attorney for me and in my name to appear at Essex County Court &
prosecute all such suits as I shall have there depending & haveing obtayned Judgmt: to
act to ye extent & what my sd Attorney shall lawfully act & doe I hereby confirm.
Witness my hand and seale this 26th day of Janry: Ano 1692/3
Signed & sealed in ye presence of us
          THO: EDMONDSON,   ROBT: YARD
          HEN: AWBREY, JNO: BATTAILE
          Vere Recordatr: Test F. MERIWETHER, Cl Cur

p.   JOHN GATEWOOD saith that the said Mare that ELIZA: LINSEY hath taken up did
144   keep cumpany with a Horse of his one sumer in BROWNS OLD FIELD and that
         ye said Mare to ye best of his knowledge dus belong unto an Orphant Girle of
ABRAHAM BROWNs and further saith not
Essex Com. Sworn to in Court   JOHN GATEWOOD
          Febry: 11th: 1692/3
          Vere Recordatr: Test F. MERIWETHER

p.   The Deposition of RICHARD JONES aged 23 years of age or theire abouts your
144   Deponant saith the young Maire that the Wedowe LENSEY hath taken up is the
         Maire which belongs to ELIZABETH BROWNE, Daughter of ABRAHAM BROWNE
deceased, to the best of his knowledge & farther your Deponant saith not
Essex Com Sworn to in Court Febry: 11th 1692/3
          Vere Recordatr. Test F. MERIWETHER

P.   Att a Court held for RICHMOND COUNTY ye 5th day of 8br: Ano 1692 Pr:sent
145   their Mats. Justices of ye Peace for the sd County
         Mr. HENRY AWBREY presenting to this Court an Ordr: of Essex Court, requesting
him to discourse ye Justices of RICHMOND COUNTY concerning laying of ye leveys, as
also to appoint a time for doing ye same, wch: this Court takeing into consideracon have
for ye ease of ye Inhabitants of each respective County, formerly RAPPA., thought fitt
& do agree that ye Claimes for this County of RICHMOND by each respective Claimer inhabiting ye said County be brought in to ye Court held for ye sd County in 9br: now next
following, where any four or more of ye sd Justices of Essex County are desired to be
present at ye bringing in and receiving ye sd claimes & that the respective Claimers
inhabiting ye County of Essex (if ye Justices of ye sd County shall think fitt) do bring in
their claimes to Essex County Court to be held in ye sd month November where four or
more of ye Justices of this County will be present; And that such Gent: in conssision as
shall be appointed by each Court together with ye Clerks of ye Courts, do bring ye
severall claimes attested, and do proportion ye same by ye whole number of Tithables of
both Counties at ye House of Capt. WM. MOSELEY at such time as shall be agreed upon by
ye Justices meeting at Essex Court in 9br: moneth of November
                         Copie Test   WM: COLSTON, Cl Cur
          Vere Recordatr: Test F. MERIWETHER, Cl Cur Com Essex

p.   Rich: ss)   These are to certifie that ye severall lists of Tithables taken and
146   returned for this County amount of One thousand tithable persons & no more
        dated ye 2d of November 1692
                                            Test   WM. COLSTON, Cl Cur
        Vere Recordatr: Test F. MERIWETHER, Cl Cur Com Essex

pp.   Virga. ss   By his Excellency
146-   Whereas their sacred Mats: William and Mary, King and Queen of England,
150   Scotland, France and Ireland, Defendrs: of the faith &c., have by their Royall
        Lettrs: Patent under the Great Seale of England bearing date at Westminster ye
first day of March, in the fourth yeare of their Reign, given and granted unto me Sr.
EDMOND ANDROS Knt. their Mats: Lt. & Govr: Genl. of Virga:, full power and authority to
constitute and appoint Judges and in case required Comissions of Oyer & Terminr:
Justices of the Peace, Sheriff & other necessary Officers, and Ministers within this
Colony; for the advance of Justice and puting ye Laws in execution; and to administer
such Oath or Oaths as are usually given for ye due execution and performance of Offices
and places & for clearing the truth in Judicial Causes. Now Know yee that I ye sd Sr.
EDMOND ANDROS, Knt., their Mats. Lt. and Govr: Genll. of Virginia, p:rsuant to their
Mats. sd Lettrs: Patents and ye Laws of this Country; have assigned you Mr. HENRY
AWBREY, Mr. HENRY WILLIAMSON, Capt. JNO. CATLETT, Capt. WM. MOSELEY, Mr. THO-
MAS EDMONDSON, Capt. EDWARD THOMAS, Mr. THOMAS HARWAR, Mr. FRANCIS TALIA-
FERRO, Mr. BERNARD GAINES, Mr. ROBERT BROOKE, Capt. JNO. BATTAILE, Mr. JNO.
TALIAFERRO and Capt. ANTHONY SMITH joyntly and severally and every one of you
Justices to keep ye Peace for Essex County, and to keep or cause to be kept all Ordinances
Statutes of England and Lawes of this Country made for th good of ye Peace and for con-
servacon of ye same; and for ye quiet rule and governmt. of ye People in all and every
the articles thereof; in ye said County according to ye force forme and effect of ye same
and to chastise and punish all p:sons offending agst: ye forme of those Ordinance,
Statutes of England & Lawes of this Countrey or any of them, in the County aforesaid;
and to cause to come before you or any of you all those p:sons who shall threaten any of
their Mats: Leige People, eitehr in their bodies or burning their houses, to find sufficient security for the Peace and for the good behaviour toward our Sovereign Lord
and Lady, the King & Queen, and all their people, and if they shall refuse to find such
security, then to cause them to be kept safe in Prison untill they find such security. I
have also assigned you and very four or more of you (whereof any of you Mr. HENRY
AWBREY, Mr. HENRY WILLIAMSON, Capt. JNO: CATLETT, Capt. WM. MOSELEY, Mr. THO-
MAS EDMONDSON and Capt. EDWARD THOMAS shall be one) to meet at ye usuall place of
Holding Court in ye County aforesd, at certaine dayes according to Law, to hear & determine all suits and controversies between party and party doing therein what to
Justice appertaineth according to ye Lawles of England and this Countrye, with power
likewise to you and every of you to take Depositions and Examinacons upon Oath for the
better manifestation of ye truth of all such matters and causes, and to keep or cause to
be kept all orders of Court, Orders of Councill & Proclamacons directed to you or
comeing to your hands from me and the Councill and to punish ye Offendrs: and
breakers of the same according to the Lawes of England and this Countrey, & further to
keep or cause the Clerk of your Court to keep Records of all Judgmts. and Controversies
decided and agreed upon by you or any four or more of you (whereof any of you shall
be one) And further I command you and every of you that you diligently mind ye
keepeing of the Peace, Statutes of England and ye Lawes of this Countrey and all and
singular other ye Premisses

I do also by virtue of these presents comand ye Sheriff of ye sd County of Essex
that at those certaine dayes and places wch: the Law all or four or more of you (whereof
any of you shall be one) shall appoint him, he cause to come before you or any four or
more of you as aforesaid such & so many good and lawfull men of his Balywick by whom
the truth in the p:rmisses may be the better known and enquired off. Given under my
hand and ye Seale of ye Colony at JAMES CITY this fourteenth day of Janry: in the
fourth year of their Mats: Reign Annoq Dom 1692
   A Commission of ye Peace for Essex County
            MILES CARY   E. ANDROS
   At a Court held for Essex County March ye 10th: Ano 1692
   The within commission was published and committed to Record
                        Test F. MERIWETHER, Cl Cur

(Pages 151 and 152 are blank)

pp.   Virga: ss   By his Excy.   A PROCLAMACON
153-   Almighty God of his Infinite Goodness & Mercy haveing many waies been
154   graciously pleased to bestow his great Blessing on this their Mats: Colony and
         Dominion of Virga: and a Genll. Assembly being called and soon to sitt to con-
sider and advice of such things as may be for the Glory of God, ye Honr. of their Mats.
and the Peace and Welfare of this Colony and the Inhabitants thereof, I Sr. EDMOND
ANDROS, Knt. their Mats: Lt. and Govr: Genll. of Virga: with the advice and consent of ye
Council do therefore hereby appoint that on Sunday the fifth day of this Instant March
prayers and supplycations be made to Almighty God at JAMES CITY for the continuance
of his Blessing and that he will be graciously pleased to give his divine assistance to ye
proceeding of ye said Genll. Assembly, And that on Sunday ye Nineteenth of this
Instant ye same be Solemnized in the respective Churches & Chappels throughout this
whole Colony and Dominion and do desire and require all Ministers & Readrs: to be
dilligent in the due p:formance of their duties according to ye times & places appointed
that all persons may joyne in their Prayers and Supplications to Almighty God in Im-
ploring his Blessing and Assistance upon this Extraordinary Occation; Given under my
hand and ye Seale of ye Colony and Dominion this first day of March in the fifth year of
the Reign of our Sovereign Lord and Lady, King William & Mary, Annoq Dom 1692/3
To the Sheriff of Essex County or his Deputy
            A Proclamacon for Prayers &c.   E. ANDROS
            RALPH WORMELEY Secr.
   The within Proclamacon was published at a Court held for Essex County March ye 10th
Ano 1692 and recorded   Test F. MERIWETHER Cl Cur

p.   This is to satisfy all whom it may concern that I ye Subscriber am God Willing
154   is bound Home for England this inshewing year in ye Ship *LORELL OF LIVER-*
         POOLE, and if any p:sons hath any business with me they may find me at ye
house of Mr. JAMES BOUGHAN. Given undr: my hand this 10th of March 1692/3
                                                        DAVID LOYD
         Vere Recordatr: Test F. MERIWETHER, Cl Cur

pp.   IN YE NAME OF GOD Amen. I JOHN JONES of the County of Essex in ye Collony of
155-   Virginia being at present weak in body but of sound and perfect mind &
160   memory praised by God, do by these presents renounceing all and singular my
         former Wills and Testaments; make and ordeigne this my last Will and Testament
in manner & forme following

Imprs. I bequeath my soule to God my Creator who gave it me; and my body to Christian buriall, hopeing through ye merits of Jesus Christ my only Saviour and Redeemer for a joyfull resurrection; and all that Estate which it hath pleased God of his Mercy to bestow upon me I give & bequeath in manner and forme as followeth

Item. I give and bequeath unto my loveing Wife, MILLICENT JONES, all that Plantacon whereon I now do live; for and dureing her life; with all ye housing thereunto belonging, and ye rents of the two Tenements which are now setled on my said Plantacon; ye one in SHARPS NECK at Five hundred a yeare for five yeares to come, ye other at my old House for six hundred ye yeare for foure yeares to come or longer if my said Wife thinks fitt and convenient to lett ye said Plantacon any longer to ye same Tennants but not to any other; I also give unto my said Wife my six Negroes wch: are three men and three Children; five of wch: Negroes I do give to her dureing her life time, ye other named Ockre, an ould man I give to her for noe longer than she doth remain a widow after my decease and then the said ould Negro to be FREE & cleare from her and all other persons whatever; & I give to my Wife one man Servant by name CHARLES ELLISON haveing two yeares to serve by condition and after my sd Wifes decease I do bequeath my said Five Negroes in manner following, viz. I give unto my God Sone, JOHN JONES, ye Sone of my Bro: RICE JONES, my Negro Harro: and to RICE JONES, the Sone of my Bro: RICE JONES, my Negro Tom; and to NICHOLAS JONES ye youngest Sone of my Bro: RICE JONES I give my young Negro James; I give unto my Coz: JOHN BROACHE, ye Sone of my Sister, MARY BROACHE, my Negro William; and I give unto my God Sone, JOHN WYATT, ye sone of my Sister, ANN WYATT, my Negro girle Joane, after my wifes decease and not before; my said Wife nor her Husband if she doth hapen to Marry, not to abuse ye sd Negroes, nor to dispose of any of them to any persons except of my said Kinsfolk before mentioned hapen to die before her, then she to have the disposeing of theire parte that doeth decease according as shee seeth fitt; the said Negroes after my Wifes decease I give unto my Cozens aforementioned and their heires forever

I give unto my Wife, MILLICENT, my Silver Tankard and Silver Salt Seller and Silver Spoons and Dram Cupp for her and her heires forever. I do likewise give unto my Wife that parcell of land wch: is in dispute between BLAISE and mee, if recovered by my Attorney at my charge

Item I give and bequeath unto my God Sone, JOHN MASSEY JUNR., one feather bed boulster & pillow that which lyeth under my bed which I now life on myselfe with rugg and blankett, I do likewise give unto my said God Sone my little long Gunn and one Iron pott of about five gallons; and the three new pewter dishes and three pewter plates and six spoones, Also I give him two cows with Calfes or Calves by theire sides, one of them to be delivered to him imediately after my decease and ye other to be delivered the yeare following; I doe likewise give him all my wearing Cloaths boath old and new, those which I now hve and those wch: I have sent for from England if they come in this shiping; And I do desire that my sd God Sone do remain and stay with his Aunt ye remaining parte of this yeare and to looke after all her business for and towards ye makeing a Cropp this yeare; And then to be cleare for himselfe; And to have all that I have hearin given to him; according as is directed

Item I give and bequeath unto my Sister, MARY BROACHE, ye Wife of JOHN BROACHE, three pounds sterling to buy her a goune & Pettecoate and one gould mourning Ring of Twenty shillings price; I bequesth unto JOHN BROACHE and to Brother, WILLIAM WYATT, eache of them a mourning Ring of Twenty shillings price to be sent for the next yeare after my death by my Wife, MILLICENT JONES, without faile & to be delivered to each of them according to my desire

I give and bequeath unto my God Sone THOMAS HOWARD, ye Sone of CHARRITY HOWARD, one Cow and Calfe to be delivered for his use ye first Spring after my death, her & her encrease forever

Item I give and bequeath unto my Wife, MILLICENT JONES, all other my Estate, English goods, household goods, moneys, debts, cattle, horses, hoggs and all other my Estate of what nature or kinde soever or in what place soever, And I do apoint and earnestly request my Loveing Bro: Mr. HENRY WILLIAMSON & Capt. EDWARD THOMAS and Mr. MATHEW LIDFORD to see that this my Will be duly performed and that noe parte of ye Estate be embesseled or made away: nor no timber to be cutt down or fall for sale off ye land whereon I now do live; by my Executrix or any that she shall marry with after my decease; And lastly I doe appoint and ordaine my beloved Wife to be my sole & absolute Executrix of this my last Will and Testament willing her to pay all my debts and Legacies above mentioned; And this I deliver to ye World as my last Will and Testament Witness my hand and Seale this 13th day of Febry: in the yeare of our Lord God One thousand six hundred ninety and two

Signed sealed and delivered in pr:sents of us

     ROBERT DEPUTY   JNO: JONES
     CHARLES ⊃ WALKER his marke
     ELIZABETH + TOUSLEY

ROBERT DEPUTY being examined and sworn saith that he saw the within named JOHN JONES sign seale and publish the within Will to be his last Will and Testament & that he was in perfect sense and memory at the doing thereof; to the best of ye Deponllants Judgmt.

Sworn to in Court this 10th day of Apll. 1693   ROBERT DEPUTY
     Test F. MERIWETHER, Cl Cur

CHARLES WALKER being examined and sworn saith that he saw the within named JOHN JONES sign seale and publish ye within Will to be his last Will and Testament and that he was in perfect sense & memory at ye doing thereof, to the best of ye Deponts: Judgmt.

Sworn to in Court this 10th day of Apll. 1693   CHARLES his marke ⊂ WALKER
     Test F. MERIWETHER, Cl Cur

ELIZABETH TOZLEY being examined & sworn that she saw ye within named JOHN JONES sign seale and publish the within Will to be his last Will and Testamt: & that he was in p:rfect sense & memory at ye doing thereof, to ye best of he Deponts. Judgmt.

Sworn to in Court this 10th: day of Apll. 1693   ELIZABETH ⊐ TOZLEY
     Test F. MERIWETHER Cl Cur

At a Court held for Essex County Aprill ye 10th Ano 1693
The within menconed Will was proved by ye Oaths of ye Witnesses & a Probat thereof granted to ye Executrix therein named

     Test Vere Recordatr: F. MERIWETHER Cl Cur

pp.   THIS INDENTURE made ye tenth day of Aprill 1693 Between RICHARD HARVIE of
161- ye County of Essex and MARY his Wife (Daughter to JOHN WHITCHURCH deced),
162   of one part and ABRAHAM STAP of ye same County of ye other parte Wittnesseth
that ye said RICHARD HARVIE and MARY his Wife for & in consideracon of one Cow and Calfe and five hundred pounds of tobo: by me in hand reced, have given and sould unto ABRAHAM STAPP his heires and assignes forever all our right title & interest & claime of & to a certaine parcell of land of about sixty acres be it more or less according to a Deed of Sale from HENRY JARMAN to JOHN WHITCHURCH bearing date ye 6th of June 1668 as will more at large appeare, wee ye said RICHARD HARVEY and MARY my Wife do hereby grant and make over from us our heires unto ABRAHAM STAPP his heires and assignes forever To have hold use & enjoy ye same with all its rights & priviledges of woods waters & water courses and whatsoever else peaceably & quietly

without any lett molestacon trouble ejection or disturbance of us ye sd RICHARD HAR-
VIE & MARY his Wife our heires or either of us our heires or any other p:son or p:sons
whatsoever claiming any lawfull claime to any part of ye demised premisses, also I ye
sd RICHARD HARVIE & MARY my Wife shall & will at ye reasonable request of the said
ABRAHAM STAPP acknowledge this our Deed or Indenture of Sale at ye next Court held
for Essex County at ye costs & charges of ye Law by him ye sd ABRAHAM STAPP to be
paid, he or they yeilding & paying to our Sovereign Lord ye King all such fess Rents or
other imposicons wch: eithr: now are or here after shall grow due eithr: by Law custome or otherwise as witness our hands & seales ye day & year abovesd.
Signed sealed and delivered in ye presents of us
   JOHN GATEWOOD,   RICHD: ℞H HARVEY
   FRANCIS GOULDMAN, THO: HUCKLESCOTT   MARY M HARVEY
   At a Court held for Essex Couty Aprill ye 10th: ano 1693
The within named RICHARD HARVEY and MARY his Wife appear'd and acknowledged ye
within specified contents to be their real act & deed, ye same was ordered to be recorded
      Vere Recordatr: Test F. MERIWETHER Cl Cur

pp.   KNOW ALL MEN by these presents that I JAMES SCOTT and MARY my Wife both
163- of ye County of RICHMOND doe for and in consideration of a valuable sume of
165   Two thousand five hundred pounds of good lawfull tobacco in caske by me in
      hand reced have granted and sold unto GEO: PROCTOR of ye County of Essex, his
heires and assignes forever, a certaine parcell or tract of land containing One hundred
acres being part of twelve hundred acres I ye sd SCOTT bought of ROBT. PAYNE ye sd
land lying in Essex County and on ye Maine Branch of COCKELSHEEL CREEKE, beginning
at a small Hickory two perches distant from a Corner post to me ye said SCOTT, thence
extending North forty four degrees East one hundred and forty eight per: to a small
Hickory by a PATH; thence South South East one hundred forty eight per: to a corner
Stake on ye South side ye Maine Branch, thence South forty four degr: West one hundred & twenty per: to a corner post to me ye sd SCOTT being by a small branch side;
thence North North West one hundred & forty eight per: to ye first station, Wee ye sd
JAMES SCOTT and MARY my Wife do hereby grant and make over from us our heires
unto ye sd GEORGE PROCTOR his heires and assignes for ever; To have & enjoye ye same
with all its rights & priviledges of all woods waters and water courses and whatsoever
else peaceably and quietly without any lett trouble rejection or disturbance of us ye sd
JAMES SCOTT and MARY my Wife our heires or either of us or any other persons whatsoever claiming any lawfull claime to any part or parcell of ye demised premises; Also
wee ye sd JAMES SCOTT and MARY my Wife do oblige ourselves our heires to make what
further assurance he ye sd GEORGE PROCTOR or his Councill in Law shall require in that
case & do further ingage ourselves to acknowledge this our Deed of Sale before ye Court
of Essex (theire to be inrouled) when thereunto lawfully called by ye sd GEORGE PROC-
TOR or his heires he or they yeilding and paying all dues or imposicons which are or
shall be charged and for further confirmacon thereof wee have hereunto sett our
hands and seales this second day of February in ye yeare of our Lord One thousand six
hundred ninety & two
Signed sealed & delivered in ye presents of
   GEORGE ANDREWS   JAMES SCOTT
   WM: W MASON   MARY M SCOTT
   At a Court held for Essex County Aprill ye 10th: ano 1693
The within named JAMES SCOTT appeared and acknowledged ye within specified con-
tents to be his real act & deed, ye same was ordered to be recorded
      Test F. MERIWETHER, Cl Cur

Also Mr. BERNARD GAINES by vertue of a power from ye within named MARY SCOTT appear'd and acknowledged her ye sd MARYs right title & interest in & to ye within menconced land, to ye within named GEORGE PROCTOR, ye same was ordered to be recorded   Vere Recordatr: Test F. MERIWETHER Cl Cur

KNOW ALL MEN by these presents that I MARY SCOTT do by these presents autho-
rise and impower Mr. BER: GAINES my true & lawfull Attorney for me & in my part &
behalfe and in my place & stead, to acknowledge and confirm unto GEORGE PROCTOR all
my right title & interest in & to a peace or parcell of land containing One hundred acres
according to a Convayance Given undr: my hand this second of Feb: 1692/3
Test GEORGE ANDREWS   MARY /\/\ SCOTT
    WM: \W/ MASON
              Vere Recordatr: Test F. MERIWETHER Cl Cur

p.   Janry: ye 29th 1692/3. I JOHN WEBSTER doath for my selfe and ye rest of the
166   Grand Jury make presentment to this Worpll. Court for ye County of Essex
          against Mr. ROBERT DEPUTY and ELIZABETH MEADS for profaning the Sabbath
day by frequently playing at Cards contrary to ye Law of God & Man as my appeare to
your Worships by ye under written evidence
The sd Witnesses sworne before me   DAVID MEREDITH
    ANTHO: SMITH   WILLIAM JEFFERYS
              Vere Recordatr: Test F. MERIWETHER Cl Cur

p.   Essex County ss. I do hereby authorize and impower JOHN EVERITT to be my
166   Atty: at Law in any Court of Record in Virginia. Witness my hand this 17th day
          of Janry: 1692/3
Test RICHARD GRIMSTEAD,   JAMES FUGEET
     THOMAS HILL
              Vere Recordatr Test. F. MERIWETHER Cl Cur

pp.   IN OBEDIENCE to an order of Essex County court bearing date ye 11th: day of
166-   Febry: 1692/3 wee Jurors whose names are hereunder written, being sworn
167   to go upon ye Land in difference between RICHARD FRYER Plt. & HENRY
          PICKITT Defendt., have in Company of EDWIN THACKER, Surveyr:, layed out a
Patent of land formerly granted unto RANDOLPH CHAMBLY dated ye 10th: day of May
1654, & sicne granted by Pattent to DAVID THOMAS & RICHARD MACUBIN dated ye 28th:
of July 1662, according to ye ancient reputed bounds thereof haveing regard to all
evidences produced by Plt. & Defendt., and wee find that the said Defendt. hath not
committed an trespass upon ye Plts. sd land. In Witness whereof wee have here unto
sett our hands and seales this 23d day of Febry: 1692/3
          WILL: YOUNG, foreman   JOHN GATEWOOD
              EDW: ADCOCKE   RALPH WHITTON
              DANL. DOBYNS   ANDREW /AO DUDDIN
              JOHN WEBB   HENRY R WOODNET
              JOHN GRIFFING   WILL /—- COVINGTON
              PHILL: PARR   JOHN /oo MICHELL
          Vere Recordatr: Test F. MERIWETHER Cl Cur
Plott A is ye beginning red Oake on ye bank by ye Creek PISCATAWAY CREEKE)
          B is an antient Cornr: red Oake
          C is a red Oake & Spanish Oake
    In Obedience of an Order of Essex County Court baring date ye 11th: day of Febry: 1692
in ye difference between RICHARD FRYER Plt. and HENRY PICKETT Deft., I ye Subscri-

ber have in company with an able Jury surveyed & layd out a parcell of land granted to
RANDOLPH CHAMBLY by Pattent dated ye 10th: day of May 1654; And since granted to
DAVID THOMAS & RICHARD MACUBIN by Pattent dated ye 28th: day of July 1662;
bounded as followeth (vizt) beginning at a small red Oake on ye bank of PESCATTAWAY
CREEKE side & runing North East by North fifty one and a halfe poles to an antient
Corner red Oake; thence South fifty degrees forty five minutes East One hundred thirty
four poles by an old line of markt. trees to ye sd CREEKE to a red Oak & Spanish Oak, &
lastly up and alongst the said CREEKE to ye place it began; including all points of high
land, being exactly measured & surveyed by ye findings and directions of ye Jury
aforesd., this 23d day of Febry: 1692/3
                                             p   EDWIN THACKER, Surveyr:
                     Vere Recordatr: Test F. MERIWETHER Cl Cur

p.   WILLM: ACRES aged about fifty five years or thereabouts saith that ye line
168   beginning at a Spanish Oake standing by PISCATAWAY CREEKE side being below
          HENRY PICKETTs Corne feild fence yt: now is was ye ancient reputed bounds of
RICKETT MACKABONE & that it was a line of a p:cell of land bought formerly of WM.
JOHNSON by RICHARD STEPHENS & further saith not
Febry. ye 23d 1692/3   WM: /X/ A ACRES
  Sworn to before mee ANTHO: SMITH
                     Vere Recordatr: Test F. MERIWETHER, Cl Cur

p.   JACOB DEBELLO aged about forty six years being a Servant formerly to RICKETT
169   MACKABONE saith that his said Master in his life time told him that his begining
          tree of his Patent stood by ye sd MACKABONEs Spring being by PASCATAWAY
CREEKE side and that the line below HENRY PICKETTs Corne feild fence that now is was a
line of a p:cell of land that was sold formerly by WM. JOHNSON ye said line begining at a
Spanish Oake and that was ye outside of his Land & that he could goe no further &
further saith not
Febry: ye 23d 1692/3   JACOB GACOMODIBOLLI DEBELLO
  Sworne before mee ANTHO: SMITH
                     Vere Recordatr: Test F. MERIWETHER Cl Cur

p.   February ye 23th 1692/3. The Depo: of THOMAS GAINES aged Sixty three yeares
169   or thereabouts saith that the line of marked trees that stands about the Land of
          RICHARD MACKABUN was Luikt & rekend to be ye reputed bounds of his land and
your Depont: doth further declare about 24 yeares or thereabout that RICKETT with ye
rest of ye adjoyning nabors did with joyent consent renew ye said line and ye said
RICKETT had fallen one or two of ye sd line trees & he did promis my Mther JOHNSON to
plant Moulbry tree in their rume & farer sayeth not
Febry: ye 23d 1692/3   THOMAS GAINES
  Sworne before mee ANTHO: SMITH
                     Vere Recoratr: Test F. MERIWETHER, Cl Cur

p.   The Depotion of SAMUELL PARRY aged 40 years or thereabouts sworn and saith
170   that ye best of my remembrance youer deponent did hear his Father say that
          those marked trees which youer deponant did shew ye Jury ware the bounds of
RICKETTs land between Mr. JOHNSON and RICKETTS and further saith not
Febry ye 23d 1692/3   SAMLL. PARRY
  Sworne before mee ANTHO: SMITH

FRA: MARENER aged forty three yeares or thereabouts saith that ye old marked line about RICKITT MACKABONEs ould feild was the reputed bounds of ye said RICKITTs land for these thirty yeares & further saith not
Febry: ye 23d 1692/3   FRANCIS F MARNER
Sworne before mee ANTHO: SMITH
        Vere Recordatr: Test F. MERIWETHER Cl Cur

p.   Wee ROBERT PLEY and JOHN ALMOND being appointed to audit ye Accots: between
170   WM. FITZ JEFFRIES and ROBERT DEPUTY do finde that ye ballance of ye Tobo:
      Accot: is due to ye sd JEEFRIES One hundred and fifteene pounds of tobacco & that
ye sd JEFFRIES is indebted to ye sd DEPUTY thirty nine shillings Witness our hands this
11th Aprill 1693
Vere Recordatr Test   ROBERT PLEY
      F. MERIWETHER, Cl Cur   JO: ALMOND 11th Aprill 1693

pp.   THIS INDENTURE witnesseth that I HENRY PIGOTT (Son of HENRY PIGOTT of
171- Rappa: River in Virga: Cooper) of his own free will and with ye consent of his
172   said Father & friends, doth put himselfe an Apprentice to NICHOLAS WARD of the
      City of DUBLIN, Merchant, to learne ye art of a Mariner and Navigator & with
him after ye manner of an Apprentice to serve from ye first day of Aprill One thousand
six hundred & eighty seven untill ye full end and terme of seven years next ensueing
fully to be compleat & ended dureing which terme ye sd Apprentice his said Master
faithfully shall serve, his secrets keepe, his lawfull commands every where gladly do,
he shall do no damage to his sd Master nor see to be done of others, but that he to his
power shall lett or forthwith give warning to his sd Master of ye same, he not not wast
ye goods of his sd Master nor lend them unlawfully to any, he shall not committ fornication nor contract matrimony within ye sd terme, he shall not absent himselfe from
his sd Masters service day nor night unlawfully, but in all things as a faithfull apprentice shall behave towards his sd Master & all his dureing ye sd terme, And ye sd Master
his sd Apprentice in ye Art of a Marriner & Navigator by ye best meanes that he cann
dureing his sd time & for ye true performance of all & every ye sd Covenants & agreemts: herein menconed each of ye said parties bindeth himselfe to ye other by these
presents. In Witness whereof ye parties above named have to these presents Interchangeably put their hands and seales ye 5th: day of Aprill 1687.
Signed sealed & delivered in ye presence of us
      KATHERINE FANTLEROY,   NICH: WARD
      FRAN: MOORE
   At a Court held for Essex County Aprill ye 10th: Ano 1693
The within Indenture was at ye request of SARAH PIGOTT, Wife of ye within named
HENRY PIGOTT, Cooper, admitted to Record
                Vere recordatr: Test F. MERIWETHER Cl Cur

p.   Mr. BROOK   March ye 6 1692/3
172   Sr. I have ordred JAMES GRIDET to be arested at ye next Court wch: is upon
      Fryday next & not knowing whether I can be there myselfe have sent ye Bill by
Mr. TEA. would desire dye favour of you as for to crave a Judgmt. for me in my absence
for if GRIGET will give in good security for ye paymt. of ye sd Debt ye next yeare & pay
ye charge you may sett ye accon lett ye accon faile if not to prosecute ye same this wth:
my exprest to yor: selfe & good wish is what ofers from ye assured freind to Concerne
                                                  GEORGE TAYLER
        Vere Recordatr: Test F. MERIWETHER Cl Cur

p. An Accot of Debts paid out of ye Estate of JON: SORELL	
173 Sold at an OUTCRY January ye first 1691	
To DAVID JENKINS for THO: INGRAM s portion	3205
To ABRAHAM AMOS a hired Servant for wages	0850
To Capt. BATTAIALE for Levies Qt. Rents &c. Ano: 1691	0528
To EVAN JONES by attachmt:	1230
To THO: GRIFFIN by attachmt:	0318
To Mr. COLSTON for Clks. fees	0068
To Mr. MERIWETHER for Clks. fees	0035
To Mr. JNO. TAVERNR: by attachmt.	0593
To Capt. ANTHONY SMITH by attachmt.	0504
To ROBERT MAYFIELD by attachmt.	0488
To AURELIA CAWTHORNE by attachmt.	0500
To ye Sheriff	0105
To Mr. ROBERT COLEMAN	0172
To my Salary at 10 lb. p Cent	0860
	9456

RO: BROOKE

Vere Recordatr: Test F. MERIWETHER Cl Cur

1692 The Estate of JNO: SORRELL dd. in tobo:		p Contra Credtr:
To severall debts by attachmts. & other accounts paid as by a		
list thereof signed by Mr. ROBT. BROOKE amounting	9456	
To ye Ballance	0722	
	10178	

By ye Estate sold at an Outcry as by severall Judgmts.   Tobo: 10178

Wee FRANCIS GOLDMAN & JOHN ALMOND being appointed to auditt & examine ye Accts. of Mr. ROBT: BROOKE intrusted with ye Estate of JNO. SORRELL do finde ye ballance due to ye Estate of ye sd SORRELL to be seven hundred twenty & two pounds of tobo: Witness our hands this 11th: Aprill 1693   FRANCIS GOULDMAN
                                            JO: ALMOND 11th Aprill 1693

        Vere Recordatr: Test F. Meriwether Cl Cur

pp.   TO ALL PEOPLE to whom this present writing shall come WILLIAM BALL of
174-   PISCATICON CREEKE in Farnham Pish in Essex County sendeth Greetings. Know
175   yee that I sd WILLIAM as well for & in consideration of ye naturall love & af-
        fection which he hath & beareth to his three Children, SARAH, EDWARD and
JOHN BALL, as for and in consideration of ye sum of Five shillings to him ye sd
WILLIAM in hand paid by ye sd SARAH, EDWARD and JOHN well & truely paid hath
given granted bargained & sold and by these presents doth fully clearely & absolutely
give grant bargaine & sell unto ye sd SARAH, EDWARD and JOHN, one young Grey Mare
branded on ye neer buttock with an eye of an OX and ye said WILLIAM BALL for ye consideracons aforesd. doth further give grant bargaine and sell unto ye said EDWARD
BALL one Cow called Dazey marked on ye right eare with a slitt and an under keele & ye
left eare cropt and ye said WM. BALL for ye consideracons aforesd. doth farther give
grant bargaine & sell unto ye said SARAH BALL one Cow called Browney marked with
an under keele on ye right eare & with two slitts & a crop on ye left, To have and to
hold ye sd Mare with all her future encrease unto ye sd SARAH, EDWARD and JOHN
BALL from ye day of the date hereof to her his or their only proper use & uses as his
her & their owne proporcon and chattells forever, And to have and to hold ye sd Cow
called Dazey withall her future encrease unto ye sd EDWARD BALL his heirs form
henceforth as his own proper goods & chattells for ever and to have & to hold ye sd Cow

called Browney with all her future encrease unto ye said SARAH BALL her Exrs. &
assignes from henceforth as her & their own proper goods & chattells forever; & ye sd
WM. BALL for himselfe his heirs doth covenant & grant to & with the sd SARAH, ED-
WARD and JOHN BALL their heirs Exrs. and assignes and to & with every of them joyntly
and severally by these presents that he ye sd WM. BALL his Exrs. & Admrs. ye said Mare
with her encrease unto ye sd SARAH, EDWARD and JOHN BALL & ye sd Cow called Dazey
unto ye sd EDWARD & ye sd Cow called Browney unto ye sd SARAH shall & will warrant
and forever by these pr:sents defend against all people whatsoever according to effect
intent & true meaning of these pr:sents In Witness whereof I sd WM. BALL hath hereunto sett his hand & seale dated this 11th day of Aprill Ano Dom 1693
Signed sealed & delivered in ye presence of
    JOHN CATLETT   WM. ◯ BALL
    F. MERIWETHER
  At a Court held for Essex County Aprill ye 11th: Ano 1693
Ye within named WM. BALL appear'd & acknowledged this within specified contents to
be his act & deed, ye same was ordered to be recorded
    Vere Recordatr: Test F. MERIWETHER Cl Cur

pp.   KNOW ALL MEN by these presents that wee ROBERT COLEMAN, JAMES BOUGHAN
176-   and FRANCIS MERIWETHER are held and firmly bound unto ye Worpll. their
177   Mats: Justices of ye Peace for Essex County in the sum of ten thousand pounds of
    good ferm merchantable tobo and cask to ye true paymt. whereof on demand
convenient in ye abovesd County we find our selves and either of us our heires and
either of our heires Exrs. & Admrs. joyntly & severally firmly by these presents; Witness our hands and seales this 10th day of Apl. Ano Dom 1693
  The Condicon of this obligacon is such that whereas ye above bound ROBT. COLEMAN is
Licensed to keep an ORDINARY in this County this ensueing yeare, if therefore ye sd
ROBT. COLEMAN dureing ye sd time doth make such provision for entertainmt. as ye Act
of Assembly enjoyns, & doth not suffer nor permitt any unlawfull gameing in his
House, and likewise on ye Sabbath day he suffer no p:son to Tiple or drink more than is
necessary, & that he charge no more for his Liquors then ye Law alows or ye Court
p:suant to Act of Assembly have appointed or putt sett down & do p:form all other things
wt:soever wch: ye Law in that case enjoyns, The ye above obligacon to be void otherwise to be & remaine of full force and virtue
Signed sealed & delivered in presence of   ROBT: COLEMAN
    (no signatures)   JAMES BOUGHAN
                                      F. MERIWETHER
    Vere Recordatr. Test F. MERIWETHER Cl Cur

p.   The Deposition of ROBT: DEPUTY aged forty five yeares or thereabouts sworn
177   saith that on or about ye later end of November last past yor: Depont: did see
    ANNE MEREDE, ye Wife of DAVID MEREDE, ride a Horse belonging to JONAS SMITH
with birdle & saddle & further saith not
Essex Cont: Sworn to in Court this 11th: of Apll. 1693   ROBEART DEPUTY
    Test F. MERIWETHER, Cl Cur

    The Deposition of ELIZABETH DEPUTY aged twenty one yeares or thereabouts
sworn saith that on or about ye latter end of November last past ye deponent did see
ANNE MEREDE ye present Wife of DAVID MEREDE ride a hors belonging to JONAS SMITH
with bridle & sadle and further saith not

Essex Com: Sworn to in Court this 11th: day of
        Aprill 1693   ELIZABH: + DEPUTY
                Test F. MERIWETHER, Cl Cur

        The Deposition of WILM. HALL aged twenty nine yeares or theirabouts is sworn
saith that on or about ye latter end of November last past ye Deponant did see ANNE
MEREDE ye present Wife of DAVID MEREDE ride a hors belonging to JONAS SMITH with a
bridle & saddle & further saith not
Essex Com: Sworn to in Court this 11th: day of
        Aprl. 1693 Test F. M. Cl Cur   WIL *N* HALL
                Vered Recordatr: Test F. MERIWETHER, Cl Cur

p.   The Deposition of JNO. COLLEYVOW Whereas yor: Deponant being in ye Howse of
178   ROBART DEBBETY, ANN MERRIDA, Wife of DAVID MERRIDA, being ye ROBART
        DEBBETY desired this ANN to goe to her Mother to borrow him some Salt, and ye
said DEBBETY did lend her a Horse and mad his one Kinsman, WILL WHEALER, to take up
ye Horse for ye fored. ANN MERRIDA to ride, & yor: Depont. did know that not long
before this horse was ROBART DEBBETYs Horse and did suppose it to be soe at that time &
further saith not
Sworne before me this 9th: of Janry: 1692
        THO: EDMONDSON   JNO. COLLEYVOW
        Vere Recordatr: Test F. MERIWETHER Cl Cur

p.   Essex County ss December ye 31th 1692
178   This day JOHN AWBREY made Complaint that WILLIAM THORUGOOD is indebted
        to him ye sd AWBREY by Bill and acct. Twenty shillings Sterling, And by
obligacon under ye said THORUGOODs hand for a Mare received and ye sd THORUGOOD
haveing departed ye Countey these are in theire Mats: name to charge & command yu
on sight hereof to seize & attach so much of ye Estate of ye abovesd WM. THORUGOOD
within this County as will satisfie ye above debt whereof you are not to faile. Given
under my hand ye day & yeare abovesd.
To ye Sheriff or his Deputy in their absence   RO: BROOKE
  to ye Constable to Execute & make return to
  ye next Court
Janry: ye 5th: 1692/3. Then executed ye within attachmt. on a black Gelding branded
on ye neare buttock wth: G T with a starr on his forehead & a white snipp on his nose,
it being part of ye Estate of ye w:thin named WM. THORUGOOD & seized for ye use of Mr.
JOHN AWBREY   p GEO: PARKE SSEC
        Vere Recordatr: Test F. MERIWETHER Cl Cur

P.   Essex County ss I do hereby authorize and impower JOHN EVERITT to be my
179   . Attry: at Law in any Court of Record in Virga: witness my hand this 9 day of
        March 1692/3
Test   JNO: COLLEYVOW   PETER *P* HUDSON
        ANN *O* FITZ JEFFREYS
        Vere Recordatr: Test F. MERIWETHER, Cl Cur

p.   Essex County ss: I do hereby authorize and impower JOHN EVERITT to be my
179   Attry: at Law in any Court of Record in Virginia. Witness my hand this 9th
        March 1692/3
Test WILLIAM JEFEY   JOSHUA NASON

Vere Recordatr: Test F. MERIWETHER Cl Cur

p.   This may certifie that I ye Subscriber am intended out of ye Country this
179   present Shiping
          Apll. 10th: 1693   WILL. COLLMAN
          Vere Recordatr Test F. MERIWETHER, Cl Cur

ACRES. William 3, 6, 7, 42, 64, 66, 85, 103.
ADCOCK. Edward 38, 41, 102.
AKUS. William 8, 19.
ALLAWAY. John 27.
ALLISON. Edward 95.
ALMOND. John 3, 29, 31, 32, 38, 42, 47, 74, 75, 104, 105.
AMOS. Abraham (Servant -105).
ANDREWS. George 101, 102.
ANDROS. Sr. Edmond, Knt. Governor Generall of Virginia 37, 76, 77, 92, 93, 97, 98.
ARMITAGE. Moses (Constable -2), 45, 47.
ARMSTRONGE. Robert 52.
AUSTIN. John 94.
AWBREY. Henry (Sheriff, Justice -1), 2, 15, 20, 23, 26, 27, (Feoffee for Town -29), 38, 46, 51, 53, 54, 55, 57, 96; John 107.
AXE. George 78, 79, 80, 81, 83, 84.

BACON. Nathaniel (President of Councill -59), (Collo: -63).
BAKER. Elizabeth 78, 80, 81, 82, 83, 84; John 28, 29, 75, 76, 77, 78, 79, 80, 81, 82, 83, 84, 85.
BALEY. Richard 94.
BALL. Edward 48, 105, 106; John 48, 105, 106; Sarah 48, 105, 106; William 18, 23, 44, 45, 48, 105, 106.
BARBER. William (Capt.., Justice Richmond Co. -26), 27.
BARKELEY. Sr. William, Knt. 65.
BARNS. John 94.
BASETT. Abgall 30.
BATES. John 16, 66; Line 90.
BATHOW. Jonathan 30.
BATTAILE. Capt. 105; John (Capt., Justice -1), 4, 8, 10, 11, 12, 14, 19, 22, 23, 26, 30, 53, 54, 60, 61, 70, 87, 91, 96; Katherine 60.
BAUGHAN (BOUGHAN). James 7, 9, 10, 13, 14, 16, 17, 20, 21, 23, 25, 26, 30, 31, 32, 33, 35, 40, 41, 53, 74, 76, 85, 98, 106; James Senr. 70; John 10.
BEAVER. Robert 45.
BECKLEY. Joseph 66.
BEEZLEY. William 3.
BELL. John (Servant -18).
BENDERY. William 38, 57.
BENNETT. Richard (Esqr.-86).
BEVERLEY. Robert 12, 59, (Yeoman -60)
BILLINGON. John 2, 38.

BLAISE -99; John 17.
BLUMFEILD (BLOOMFEILD). Elizabeth 10, 12, 17, 18, 22, 24; Samuel (Capt. -10), 18, 24, 50, 51.
BOOKER. Richard (Capt.-22), 71, 72, 73.
BOOTH. Henry 13; Humphry 35, 50.
BOWLER. James 4, 5, 23, 89, 90.
BOWLES. John 27.
BRACEY. Edward 25.
BRADLEY. Abraham 95; Daniel (Capt. Commander *Richard & Mary)*, 57
BRAISIER. John 16, 34, 43.
BRANCHES: Bridge 61; Brookes Spring 65; Crumple Quarter 61; Horse 90; Long 73, 85; Midle 74, 85; Muzenseen 51.
BRISINDON. Richard 3, 32, 48.
BROACHE. John 99; Mary (Jones -99).
BROADLEY. Abraham 4.
BROKENBURROW. William 27.
BROOKE(S). George 65; Richard 3; Robert (Justice -1), 9, 17, 20, 26, 35, 39, 44, 47, 55, 57, 67, 69, 87, 105, 107.
BROTHERS. William 5, 8.
BROWNE. Abraham 96; Daniel 2, 5, 19; Elizabeth 7, 10, 33, 96; Francis 29, 38, 42, 43, 44, 45, 73, 74; Francis Senr. 70; Old Field 96; William 4.
BRYAND. John 30.
BUCKNER. John 51, (Clerk, Gloucester Co. -94).
BURNETT. John 10, 52, 53, 74; John (Elder) 10, 53; Lucy 6.
BUSH. Richard 3, 6.
BUTCHER. Line 90.
BUTLER. Thomas 66.
BUTTON. Robert 76, 77, 78, 79, 81, 83, 84; Thomas 75, 77, 78, 79, 81, 82, 84.

CADE. Lettis (Letticia) 12, 62; Robert 5, 12, 14, 61, 74.
CAMBELL. Ann 27.
CAMMILL. John 7, 16, 18, 25; Sarah (Killman -25).
CARTER. Richard 13, 18.
CARTY. Denis 70.
CARY. Miles 92.
CATLETT. John (Capt. Justice -1), 8, 26, (Feoffee of Town -29), 30, 31, 42, 51, 52, 54, 55, 84, 91, 106; William 10, 12, 17, 18, 51.
CAUTHORNE. Aurelia 105; Richard 30.
CHAMBERS. Elizabeth 30.

CHAMBLY. Randolph 41, 102, 103.
CHENEY. William 43.
CHILTON. Edward 4.
CHUBBS. William 2.
CLAIBORNE. William 13, 58, 59.
CLAPHAM. William 30.
CLARKE. Thomas 29; Ursula (Servant -30).
CLEMENTS. Benjamin 24.
CLOUTSOME. Mary 29, 89; Thomas 29, 87, 88, 89.
CLOWSON. Thomas 14, 19, 22, 23.
COATES. Samuell 34, 58, 59.
COGHILL. David 22, 71, 72, 73; Line 59; James 71.
COGWELL. James 23, 70; Mary 8, 22, 70.
COLE. William (Honble. Secry. of Va.-1), 59.
COLEMAN (COLLMAN). Robert 4, (Ordinary -5), 6, 11, 17, 19, 25, 26, 27, 34, 42, 45, 48, 65, 74, 96, 105, 106; William 66, 108.
COLLENERY. Edmond 30.
COLLERRELL. John 30.
COLLEYVOW. John 107.
COLSTON. Mr. 105; William 7, (Clerk Rappa. Co. -27), (Burgess -28), 51, 53, 57, 96, 97.
COMPTON. William 29, 90.
CONELE (CONNELLEY). Edmund 29, 75, 88, 89.
CONSTANTINE. William 63.
COOPER. Ann 31; George (Capt. -24); Thomas 3, 46, 48, 70; Thomas Junr. 32; Thomas Senr. 32.
COPELAND. Nicholas 2, 5, 23, 70, 75, 89; William 16, 34, 39.
COPNALL. Simon 7, 32.
CORKER. James 14.
COTTON. Robert 93.
COUCH. Thomas 18.
COUNTIES: Gloucester 14, 57, 60, 71, 77, 78, 79, 80, 81, 94; King & Queen 2, 3, 13, 58, 59; Middlesex 12; New Kent 50, 59; Rappahannock 2, 8, 16, 19, 25, 27, 39, 40, 50, 51, 52, 57, 59, 65, 71, 74, 76, 78, 79, 80, 83, 90, 96; Richmond 20, 26, 28, (Discourse on Laying leveys -96), 101.
COVINGTON (COVENTON). Richard 2, 3, 5, 6, 9, 13, 34, 44, 45, 58, 95; Thomas 19, 47; William 10, 19, 22, 24, 41, 56, 102; William Senr. 5, 58, 59.
COX. William 63.
CRABB. Hugh 2.
CRASKE. John 32.

CREEKS: Apamatrix 63; Cockelshell 101; Gilsons 76, 78, 83; Golden Vale 51; Occcupacon 69, 76, 78; Occopace 59; Pescatacon 85, 105; Piscataway 2, 8, 19, 52, 53, 61, 64, 65, 70, 102, 103.
CREEMER. William 4.
CRESFEILE. Edward 12.
CRIME & PUNISHMENT. Act for Suppressing Sin 38; Action of Trespass 8, 19, 36; Carry away Servt. Woman 20; False Pack Tobacco 5; Having bastard Child 7, 9, 30, 70; Not keep Covenants 14, 15; Playing Cards on Sabbath 38, 102; Refusing to serve on Grand Jury 5, 8; Runaway Servant 30; Steal Hog 3; Stole tobacco 13; Take up horse 33, 34, 45; Whipping post 6.
CRISPE. Thomas 32.
CROOKE. John 30.
CROW. Thomas 3.
CRUMSURE. Ann 30.
CRYMES. William 13, 14, 18, 20, 21, 23, 32.
CURRY. Henry 11, 15.

DALLE. Petter 30.
DANGERFEILD. John 2, 37.
DANIELL. James 30.
DAVIS. John 32, 46.
DAY. John 38; Thomas 3.
DEANE. John 27.
DEBELLO. Jacob Gacomodibolli 103.
DEBNAM. Mary 60.
DELABELLO, Jacob 27.
DENAIN. Alexander 12, 48, 62, 63.
DEPUTY. Elizabeth 49, 106, 107; Robert 33, 34, 35, 36, 37, 38, 39, 42, 43, 45, 48, 49, 100, 102, 104, 106.
DEVALL. John 26.
DICK. John 44.
DICKSON. Michael 38.
DIXSON. John 32.
DOBBINS. Daniel 2, 5, 26, 38, 41, 102; George 35, 44.
DOBOLLOW. Jacob 31.
DOHHODY. Jane (Marriage -57).
DONIPHAN. Alexander 27.
DOORS. John 12.
DRACUS. Edward 7, 46.
DRAINS. Edward 31.
DRILL. Ann 42; Jonathan 3.
DUDDIN(G). Andrew 3, 41, 102.
DYER. Henry 30.
DYES. Francis 10, 12, 18.

EARINGTON. John 32.
EDMONDSON. Mr. 18; Thomas (Justice -1), 23,
  26, 31, 33, 65, 96, 107.
EDWARDS. W. (Clerk Con.-56), 69.
ELLISON. Charles (Servant -99).
ELLITT. John 15, 18, 23, 24.
ELLSER. Elizabeth 18.
EVANS. Benjamin 91, 92; Elizabeth 91, 92;
  Henry 91, 92; John 30, 71, (Will of -91), 92;
  John (Younger) 91, 92; Rees 4, 10, 12, 15, 52,
  90; Sarah 91, 92; Susan 91, 92; Susanna 30,
  92; Thomas 17, 91.
EVERIT (EVERETT). John 30, 32, 33, 34, 35,
  38, 39, 43, 45, 46, 102, 107.
EVERS. Farratt 3.

FACK. Ann 30.
FANTLEROY. Katherine 104.
FEAGLE. Richard 4.
FERGESON. John 19.
FERRIES: Piscataway 27; Southins 27;
  Totaskey 27.
FINCH. Richard (Capt. Comandr: *Henry Prise,*
  -67).
FITZJEFFRIES. Ann 107; William 42, 43, 104,
  107.
FORBES. Alice 7, 16, 18, 25, 26, 32, 47;
  Arthur 47.
FORTH. John 58.
FOSTER. John 28, 82, 83; Robert 28, 79, 80,
  81; Thomas 36, 40.
FOY. Ann 30.
FRANCIS. Walter 27.
FRANKLAND. Thomas (Post Master Generall -93).
FRANSOM. Cornelius 47.
FREEMAN. Edward 62, 73, 74, 85; John 32;
  Mr. 61; Richard 29, 73, 74, 85, 86;
  William 29, 61, 62, 73, 74; William (Younger)
  85, 86.
FRENCH. Hugh 7, 14; Margaret 14.
FRYER (FRYAR). Richard 3, 7, 8, 15, 19, 24, 36,
  41, 42, 102.
FUGEET. Dorothy (Pettitt) 39, 40; James 35, 39,
  40, 43, 102.
FULLERTON. James 8, 12, 19, 64, 70;
  James (deced) 8, 19, 64.
FULLINGTON. James 6, 7.

GAINES. Bernard (Justice -1), 23, 26, 38, 54, 91,
  102; Daniel 78; Katherine 39, (contd)

GAINES (contd.) Margrett 52; Thomas 10, 13,
  19, 33, 34, 35, 39, 40, 42, 44, 45, 52, 53, 103.
GARNETT. John 28, 77, 78, 79, 83; Line 83.
GATEWOOD. John 33, 41, 43, 96, 101, 102.
GEORGE. Francis 30; Mr. 42.
GITTINGS. David 60, 61.
GLASSCOCK. Thomas 27.
GOBETT. Susana 30.
GOGGIN. Thomas 32.
GOLDON. Richard 30.
GOOD. Richard 59.
GOODRICH. Benjamin 6, 8; Joseph 4, 6, 11, 17.
GORE. Henry 32.
GOSS. John 2.
GOULDMAN. Alice 25; Francis 34, 46, 47, 101,
  105; Thomas 25, 29.
GOVIRE. Robert 94.
GRAVES. Thomas (Servant -18).
GRAY. Abner 33; William 59.
GREDIT (GRIDET). James 4, 46, 104.
GREEN(E).Richard 27; Samuel 2, 16; Thomas 3, 6.
GREENSTED (GRINSTED). Richard 10, 11, 14, 16,
  19, 20, 24, 26, 31.
GREGORY. Richard 13, 60, 66, 67.
GRIFFEN (GRIFFIN). John 30, 35, 102;
  Samuel 4, 9, 35; Thomas 4, (Servant -8), 9,
  20, 69, 105.
GRIFFES. Margaret 30.
GRIFFING. John 41.
GRIMES. Charles 60.
GRINSTED. Richard 13, 102.
GROVE. George 42.
GWINES. Ann 30.

HALFORD. John 60.
HALL(E). Peter (Mercht. Liverpool -49);
  Richard 19; William 49, 107.
HALSEY. Robert 4, 11, 14, 19, 32, 57.
HAMILTON. Andrew Esqr. (Manage Generall
  Post Office -93).
HARDING. William 3.
HARPER. John 12, 44, 45, 48, 61, 62, 63;
  Lydia 12, 63; Thomas 61, 62, 70, 73, 85;
  William (Constable -2).
HARRIS. Thomas 27.
HARRISON. Andrew 3, 6, 7, 13, 14; Daniell 92.
HARVEY. Mary 37; Mary (Whitchurch 100, 101);
  Richard 37, 100, 101.
HARWAR. Samuell 32; Thomas 65, (Justice -97).

HARWOOD. Phill: (Capt. -6).

HASLEWOOD. Ann 30, 45, 91; Elizabeth 30; George 3, 4, 30, 42, 45, 47, 91; John 51.

HASELL. John 30.

HAWKINS. Thomas (Majr.-87), 88.

HAYES. Thomas 78, 79, 80, 81, 83, 84.

HAYWARTON. Thomas 58.

HENLY. Jos: 26.

HEYWARD. John 52; Peter (Deputy Post Master -93).

HILL. Leonard 3, 7, 8, 13, 18, 21, 24; Thomas 102.

HILLIARD. Thomas 8, 51, 52.

HINDS. Thomas 3, 5, 6.

HINE. John 50, 51.

HODGES (HODGIS). Arhtur 32; Mary 5.

HOLDING. Rachel (Servant -7), 10.

HOLT (HOULT). John 44; Land 53; Richard 3, 6, 10, 52; Richard Junr. 10, 48.

HOWARD. Charrity 99; Thomas 99.

HOWARTON. Thomas 26.

HOWLETT. William 28, 84, 85.

HUCKLESCOTT. Mary 88, 89; Thomas 3, 11, 14, 20, 23, 24, 31, 36, 46, 71, 88, 89, 90, 92, 101.

HUDSON. Peter 46; William 42, 44, 45.

HUTCHINS. Richard 7, 8.

HUTSON. John 30, 90, 91; William 90.

INDIANS. Doegs Land 60; Indian Path 64; Mattaponey Path 75; Old Assuamansockek Foot Path 58.

INGRAM. Dorcas 14; Thomas 105.

JACKSON. Patrick 16.

JAMES. Francis 27.

JARMAN. Henry 100.

JEFFREYS. Edward 6, 9; William 33, 34, 36, 37, 44, 45, 102.

JENKINS. David 13, 14, 105.

JENNINGS. Francis 30.

JOHNSON. Martin 20, 24, 26, 36, 40, 69; Robert 21; William 3, 13, 33, 44, 45, 65, 85, 103.

JONES. Edward 27, (Sub Sheriff -27); Evan 9, 57, 105; John 6, 9, 26, 30, 32, 37, (Will of -98, 99), 100; John (Son of Rice -99); Millicent 37, 99, 100; Negro slaves mentd. 99; Nicholas 99; Rice 99; Rice (Son of Rice -99); Richard 6, 9, 36, 96; Walter 71; William 38.

JOURNEY. William 61.

JUSTICES. Henry Awbrey 1, 97, 98; Capt. John Battalle 1, 8, 11, 17, 22, 29, 37, 97, 98; Robert Brooke 1, 8, 11, 22, 28, 29, 37, 97, 98; Capt. John Catlett 1, 8, 17, 28, 29, 37, 97, 98; Thomas Edmondson 1, 2, 11, 17, 22, 29, 37, 97, 98; Bernard Gaines 1, 8, 17, 22, 37, 97, 98; Thomas Harwar 97, 98; Capt. William Moseley 1, 8, 11, 22, 28, 37, 97, 98; Capt. Anthony Smith 1, 2, 22, 28, 37, 47, 98; Francis Taliaferro 29, 37, 97, 98; John Taliaferro 11, 37, 97, 98; Capt. Edward Thomas 1, 2, 8, 29, 37, 97, 98; Henry Williamson 1, 2, 37, 97, 98.

KELSICK. Richard (Comdr.-37, 38).

KEMBALL. Joseph 26.

KILLMAN. John 25; Mary 25; Sarah 25.

KING. Benjamin 6; John 10, 13, 16, 20, 21, 25; Mary 5, 10; Richard 5, 9, 10, 22, 24, 42; Robert 8; Thomas 30.

LACKLAND. Richard 38.

LACY. Frn: 33.

LAMBERT. Thomas 71.

LAMBETH. George 21.

LANDRUM. John 13.

LASH. Henry 30.

LAWRENCE. Ann 56; Edward 56; Mary 56.

LEAKE. William 3, 6, 7, 8, 13, 25, 31, 43, 46, 66, 67.

LEIGHTON. Richard 48, 49, 50.

LEVERIT. Toby 32.

LEVEY. Laying for Essex & Richmond Co. 26, 27.

LEWIS. Thomas 27.

LIDFORD. Mathew 100.

LINCH. Elizabeth 9, 10, 15, 18, 21, 26, 33, 34, 36; William 10, 18.

LINSEY. Elizabeth 3, 96.

LOBB. William 22, 72, 73.

LOCKETT. William 43.

LOITON. Judith 33; Richard 33.

LONG. Henry 6, 33, 34, 39, 43.

LOVELESS. Roger 32, 48.

LOVEN. John 69.

LOYD. Coll: 27; David 11, 15, 47, 67, 74, 98; Thomas 27; William (Colo:) 29.

LUMKIN. Robert 3.

MACARTIE. Dennis 22, 24, 27.

MACKABONE. Rickett 103, 104.

MACUBIN. Richard 102, 103.

MAGUFFIE. John 17.
MARMADUKE. Thomas 6.
MARRINER. Francis 45, 104.
MARSH. Benjamin 21, 70; William 31.
MARWOOD. James 82.
MASON. William 101, 102.
MASSEY. John Junr. 99.
MATHER. Hugh 43, 44, (Mercht. Liverpool -49).
MATHEWS. Benjamin 33; Richard 4, 31.
MAUSBIN. Richard 41.
MAYFIELD. Robert 105.
MAYO. Vallentine 30.
MAZY. Martin 47.
MEADOR. John 19, 26; Thomas 2.
MEADS. Elizabeth 7, 9, 34, 102.
MEREDITH (MEREDE). Ann 106, 107;
   David 102, 106, 107.
MERIWETHER. Francis (Clerk of Essex Co. -1),
   3, 12, 17, 21, 27, 35, 44, 50, 55, 57, 59, 66, 78,
   91, 97, 106, 108; Mr. 105.
MERRIDAY. Ann 45, 49; David 33, 34, 35, 36,
   39, 45, 49.
MERRITT (MERRIOTT). William 17, 20, 24, 31, 34.
MERTEER. John 38.
MICHELL. John 41, 102.
MICOU. Paul 32, 35.
MILLER. John 82.
MILLS. John 9, 10, 15, 18; Robert 19.
MITCHELL. John 5, 42.
MONJOY. Richard 30.
MOODIE (MOODYE). John 20, 70, 71.
MOORE. Francis 104.
MORGAN. John 3, 37.
MORRIS. George (Majr., Surveyor -64),
   William 32.
MOSELEY. William (Capt., Justice -1), 2, 23, 26,
   29, 31, 39, 53, 54, 57, 59, 66, 75, 76, 84, 87,
   94, 96.
MOSS. Henry 13; John 3, 5, 6, 19; Robert 5.
MUNDAY. Thomas 26.
MUSCOE. Salvator 82.
MYNE(S). Robert 22, 72, 73.

NASON. Joshua 9, 16, 30, 34, 48, 95, 96, 107.
NEAL. Thomas Esqr. (Manage Generall Post
   Office -93).
NELSON. John 10, 12, 18; Mathew 10.
NEWBELL. James 32, 34, 46, 48.
NEWTON. Edward 27.

NICHOLSON. Honble. Francis Lt. Govr., 1, 4, 53,
   54, 55, 56, 63, 67, 68.
NOELL. Cornelius 29, 75, 87, 88, 89;
   Daniel 75, 89, 90.
NORMENT. Josue 59.
NORTH. Abraham 36, 46, (Marriage -94);
   Anthony 46; Richard 30; Sarah 36, 46.

OCKRE. Ould Negroe to be free 99.
ONGLEY. Mary 20.
ORCHARD. James 3, 27.
OUGLEY. Mary 70.
OWEN. Hugh 12, 59, 60.

PAGE. Line 88; Thomas 87, 90.
PAGETT. Edmond 26.
PAINE (PAYNE). John 51; Robert 43, 101;
   Thomas (Constable -2), 33, 47.
PANTREP. Ann 31.
PARISHES: Elect Vestry 39; Kingston 77, 78,
   79, 80, 81; St. John 58; St. Marys 2, 51;
   Sittingburne 2, 22, 39, 51; South Farnham 2,
   30, 58; Ware 60.
PARKE. George (Sub Sheriff -1), 3, 7, 17, 27, 35,
   39, 44, 47, 54, 55, 57, 67, 69, 70, 76, 94, 96,
   107; Thomas 32.
PARKER. Jeremiah 17, 69; John 69;
   Thomas 50, 51, 69; Thomas Senr. 17, 69.
PARR: Phill: 6, 12, 13, 18, 21, 24, 34, 36, 41,
   43, 44, 45, 47, 65, 102.
PARRY. Samuell 103.
PATENTS: Bennet 86; Button 75, 77, 79, 81;
   Chambly 41, 102; Fullerton 19, 64; Gaines 53;
   Good 59; Grimes 60; Hutson 90; Macubin 102;
   Noell 87, 88; Owen 59; Page 90; Prosser 51;
   Thomas 102; Vicaris 59; Ward 75;
   Welding 90.
PATRIDGE. John 27.
PATTISON. Thomas 65.
PAVEALE. Walter 74.
PAVEY. Walter 4.
PECKETT. William 49.
PEIRSIL. Danniel 33.
PELL. Christopher (Servant -37).
PENDLETON. Phill: 7, 8.
PENNE. John 86.
PERSEFULL. John 30.
PETTIS. Dorothy 40; Thomas 40.
PETTITT. Dorothy 39, 40; Katherine 39;
   Thomas 39, 40.

PHELPS. Thomas 9, 32, 36.
PICKETT. Henry 2, 10, 11, 15, 33, 34, 36, 41, 42, 67, 102, 103; John 5.
PIGG. Elizabeth 31; John 31.
PIGGETT. Henry 13, 43, 104; Henry (Elder) 43, (Cooper -104); Sarah 43, 104.
PITTS. John (Constable -2).
PLACES. Browns Old Field 96; Buttons Range 76, 77, 79, 80, 81, 82, 83, 84; Christ Church Hospital 68; Colemans Ordinary 106; Doegs Land 60; Easterne Shore 63; East Jarsey 93; Fort 63; Glovers Neck 65; Hobses Hole 33; Maryland 93; Moejack Bay 63; Pimonkey Neck 58; Rotten Marsh 69; Sandy Point 63; Sharpes Neck 99; The Best Land 58; Town Land in Essex County 29; Tyndalls Point 67.
PLEY (PLEA). Robert 9, 11, 42, 44, 45, 48, 49, 104.
POTTER. Abednineck 16, 66; Rachel 16, 17.
POWELL. John 16, 21, 42.
PRESSON. Henry 78, 79, 80, 81, 83, 84.
PRICE. John 6,7, 8, 12, 19, 64, 70; Thomas 50; William 34, 39, 43, 44.
PROCLAMATIONS & ACTS. Acts of Assembly 1, (Published -38), (Dissolved -92); Acts of Suppressing Sins 38, 68; Appointing Places for Ships 63, 64; Apprentices Bound by Christ Church Hospital 68; Assembly dissolved 92; Clerks impowered to appoint Deputies 56; Commission of Place 1, 3, 7, 22, 76, 77, 97, 98; Lycences for Marriage 68; Order of Councill 1, 17, (to John Baker -77); Post Office 93; Powder to be used only for defence 56; Paryers for Divine Assistance 98; Publick Thanksgiving 22, 77; Seaman 17, (Runaway 67, 68); Sheriff 1, 53, 54.
PROCTOR. George 38, 101, 102.
PROSSER. Elizabeth 51; John 51.
PUE. Mary 29.
PURVIS. David 30; John (Capt. -3).
PUTLEY. Mary 30.
PYELL. Henry 29.

RACKLY. John 47.
RADLY. Thomas 48.
RHODES. Richard 25.
RICHARDS. John 10, 56.
RICHARDSON. Antony 94; James 95; Robert 9.
RIVERS. Coratomen 63; Elizabeth 63; James 63; Lower Machotinck 63; (contd)

RIVERS (contd) Nansemond 63; Peanketanck 63; Potomack 63; Rappa: 63; Warwick 63; Wicocomico 63; Yorke 63.
ROADS & PATHS: Indian 64; Mattapony Path 75; Main 3, 91; Old Assuamansockek Foot Path 58; Paths 53, 101; Range 76, 84; The 71.
ROBERTS. Willit 94.
ROBINS. Rebecca 33.
ROBINSON. Christopher 21, 24, 31, (Sec: 77); Max: 27; Richard 31, 35, 38, 39, 47.
ROME. David 30.
ROSON. Thomas 71.
ROWZEE (ROWSEY). John 69; Lodiwick 2, 69, 94, 95; Sarah 36, 46, (Marriage -95).
RUDDERFORD. Margaret 66; Robert 17, 66.
RUNS: Hoskins 91; Occupation 75.
RYDER. William 22, 72, 73.

SADLER. Thomas 71.
SAINT JOHN (ST. JOHN). Thomas 2, 34, 45.
SALLIS. Samuell 2, 30.
SAVAGE. John 2, 5, 65.
SCOTT. James 101; John 13, 14, 18, 20, 21, 23, 24, 32, 38, 44, 45, 47, 72, 73; Mary 38, 101, 102.
SEARLE. John 8, 47, 69.
SEYMOUR. John 16, 17.
SHEFFIELD. Benjamin 3, 7, 8, 13, 18, 21, 24.
SHEPARD. Jere: 46; Thomas 8.
SHERWOOD. William 6.
SHIPLEY. Alice 21.
SHIPS & VESSELS. Henry Prise 67; Lorell of Liverpoole 98; No Persons to go on Ships until known what she is 64; Places for Harbours for Ships 63; Resolution 37, 38; Richard & Mary 57; Runaway Seaman 67, 68.
SHORT. Thomas 33.
SLAUGHTER. Francis 91.
SMITH. Anthony (Capt., Justice -1), 3, 26, 33, 36, 38, 41, 70, 102, 103, 104, 105; Elizabeth 11, 34, 60, 61; James 45, 58, 59; John 11, (Marriage -57), 60, 61, 94; John Senr. 5; Jonas 33, 34, 49, 106, 107; Thomas 7, 9, 33; William 8, 21, 27, (Capt. -32), 51, 52, 72; William Junr. 27.
SMITHER (SMYTHER). William 28, 29, 81, 82.
SOLMON. John 26.
SOPER. John 8.
SORRELL. John 9, 12, 17, 20, 57, 67, 69, 105.
SOUTHERNE. John 5, 10, 11, 13, 14, 16, 19, 20, 24, 31, 94.

SPENGE. John 30.

SPICER. Arthur (Capt.-14), 15, 17, 18, 19, 22, 23, 24, 25, 26, 27, 31, 32, 43; Capt. 13, 16, 21.

SPIERS. John 30.

STANDRIDGE. Thomas 95.

STAP. Abraham 100, 101.

STEPHENS (STEEVENS). Richard 12, 61, 62, 103.

STEPP. Abraham 37.

STIMSON. John 10, 11, 12.

STOAKES. Richard 2.

STOESLEY. Thomas 30.

STONE. Coll: 27; John 27.

STOPFORD. Martha 43.

STORY. Joshua 60.

STRANGE. Joseph 30.

STROTHER. William 6.

SUTTLE. Francis 27.

SWAMPS: Main 58; Richard Taylors 3.

SWAN. Alexander (Capt., Justice Richmond County -26).

SWETMAN. William 34.

SYNOCK. Robert (Doctor -16), 66.

TALBOT. Richard 4, 5, 7.

TALIAFERRO. Charles 26; Francis 4, 8, 30, 31, 33, 52, 61, (Justice -97); John 4, 11, 15, 30, 60, 61, (Justice 97); Richard 12.

TANDY. Silvester 20, 26.

TAVERNER. John 9, 12, 13, 14, 15, 16, 17, 20, 21, 22, 35, 67, 70, 105.

TAYLOR. Daniell 56; George (Justice Richmond Co.-26), 46, 104; James 13, 16; Lorana 7; Richard 2, 3, 21, 26, 33, 34, 36, 38; Thomas (Servant -2), 13.

TEAY (TEA). Mr. 104; Robert 11.

TEMERTON. David 29.

THACKER. Edwin (Surveyor of Lower part -9), 12, 19, 41, 44, 53, 64, 102, 103; Samuel 47, 57.

THOMAS. David 41, 102; Edward (Capt. Justice -1), 4, 5, 7, 10, 12, 17, 20, 24, 26, 28, 29, 30, 31, 36, 37, 38, 40, 53, 54, 55, 70, (Mercht. -86), 87, 91, 100; John 30; Robert 11, 21, 24, 31, 95.

THORNTON. Francis 42.

THOROGOOD. William 38, 107.

THORPE. Thomas 5, 33.

TODD. Elizabeth 36, 40; William 36, 40.

TOMLIN. Rebecca 26, 32, 35; Thomas 3; William 17, 31, 46.

TOSTLY (TOUSLEY). Elizabeth 100; Thomas 94.

TRAVERS. Samuell (Capt. -10), 12.

TURNER. Bryant 31, 32.

VANDERCRUIT. Bartho: 47.

VAUSE. Ann 29, 86, 87; Vincent 29, 86, 87.

VAWTER. Bartholomew 30, 90.

VEALE. William 25.

VERGITT. John 72, 73.

VICARIS. Thomas 23, 59, 70.

VICARS. Mr. 87

WAIGHT. Robert 52.

WALKER. Charles 100; Thomas 27.

WARD. Bryan 26, 29, 74, 75; George 20, 70, 71; Mary 6, 74, 75; Nicholas 43, (Mercht. of Dublin -104); Samuell 6.

WARKEMAN. Elizabeth 31, 32.

WATERMAN. Elizabeth 29.

WATERS. John 10, 11, 15, 25, 31, 33, 35, 36, 40, 57,, 74; John Jr. 12, 65.

WATKINS. Thomas 3, 5.

WATSON. John 20, 26, 33.

WEARE. John 89.

WEBB. John 41, 102; John Senr. 42; Robert 7; Thomas 5.

WEBSTER. John 2, 3, 5, 6, 65, 102.

WEILDING. Samuell 90.

WELLS. Stephen 21, 70.

WHEDEN. Edmond 30.

WHEELER (WHEALER). Thomas 5, 19, 57; Will: 107.

WHITCHURCH. John 100; Mary 100.

WHITE. Chillion 22, 72, 73; Jeremya 50, 51.

WHITTON. Elizabeth 25; Ralph 3, 6, 8, 9, 16, 20, 21, 25, 30, 32, 34, 35, 41, 46, 47, 95, 96, 102

WILLCOK. John 30.

WILLIAMS. Henry 30; John 5, 9; Shadrick 28; Thomas 33.

WILLIAMSON. Henry 4, 16, 26, (Feoffee in Trust conveying Town Land -29), 86, 100; John 11

WILLKISSON. John 30

WILSON. David 13, 17, 26, 31, 34, 44, 45, 46, 47; Elias 27; George 26; Richard 29.

WILTON. Mary 29, 90; Richard 29, 33, 90.

WOOD. John (Constable -2); Thomas 6, 9, 16; 70; Thomas Junr. 21; Thomas Senr. 20.

WOODNOT. Henry 8, 16, 41, 102.

WORMLEY. Esqr. 27; Ralph Esqr. 98.

WRIGHT. Matrum 76; Mr. 79, 84.

WYATT. Ann (Jones -99); John 99; William 99.

YARD -35; Robert 35, 96.

YEATS. Katherine 30.

YOUNG. William 13, 15, 19, 24, 36, 41, 94, 102.

www.ingramcontent.com/pod-product-compliance
Lightning Source LLC
Chambersburg PA
CBHW080337270326
41927CB00014B/3255